Leicester ●

Kings Lynn ●

Sandringham

Norwich ●

Barnwell

Gatcombe

Oxford ●

Windsor

London

Broadlands

Winchester ●

uthampton

Portsmouth

Osborne

N

ROYAL FARMERS

Books published by Ralph Whitlock include

SOMERSET
WILTSHIRE
WHITLOCK'S WESSEX
GENTLE GIANTS
BULLS THROUGH THE AGES
EXPLORING RIVERS, LAKES AND CANALS
A SHORT HISTORY OF BRITISH FARMING
FARMING AS A CAREER
FARMING FROM THE ROAD
AGRICULTURAL RECORDS
THE EVERYDAY LIFE OF THE MAYA
THE WARRIOR KINGS OF A SAXON ENGLAND
THINKING ABOUT RURAL DEVELOPMENT
THE FOLKLORE OF DEVON
A CALENDAR OF COUNTRY CUSTOMS

ROYAL FARMERS

RALPH WHITLOCK

MICHAEL JOSEPH   LONDON

First published in Great Britain by Michael Joseph Ltd., 44 Bedford Square,
London WC1
1980

ISBN 0 7181 1752 2

Filmset and printed in Great Britain by
BAS Printers Limited, Over Wallop, Hampshire
and bound by Hunter and Foulis Limited, Edinburgh

To my multi-national grandchildren

JONATHAN (*English*)
MARK (*American*)
MARY-JANE (*English*)
GRAHAM (*English*)
STEVEN (*English*)
DANIEL (*Canadian*)
CARLA (*Canadian*)

Contents

My thanks are due to all those who have helped with the collection of illustrations for *Royal Farmers*. I am particularly grateful to Her Majesty the Queen for permission to reproduce photographs nos. 6, 7, 8, 9, 11, 12 and 13 from the book entitled *The Prince Consort's Farms*, and photographs nos. 3 and 4 which were obtained from the Royal Library at Windsor Castle.

I should also like to thank *The Field* for the opportunity to have access to their files and to borrow photographs nos. 14, 16, 22, 23, 41, 43, 44, 45 and 46.

List of Illustrations

Acknowledgements

The germ of the idea for this book appeared when, while studying the life of King George III, I became impressed by that sadly misunderstood monarch's agricultural activities. That the contributions of 'Farmer George' to the great farming revolution which occurred in his reign should have been so neglected by agricultural historians seemed to me an incomprehensible omission that should be rectified.

Reading further, I found that the Prince Consort, some forty or fifty years later, had played a similar leading role in promoting the agricultural developments of the mid-nineteenth century. His work too has been largely neglected and forgotten. Sandwiched between them I discovered King William IV, who, in spite of his naval background, was so deeply immersed in the affairs of his farm at Bushy Park that his letters frequently give them pride of place.

King Edward VII and King George V had a deep love of fine livestock and the life of the countryside, and in the management of the Royal Estates in wartime George VI set, as in so many other matters, a right royal example. At Sandringham, Balmoral, Windsor, Gatcombe, Barnwell, Broadlands and Stoke Climsland our present Royal Family run their respective farms with an efficiency which the pioneering King George III would have envied and the Prince Consort profoundly approved.

I would like to express my gratitude to H.M. the Queen for graciously approving this project of writing a book on Royal Farmers, and for granting me access to the Royal Archives at Windsor.

I would also like to express my grateful thanks to other members of the Royal Family for granting permission to visit and write about their farms. Queen Elizabeth the Queen Mother afforded me full facilities for preparing the short chapter on Longoe Farm at the Castle of Mey. At Gatcombe Captain Mark Phillips spent half a day showing me around his new farms. H.R.H. Prince Alice the Duchess of

Gloucester gave me much help in preparing the chapter on Barnwell and supplied several personal photographs of her husband and family. H.R.H. the Duke of Gloucester also met me at Barnwell and gave me a full résumé of his farming activities and the history of the Estate, as did the late Admiral of the Fleet, Earl Mountbatten of Burma, when I visited Broadlands.

I want to express, too, my sincere thanks to the many officials of the royal household and estates who have helped me so generously and patiently dealt with my many enquiries. I would like to express my appreciation of the great assistance given by those who have lent or procured books and documents for me, and in particular the staff of Yeovil Library who have dealt with courteous equanimity with the most extraordinary requests. My gratitude is also due to Betty Fieldhouse and Jacqueline Dean who have typed, and re-typed, and re-typed the manuscript. And to my wife, Hilda, who has shared all the work but who has enjoyed some compensation in visiting the royal farms with me.

Finally, I am most grateful to all those publishers who have given their permission for extracts from their publications to be included in *Royal Farmers*.

Introduction

by H.R.H. Prince Philip, Duke of Edinburgh

It is self-evident that of all the things produced by man, food is essential to life itself, but it was the deliberate cultivation of food resources which made it possible for human groups to develop from primitive nomadic tribes into settled, prosperous and civilised communities. Inevitably the most successful cultivators became leaders and naturally successive leaders continued to be cultivators.

This book traces the story of the development of agricultural cultivation and the systems of land tenure in this country through the ages and is full of fascinating detail about the individual contributions of Kings and Princes. It is particularly fascinating for me as I find myself to be the current custodian or trustee of this tradition.

That there should have been vast changes in agricultural practice and land tenure in this country over the last thousand years or so is not particularly surprising, but when the last fifty years comes to be seen in the perspective of history it will be obvious that no other similar period has witnessed quite such dramatic changes.

When I first went to Sandringham over thirty years ago, some of the tenanted farms were still being worked by horses. Gangs of female labour were contracted to lift the vegetable crops. Sugar-beet was hoed and topped and tailed by hand, and produce in general was bought and sold in local markets, a pattern not much changed in 200 years. On the other hand the picture of the highly intensive mechanised agricultural industry of today could not be more different.

In 1952 The Queen succeeded her father and inevitably the duties and responsibilities of the sovereign fully occupied her time and energy, although she has never lost her interest in the farming and other activities on the Estates, and the supervision of the thoroughbred studs is entirely in her hands. It therefore fell to me to

13

assume the general responsibility for the Sandringham and Balmoral Estates, and as Ranger of Windsor Great Park, to begin that ambivalent relationship which always exists between someone in a titular position and an autonomous semi-Government department. Suggestions, gentle persuasion and a good personal relationship with the Deputy Ranger is about the extent of the Ranger's influence, supported only by the fact that he is resident on the place.

In spite of these limitations it is possible to achieve quite a lot. Indeed King George VI's enthusiasm for gardening and his close understanding with Sir Eric Savill, the Deputy Ranger of his time, produced amongst other things the magnificent valley and Savill Gardens in the south-east corner of the Park.

In my time, Smith's Lawn, which used to be the training gallops for Barnard Smith, the Duke of Cumberland's racing trainer, again echoes to the thud of hooves with its flourishing Guards' Polo Club, started in 1955, and more recently the monthly meetings of the Windsor Park Equestrian Club, and more recently still with the competitors in the 1978 National Driving Championships.

For some time it was becoming increasingly evident that the cultivation of that part of the Park north of the 'Copper Horse', first ploughed during the last war, was not a viable proposition, and furthermore the tractors were doing considerable damage to the rides and tracks. It seemed to me that the solution would be to make the area back into parkland and to stock it with deer. The first stage of this 'reclamation' is currently taking place and the first batch of nineteen hinds from Balmoral were introduced to their new home on the evening of 2 February, 1979.

As we are tenants of Shaw and Prince Consort Farms in the Home Park, the situation there is rather different, and the decision to retain the Jersey and Ayrshire milking herds was one we could take without having to get the 'landlord's' approval.

Responsibility for Sandringham and Balmoral has been rather more direct and the challenge, particularly after six years of war, to modernise, and more recently in the face of inflation, to contain costs and increase revenue has been daunting. However, after twenty-six years it is very satisfying to see the fruits of the forestry programmes on both Estates introduced in the early fifties and of the other successful enterprises. There have naturally also been some failures.

The details of cropping programmes and the selection of agricultural machinery are better left to the professionals. I have taken the line that I can make a more valuable contribution to the discussion of broad policy issues particularly in relation to national and international trends in agriculture, and such things as closing down and starting new enterprises, taking farms in hand, housing and similar matters.

There is one point of detail which I have consistently advocated. In all forms of 'double-cross' beef production, I have always maintained that the bigger British beef breeds are just as successful as the more fashionable exotics. But I do not always win, witness the Charolais and Simmenthal in addition to the Devon, Hereford and Lincoln Red bulls at Sandringham and the Blondes at Balmoral.

It was largely as a consequence of the Highland cattle, which I introduced to Balmoral in 1954, that we later went in for the then newly developing Luing Cattle as they are derived from a Highland-Shorthorn cross. Sadly my plan to combine the beef operations on the two Estates had to be abandoned for various, but what I still maintain were not convincing, reasons.

Beef cattle are not the only livestock at Balmoral. In 1972 my old friend Lord Buxton wanted to get rid of his flock of Soay sheep and I offered to give it a new home. The adventures caused by those semi-wild sheep since they arrived at Balmoral would fill a book on their own. What would happen should we attempt some form of deer-farming remains to be seen.

Although not strictly speaking anything to do with farming, the re-designing of gardens and landscapes is something that has to go on as dictated by natural ageing, developing farming techniques and financial resources. I find it a most agreeable challenge and there is nothing more satisfying than to see the designs for the East Terrace and the small garden on the south slopes at Windsor and the almost totally re-designed gardens at Balmoral take shape and fill out with maturity.

At Sandringham woods have to be cut and replanted, but avenues and vistas have also been established and long-term plans made for the future of the park. It has not always been easy to find convenient places for amenity planting on the open cultivated land, but where it has been possible the results have been most rewarding. Perhaps the most difficult problem is the replanting of trees on land under permanent pasture or where the land has recently been taken into cultivation. The massive oak trees are a great feature in the landscape but highly inconvenient from a practical point of view.

The spin-off from a fairly close involvement in agriculture has been particularly interesting for me. In 1957 I was invited to be President of the Royal Agricultural Society of England, although I did not give the job anything like as much time and attention as I should have liked to have done, particularly as it came at the time when the Society was considering whether to continue to change the site of the annual show or whether to settle somewhere permanently. I was invited to fill the post again in 1963 just after the Society had settled in at Stoneleigh and I have only recently accepted the invitation to preside in 1980.

Arising from my connection with the R.A.S.E. was my involvement in the foundation of the Royal Agricultural Society of the Commonwealth, a brainchild of an Australian friend, Mr Sam Hordern. Still perhaps not as well known as it deserves to be, the conferences which it organises for the member Agricultural Societies of the Commonwealth are, in my opinion, among the most valuable agents for Commonwealth co-operation, and with an even more important potential for the future as more Agricultural Societies are formed in the so-called 'third world' countries and become members and send representatives to the conferences.

One of the reasons that I became so closely involved with the conservation of nature was my first-hand experience of the devastating effects of the use of the very poisonous chemicals introduced into agriculture in the 50s and the immense power of modern machinery in the reclamation of marginal land. The few remaining areas of uncultivated 'breckland' on Sandringham vanished within a few years and the vastly improved drainage on the marshland completely changed the character and the wild populations of that area. It was not difficult to imagine what this meant when scaled up into national and world terms. It was largely for this reason that I retained thirty acres of the newly reclaimed salt marsh as a sanctuary.

The management of land is a very long-term business and the best results can only be achieved if there is confidence in continuity. We are enjoying the gardens and avenues and amenities planted by previous generations and it is because I feel myself to be a temporary custodian that I am planting for future generations. It is not the ownership that matters, it is the sense of responsibility for the well-being of an Estate in every way and so much enhanced by the feeling of continuity between generations of the same family. This kind of responsibility and emotional attachment cannot exist in the same way in professional management which is inevitably even more transient than ownership. Since I became involved we have had three Keepers of the Privy Purse, four Factors at Balmoral, two Agents at Sandringham and three Deputy Rangers at Windsor.

Whatever it is I can only say that I find the urge to improve and to develop the Estates is as strong in me as in any of my predecessors.

1

MONARCHY IN THEORY AND PRACTICE

THE ANOINTED MONARCH

Kingship was a sacred vocation from very early times. The king was not only crowned – more important, he was anointed in a religious ceremony that was at least as significant as the consecration of an archbishop. As regent of God on earth, the king was entitled to reverence as well as obedience. And just as the earth belonged to God, so, as far as his kingdom was concerned, everything and everyone in it belonged to the king. He could graciously give of his bounty and he could take away.

The theory was crystallised and translated into ruthless practice in England by that vigorous monarch, William the Conqueror. Under the feudal system, which he imposed rigidly upon a nation that was already loosely organised on similar lines, every man had a master. In return for certain specified services the cottager held his land from the lord of the manor, the lord of the manor from some great noble, and the noble from the king. An aristocrat who lorded over half a dozen counties would kneel before his sovereign and, by placing his hands in his and performing homage, would acknowledge that in theory at least, (and in practice where a monarch of the calibre of King William I was concerned), all that he possessed was held by permission of the king. The Domesday Book was in effect a magnificent, pioneering attempt to make an inventory of all his property. So, through all the vicissitudes of the medieval centuries, we see the king making grants of land, houses, timber, offices, charters and anything else desired by his subjects. Everything was his to dispose of.

Although much of the land of England thus came to be controlled only indirectly by the king, he retained much of it under his direct authority. The royal forests, accounting for approximately one sixth of the total area of the realm, were a notable example. The deer there, which provided the royal household with much of its meat, were protected by draconian forest laws. Also scattered throughout the country were many royal manors, which were farmed for the king's benefit.

THE KING AS LORD OF THE MANOR

In cases where the king himself was the lord of a manor he naturally delegated his authority, in his absence, to a seneschal or steward who lived in the manor-house and administered the estate. Under him a bailiff farmed the demesne farm, which usually occupied an enclosed area comprising some of the best land but also a number of strips in the common fields. Sometimes, when a steward had charge of a number of manors, the bailiff lived in the big house and was the visible representative of supreme authority. The bailiff was naturally appointed by the king or his steward, but he had under him an assistant, known as a reeve, who was in theory elected by the other farmers.

These other farmers were all tenants, each holding a number of strips in the common fields according to his status. In early times cash rents were rare, the commonest form of payment being by service. Each tenant, again according to status, had to work a specified number of days on his lord's farm. As their elected representative, the reeve had to help the bailiff in determining just what services were required from each man and in ensuring that everyone did whatever was expected of him. In addition, he had to see that the implements, which were often communally owned, were kept in good repair, and he had to supervise the work of independent specialists, including the manorial shepherd, oxherd, swineherd, cowherd, hayward, woodward, dairymaid (or cheesemaker) and often beekeeper.

At the royal manors, therefore, the king was by delegation involved in farming, a fact which had practical significance as he was not always an absentee landlord. A consideration of the implications of life before the age of shops will indicate why this was so.

Food was normally consumed where it was grown. There were few facilities for transporting it for considerable distances. Medieval records frequently remind us that a local failure of crops meant famine for the locality concerned; there was little chance of making good the deficit by importing food from elsewhere.

For a king with his court and his large household, it was impossible to remain for long periods in one place – royalty in early and medieval times was therefore essentially peripatetic. The royal household spent the year moving from royal manor to royal manor around the kingdom, remaining in each of them just long enough to eat up the accumulated provisions. The phenomenally energetic Henry II supplies an outstanding example of this way of life. Possessing the allegiance of at least half of France as well as of England, Wales and Ireland, he spent his Christmasses at places well dispersed around his domain, such as Bordeaux, Dublin, London, Tours and York.

A contemporary writer, Peter of Blois, who was a courtier in King Henry's entourage, gives a graphic account of what went on:

> If the King has decided to spend the day anywhere, especially if his royal will to do so has been publicly proclaimed by herald, you may be certain that he will get off early in the morning, and this sudden change will throw everyone's plans into confusion. . . . You may see men running about as though they were mad, urging on the pack-horses, driving chariots one into another, and everything in a state of confusion. . . . His pleasure, if I may dare to say so, is increased by the straits to which his courtiers are put. After wandering about three or four miles in an unknown forest, frequently in the dark, we would consider our prayers answered if we found by chance some mean filthy hut. Often were there fierce quarrels over these hovels, and courtiers fought with drawn swords for a lodging that it would have disgraced pigs to fight for.

As far back as the time of the early Saxon monarchy, steps had already been taken to commute the obligations of the manor to a fixed charge, albeit in kind rather than cash. Thus, to give an instance from the reign of Ina, King of the West Saxons from 689 to 726, 10 hides of land (a hide being sufficient to support a farming family for a year, and in general the equivalent of about 120 acres) were required to pay the rent in food whenever the King chose to visit the royal manor: namely 10 vats of honey, 300 loaves of bread, 12 ambers of Welsh ale, 30 ambers of clear ale, 2 adult cows or 10 wether sheep, 10 geese, 10 hens, 10 cheeses, an amber of butter, 5 salmon, 100 eels and 20 pommels of fodder. (The exact equivalent of an amber is not known, but in the thirteenth century, long after the time of Ina, it was 4 bushels.) Doubtless, the more infrequent the royal visits the better the peasantry were pleased, though perhaps the stewards exacted the tribute regardless. The advantages to the royal commissariat of being able to reckon on stipulated items of provisions rather than having to rely on what they found on arrival are obvious. Nor was it only royal manors which were subjected to royal visitations. The king had a right to demand hospitality from any of his subjects, and it was naturally deemed an honour for any noble house or great ecclesiastical establishment to entertain the king, though for many of them it must at times have been an honour they would gladly have dispensed with. Indeed, as late as the reign of King Henry VII, visits from the King and his court were deliberately used as a device to curb the power of uncomfortably influential subjects. The royal party would stay long enough to ensure that the worried but hapless host was financially crippled for a generation or so.

Throughout the Middle Ages, monarchs juggled with grants and impositions in the endless struggle to cater for the daily needs of their immediate dependants. Historians, recognising the normal impecuniosity of medieval kings, are generally preoccupied with its effects on foreign policy, but the supply of ale and victuals for family, courtiers, retainers and hangers-on must have been an even more pressing and perennial problem.

FARMING THE FORESTS FOR MEAT

The provision of supplies to the catering department of the royal court involved more than growing crops and rearing farm livestock. An important item of meat until quite recent times was one which rarely appears on menus today, namely venison. Medieval hunting was very similar to the game-cropping practised today in most countries where big game exists. A surplus of animals was culled but a sufficient breeding stock was left to maintain the numbers. That is precisely what happens to the red deer of Balmoral today.

The savage forest laws of early times may thus be seen in a different perspective. It was not so much that poachers interfered with the king's sport as that they were robbing him of his dinner, which was naturally an appalling crime.

Medieval hunting was not normally the counterpart of modern stag-hunting. It was not a matter of careering over the countryside on horseback, in the wake of baying hounds. In spite of the term 'chase', as applied to royal forests, the deer were not as a rule chased, though contemporary pictures show that this sometimes happened. The technique was rather that of pheasant-shooting or grouse-shooting. The deer were driven by a curving line of beaters to where the sportsmen, armed with bows, waited in concealment at the woodland edge.

D. Grinnell-Milne, in *The Killing of William Rufus*, has worked out exactly how the hunt was organised on that day when the King met his death in the New Forest. He writes:

> For this sort of hunting there are obviously a few simple but essential requisites. First, and most obvious, the hunters must stand downwind of the quarry. Then there must be a thicket in which the deer are known to be lying, and an open space to which they can be driven by beaters working from upwind. Facing this open space there must be another wood, on the fringe of which the hunters must be able to stand concealed but with an unobstructed line of sight. . . .

He puts the maximum range at which an arrow from a longbow could be expected to hit a moving target at about fifty yards.

The hunt would be under the direction of the Chief Hunter, a court official with the status of a knight. He would delegate the detailed operations to a keeper – a local man who had charge of the 'Walk' which was to be hunted. The keeper would assemble a party of local beaters, forest peasants, and line them up along the far side of the selected wood. Attached to this party there would normally be several huntsmen each with a few hounds on leash. Their duty was to select some good fat bucks from the startled deer and to allow the others, especially the does in calf, to double back and escape.

The Chief Hunter would also organise the shooting party, allocating stands to each huntsman and sending a local man with him, to act as guide and 'bearer'. Each huntsman would, in addition, have a personal attendant, to carry spare arrows and bowstrings and to serve generally as a loader at a modern pheasant shoot.

The entire operation was, in short, a highly professional exercise, designed more to provide the court with meat than the king with sport, though doubtless he derived a good deal of enjoyment from it. As Grinnell-Milne rightly points out,

> compared to stringy beef and tough old mutton, a well-hung haunch of venison was a delicacy more favoured then than now. The skins too had more widespread uses; for mats, hangings and bed coverings, for deerskin jackets and buckskin breeches, for soft heuse and ankle-boots, and thongs for the countless purposes of tying and binding. Even the antlers retained their ancient value as primitive picks and shovels and also to this day, as shafts for knives.

Even as late as the sixteenth century, Queen Mary I dealt with the deer in Windsor Forest in a characteristically ruthless manner, which had the effect of producing a good bag of meat. Shortly after her marriage in July 1554, she had nets four miles long erected through the forest, set huntsmen and hounds to drive the deer into them, and slaughtered them wholesale. It seems that by that date the method was regarded as somewhat unsportsmanlike, although netting deer was commonly practised by poachers.

Nevertheless, it is true to say that for most of history the deer in the royal forests were 'farmed', just as the cultivated land of the manors was farmed, and for the same purpose, namely to supply the royal household with food. This principle of providing meat for the royal household from the royal estates is still followed today.

ROYAL INTEREST IN THE END PRODUCTS OF FARMING

Apart from promulgating laws to preserve a healthy stock of deer, there is little evidence of any medieval kings displaying an interest in agricultural improvement. The more vigorous of them were more inclined to afforest farmland in order to increase the stock of deer, as for instance King Henry II, who extended the Forest of Windsor over most of Surrey. All had numerous manors scattered throughout the country, and sundry tallies of the farm stock on some of them have survived. If, however, any of the medieval kings knew about or displayed interest in agricultural activities, the records have not survived. Their interest was probably confined to the end products. Besides food, one of those products was wool, one of the main sources of prosperity in medieval England and therefore of considerable interest to the king.

THE INTEREST OF MEDIEVAL AND TUDOR MONARCHS IN HEAVY HORSES

Although medieval monarchs took an undoubted interest in the breeding of heavy horses, their motives were military rather than agricultural. Even in early times, however, there was a spin-off for agriculture, chiefly of mares and old war-horses, for armoured knights demanded stalwart young stallions. William FitzStephen, writing in 1171 of the horse sales held every Friday at Smithfield, says, after describing the behaviour and appearance of the 'sumpter horses',

> In another part of the field stand by themselves the goods proper to rustics, implements of husbandry, swine with long flanks, cows with full udders, oxen of bulk immense, and woolly flocks. There stand the mares fit for plough, dray and cart, some big with foal, and others with their young colts closely following.

In the hope of selling them for war-horses, horse-breeders in those days did not castrate their stallions, a practice which must have resulted in the perpetuation of a mediocre type of animal, the progeny of mediocre sires. To counteract this downhill tendency, sundry medieval monarchs imported heavy stallions from Europe. One of the biggest of the early importations was negotiated by King John, who in about 1200 brought over 100 black Flemish stallions, probably ancestors of the Shires.

Other major importations were engineered by King Edward III during his long reign (1327–1377), the initial incentive being the need to replace vast numbers of horses slaughtered at the Battle of Bannockburn. For some years after that major defeat, horses were so scarce in England that their export was forbidden, especially to Scotland. Indeed, from that time onwards until the reign of King Henry VIII, a series of Acts controlling or prohibiting the sale of horses outside the country was passed. In 1532 the penalty for exporting a stallion was fixed at the huge sum of £40. Later in his reign King Henry VIII attempted more positive action by importing stallions to improve the English stock.

King Henry's ideas were logical and well intentioned but were doomed to only partial success. In his time much of England was still unfenced common land, where cattle, sheep, pigs and horses grazed together. Nor was the practice of gelding at all widespread, not having any effect on horses in England until it was introduced in the reign of King Henry VII. So horse-breeding tended to be a haphazard affair. Recognising the difficulties, King Henry had his law apply only to parks which were at least a mile in circumference and from where the domestic livestock of peasants was excluded. A park of one mile in circumference was required to keep 2 brood mares of at least 13 hands; a park of 4 miles in circumference, 4 brood mares, and so on. Wilfully allowing the mares to be served by a stallion of less than fourteen hands was punishable by a fine of 40 shillings. Northumberland, Durham, Cumberland and Westmorland were specifically excluded from the Act, for the shrewd reason that they were too near the border with Scotland, a country with an even greater shortage of good horses.

This was in 1535–36, the provisions of the Act coming into operation in May 1537. In 1540 another and more far-reaching Act banned any stallion of less than fifteen hands from any pastureland where mares were commonly kept. It also decreed that at every Michaelmas there should be a general round-up of all mares and their progeny, for the purpose of eradicating all undesirable stock. Those to be eliminated, by slaughter, included any female 'thought not to be able, nor likely to grow to be able, to bear foals of reasonable stature' and any horse at all, including geldings, thought unlikely to be able to perform 'profitable labours', but exact measurements were not specified.

None of these laws seems to have had much effect. At the local level there was probably insufficient interest to ensure that they were enforced. Somewhat similar though less comprehensive measures, taken by King James V of Scotland at about the same time, met with even less success. Queen Elizabeth I attempted for a few years to maintain her father's policy regarding horses, but her good intentions were smothered by apathy, prejudiced opposition and the pressure of other more urgent matters, and horse-breeding was allowed to lapse into its former state of haphazard inefficiency. The only other monarch until King George III to display any interest in heavy horses was King William III who, soon after coming to the throne, imported a number of heavy black stallions from his native Netherlands.

KING JAMES I AND THE MULBERRY TREES

King James I indulged in one agricultural, or rather horticultural venture, which in fact proved to be abortive. Soon after his accession, he became fascinated by accounts of the flourishing silk factories of France. The secret of silk manufacture had been brought to Europe in the reign of the Roman Emperor Justinian (527–565) and had long been thoroughly established in Mediterranean countries, but it had not spread to Britain. King James saw no reason why this omission should not be rectified.

He therefore sent a royal letter to the Lord Lieutenants of every county, commending the idea to them and urging them to get busy planting mulberry groves, to provide leaves for the silkworms' food. Supplies of trees would shortly be arriving and would be available at six shillings per thousand, delivered to the purchaser. To further the scheme the King licensed a printer, William Stallenge, to publish a book, *Instructions for the planting and increase of Mulberry Trees, breeding of Silkworms and the making of Silk*, which the participants were also expected to buy.

Near his palace at Westminster King James discovered an area of wasteland which he decided would make an admirable mulberry orchard, so he set William Stallenge to work, levelling, enclosing it with a wall and planting it with young trees. Stallenge collected a fee

The mulberry tree planted by King James I at Broadlands in 1607 *Edward Haydon Wood*

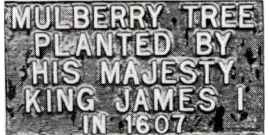

of £935 for the job. The mulberry orchard occupied the site where Buckingham Palace now stands.

King James also enthused with the passion of a missionary about the virtues of his mulberry trees on his journeys around his kingdom. At Broadlands, a venerable mulberry tree still bearing fruit was planted by him on a visit in 1607. It is alleged that when he got back to London he promptly sent a bill for the trees down to the St Barbes, then the owners of Broadlands.

Unfortunately, the ambitious project failed. The reason usually advanced is that the King was badly advised and planted the wrong sort of mulberry – the black mulberry instead of the white. The latter has softer and more succulent leaves and is a native of tropical and Mediterranean climates; it could hardly have succeeded in Britain. Silkworms dislike the hard leaves of the black mulberry. Some writers have doubted whether King James' advisers could have been so ignorant, so perhaps one may suspect ulterior motives.

King Charles I continued to pay an annual stipend for the upkeep of the mulberry gardens and the silkworms. During the Commonwealth the property changed hands several times but seems to have developed as a pleasure resort. John Evelyn describes the gardens as 'the only place of refreshment in town for people of the best quality to be cheated at; Cromwell and his partisans having shut-up and seized on Spring Gardens.' In the years following the Restoration they became one of the most popular pleasure parks in town. Booths selling wine and food, including mulberry tarts, were erected among the trees, offering a modicum of privacy to couples engaged in illicit intrigues. The gardens even had a play written about them (*The Mulberry Garden* by Sir Charles Sedley), but the unlucky and doubtless hungry silkworms, for which they were planted, seem to have faded into oblivion.

The mulberry avenue in the Home Park, Windsor Castle is probably the only one still flourishing in England.

THE ROYAL ESTATES IN THE CHANGING ECONOMY OF THE TUDORS AND STUARTS

Medieval monarchs were constantly short of money. This was largely due to the fact that there were no theoretical limits to their liability. If everything in the realm theoretically belonged to the king, it followed that he was expected to meet all the expenses, including those of the Army and the civil service. As modern millionaires have discovered, it is one thing to possess impressive assets but quite another to transform them into ready cash. In short, throughout most of history the kings of England had a cash flow problem.

Fortunately there were ways out of the difficulty. For example, the appointment of bishops, abbots and other ecclesiastical dignitaries was the prerogative of the king. What could be simpler, in times of financial stress, than to allow a bishopric or abbacy to remain vacant for a few years and to pocket the revenues. King William II, for one, employed these tactics extensively. King Henry VII, that past-master of administrative subtleties, was an expert at concocting ingenious schemes for extracting income, under the guise of fines, 'benevolences' or whatever, from the nobility, while at the same time unloading on them (and especially on the lower ranks of country gentlemen) new responsibilities for the maintenance of law and order. Under King Henry the new Justices of the Peace had plenty of responsibility and considerable authority, but no pay.

Nevertheless the financial problems of royalty persisted. Queen Elizabeth I was glad to receive a share of the piratical booty brought back by Sir Francis Drake from the Spanish Main, while the acute shortage of cash in King Charles I's exchequer was one of the factors which led up to the Civil War.

In the relatively settled state of internal affairs that prevailed under the Tudors, the possession of a landed estate began to be regarded as a most desirable asset. A country house surrounded by broad acres was a tangible investment for new capitalist merchants who had amassed money by trading. A man might retire there and spend the evening of his life enjoying the revenue from farms let out to tenants. After King Henry VIII had eliminated the great ecclesiastical estates the number of lay landowners who operated on such terms was vastly multiplied. The natural consequence was that the demand for land increased, causing rising prices and correspondingly higher rents.

The system provided a strong contrast with the older one of service tenancies, whereby a man or an institution (such as an abbey) held an estate by virtue of certain customary or statutory services. Where an estate had been granted by a monarch in return for services rendered in the past, the annual service subsequently required could be reduced to a token, such as a couple of deer, or a butt of wine, a pair of white gloves or even a single rose. This older system belonged to an age when the political power of a monarch depended largely on the strength and loyalty of his retainers. An estate owner who held valuable property by grace and favour of the king could generally be relied upon to support his monarch in any political upheaval.

The service tenancy system and the cash rental system existed side by side and often interlocked. From the royal point of view, the service system had much to recommend it and was considered to work satisfactorily. However, a man who held an estate under a service tenancy from the king would see no reason why he should not charge his own tenants an economic rent. Thus his income increased while his own rent remained static. The arrangement tended to bind him more closely than ever to his sovereign and patron, who had given and could also take away, but the king himself derived no financial benefit from the rising rents. On the contrary, in times of inflation (and it would be difficult to pinpoint a time when inflation was not prevalent), the king would often have to sell off land to provide ready cash.

It was in response to this dilemma that King James I initiated a scheme for draining part of the Fens. His son, King Charles I, was also quick to grasp the potentialities of the Fenland reclamation scheme of which the Earl of Bedford was the chief investor and in which Vermuyden was employed. King Charles intended to have first share of the new land, and the hostility he provoked from the fenmen threatened with dispossession and the destruction of their traditional way of life was reflected later in the resolute support given by the inhabitants of the Fen country to Cromwell and the Commonwealth.

To that extent King Charles may be said to have interested himself in agriculture. He coveted the revenues which would accrue from the new land. Nevertheless, after the Restoration, the plans in which he had been deeply involved were revived and put into practice, so some small credit may be allowed him for producing the fertile fields of fenland in Cambridgeshire, Lincolnshire and Norfolk.

THE CIVIL LIST

The royal finances were eventually placed on a more solid foundation in the reign of King George III by the institution of the Civil List. Under this arrangement the monarchy surrendered most of the landed estates it still possessed, including Richmond and Windsor Park, but excluding the lands of the Duchies of Cornwall and

Lancaster, in return for an annual cash grant to meet household expenses. The relinquished lands were entrusted to a new authority, the Crown Estates, which administered them on behalf of the Government.

This state of affairs still obtains. It has the disadvantage that when inflation becomes rampant, as in the late 1960s and early 1970s, Parliament has to be asked for an increase in the Civil List, a request that is almost certain to produce a political flurry. Thus in 1970 Prince Philip's entirely justified warning that the monarchy was about to go 'into the red' heralded a violent controversy about the royal finances. In the end, the Civil List was approximately doubled, from £475,000 per year granted at the beginning of Queen Elizabeth II's reign to £980,000. This sum has to cover all the expenses and salaries of the royal household, from the gardeners and footmen to the members of the Royal Family (though excluding the Queen herself, who has decided to forego any payments from the Civil List), as well as providing a reserve against continued inflation. However, it is worth noting that the income of the Crown Estates, on which the bargain was originally based, now exceeds £6 million annually, so the nation is £5 million or so to the good.

THE LANDED GENTRY ON THEIR ESTATES

After the Civil War with fewer outside distractions, the landed gentry set about exploiting and developing their estates. Just as in the Middle Ages landowners tried, by granting charters for fairs and markets, to attract trade to their estates in the hope that a new town would evolve (Devon in particular had numerous examples of this form of private enterprise), so the eighteenth-century landowners fostered the growth of new industrial towns on their estates. Those whose property lacked reserves of coal, iron or some other profitable commodity turned their attention to the improvement of yields from crops and herds. Capitalism was in the ascendant. Vast accumulations of capital were being amassed by the merchants who had become aware that an almost unlimited market for surplus manufactured goods existed overseas. And, contrary to the state of affairs over most of the Continent, no real gap existed between the nobility and the merchant. Owing to the law of primogeniture, the younger sons of noble families had long been accustomed to go into trade, while many a rich merchant purchased a country estate for his retirement, his heirs in due course intermarrying with neighbouring families.

THE COMMON-FIELD SYSTEM OF FARMING

To obtain maximum and efficient production from agriculture,

Affability

32

drastic changes were needed. Although enclosures of land went on throughout the Middle Ages and accelerated a little in the time of the Stuarts, in the early eighteenth century by far the greater part of England was still unenclosed common land. The old three-course system of the feudal economy still persisted – this involved the division of the cultivated land of a manor or parish into three large fields. Each of these was in turn devoted in successive years to two straw crops (usually wheat in the first year and barley in the second) and a fallow. Each large field was subdivided into baulks or strips (which may still be traced in innumerable fields) of approximately one acre. Strips were allocated to the village peasants in accordance with tradition and custom, some being entitled to dozens and others to only two or three. Each tenant had his share of the better soil and of the poorer stuff, with two strips hardly ever adjoining. In many places the strips were reshuffled each year, and in any event, no departure from the conventional rotation was permitted except by general consent.

The two great fields devoted to straw crops were fenced off at Lady Day, to keep out straying livestock. After harvest however, the fences were removed to give animals free access. During the summer, the flocks and herds grazed both the fallow field and the encircling common or waste land, of which most parishes had a considerable quota.

Cattle, sheep and other livestock were privately owned but kept in communal herds and flocks. Sheep were pastured for the summer on the common lands and tended by a village shepherd. Cattle were in the charge of a cowherd, pigs of a swineherd, geese of a goose-girl. An early writer (Thomas Davis, of Longleat, Wiltshire) comments wryly on 'the neglect or partiality' of the shepherd. He also lists the chief disadvantages of common-field husbandry as (a) 'the obligation of ploughing and cropping all kinds of soil alike'; (b) 'the almost total preclusion that a common flock makes to any improvement of the sheep stock'; (c) 'the difficulty, and in some instances the impossibility of raising sufficient hay or green winter food for the flock'; and (d) 'the additional number of horses necessary in occupying lands in detached and dispersed situations'. All of these were cogent arguments for a change in the system.

It is only fair to note that some modern students have objected to the idea that innovations were impossible under the old order. They point out that by the end of the seventeenth century, clovers, sown grasses, some root crops, notably turnips, and even sainfoin were widely cultivated, and they can quote examples of agreements by tenants of common-fields to sow their land to the new crops. However, tenant farmers tended in general to be conservative, and one or two stubborn diehards could wreck intelligent attempts at improvements. M. A. Havinden, writing in 1968 on *Agricultural Progress in Open-Field Oxfordshire* for The British Agricultural History Society, quotes the following instance of progress in farming in 1673:

> It seems that the lord of the manor of East Chadlington, who was a London vintner named Sir William Rollinson, had sown certain of his strips in the open fields, with sainfoin. His tenants agreed to give him right of way to move his sheep and cattle from his enclosed pastures to be tethered on these strips whenever he wished. He, in his turn, agreed to let the tenants' livestock graze his sainfoin from 1st August until the following 20th March, when it was to be fenced off with hurdles and allowed to grow for hay.

It will be noted however, that despite the enlightened attitude of the tenants, it was the landlord, a tradesman from London, who initiated the improvement.

As for livestock, bulls, rams and boars were usually provided at the joint expense of the commoners and turned loose on the commons to mate as they would. Some manors were naturally more progressive than others, investing in a worthwhile sire, while others would settle for the cheapest scrub male available. But the system militated against any consistent breeding policy.

AGRICULTURAL CHANGES IN THE SIXTEENTH AND SEVENTEENTH CENTURIES

A new style of farming was practised in some parts from the middle of the sixteenth century onwards, and by the latter part of the seventeenth century had taken over most of the land then enclosed. It went by the name of 'Up-and-down Husbandry' but would be instantly recognisable to modern farmers by the alternative names of 'ley farming' or 'alternate husbandry'. Briefly, it is a system of extended crop rotation, whereby each field is subjected to a period of years under grass followed by a period of years of arable cropping.

Among the chief factors which led to its development was the introduction of two new crops, clover and turnips. Both had been developed as farm crops in the Netherlands, though turnips had long been cultivated as a garden crop. The credit for introducing clover into the farm rotation is usually accorded to a Surrey landowner, Sir Richard Weston, in about 1645. He also experimented with turnips and flax, though the incorporation of turnips and clover into the celebrated Norfolk four-course system was perfected by Viscount Townshend in the following century.

ENCLOSURES

The stage was now set for a rapid acceleration of the system of enclosures, a process which was not, as some are inclined to think, invented in the eighteenth century but had been going on, on a piecemeal scale, throughout the Middle Ages. As illustrated in the chapter on Windsor, under a weak or preoccupied government as in the reigns of King Henry III and King Edward II, local people, from magnates to squatters, took advantage of the relaxed control to enclose plots of land in the common fields or woodlands. Often enough, the accession of a more energetic monarch resulted in the enclosed land being demanded back again, no doubt to the chagrin of the encroachers, though at other times the king himself would give permission for enclosures.

There were obviously great advantages in the permanent ownership of a block of land in a ring fence instead of the annual tenure of strips of land in the common fields. Under the old system innovations and improvements were impossible unless a whole group of neighbours could be persuaded to co-operate. Furthermore, the old system took no account of the fact that farming is a long-term business which does not necessarily produce dividends in the first year. Good husbandry requires the constant replenishment of the soil to increase fertility. A good farmer using enlightened methods leaves his land in a better condition than he found it, but a system which required him to occupy a different plot of land every year left him little incentive to enrich the plot he was due to hand over to his perhaps feckless neighbour.

Apart from the open fields with their one-acre strips, every manor was a hotch-potch of interlocked holdings, mostly small, and the scene was further complicated by the existence of numerous rights, dues and privileges which often conflicted with one another. The countryside was ripe for a drastic reorganisation of land ownership. The class which now became interested in the necessary changes was precisely that class which had the power to effect them. This it proceeded to do, efficiently and ruthlessly.

At the beginning of the eighteenth century the process was already achieving a little momentum. Between 1702 and 1762, 246 private enclosure Acts, dealing with some 400,000 acres, were passed by Parliament. After the middle of the century the tide rose to flood level. Between 1761 and 1801 Parliament dealt with 2000 Acts, covering well over 3 million acres, mostly in the south, east and midlands. From 1801 to 1844 almost the same number of Acts were concerned with a further $2\frac{1}{2}$ million acres, culminating in the General Enclosure Act of 1845.

The principle on which the enclosure acts operated was theoretically equitable. All the land in the parish was shared out in proportion to the existing holdings and rights. Account was taken of the number of acre strips each household had in the open fields, the extent of enclosures already in existence, and the numbers of cattle, sheep, pigs and geese each householder was entitled to keep on the common. In practice the distribution badly affected the poorer peasants who may have been able to eke out a living on an acre or two supplemented by grazing, pannage, firewood and other perquisites from the common but who now found life impossible on the couple of restricted acres allocated to them. In many instances they had to sell their little holdings to their bigger neighbours in order to find the cash for their share of the legal expenses.

Nevertheless, in spite of the undoubted hardships caused, the enclosures are seen in the perspective of time as being essential to agricultural progress. They provided the necessary framework for the introduction of new crops with a more efficient system of rotation, the improvement of livestock and all the other developments of the agricultural revolution which swiftly followed.

King George III, the enthusiastic 'Farmer George', living through these turbulent times and keeping well abreast of developments, initiated his own enclosure schemes by taking in hand large sections of Windsor Great Park (as described in Chapter 5).

THE AGE OF IMPROVEMENT

To the profound internal peace that characterised the eighteenth century and the enclosures which made progress possible must be added the fact that large numbers of able landowners were forced by political considerations to concentrate their energies on their estates. The reigns of the first two Georges were marked by the ascendancy of the Whig party, to the virtual exclusion from political life of their adversaries, the Tories, to which most of the big landowners belonged. Apart from other considerations, the Tories were widely suspected of favouring the exiled Stuarts, and doubtless many of them, in private gatherings, drank toasts to 'the king over the water'. Yet when in 1715 and 1745 the chance came to reveal where their loyalties lay, very few of them were willing to risk land and estates in a new civil war. Under the new Hanoverian dynasty, with its limited knowledge of and interest in British politics, they found that if they stayed away from Westminster leaving Sir Robert Walpole to manage the affairs of state, they could do much as they liked on their own estates, an arrangement which suited them very well. The diversion of such a reserve of restless intelligence and energy to the economic problems of the countryside soon made its impact.

The great agricultural improvements of the eighteenth and early nineteenth centuries can be grouped under three headings:–

1. New crops and crop rotations, linked, of course, with the reorganisation of land tenure which made them possible;
2. New tools, machines and methods of cultivation;
3. New breeds of livestock, developed by improved methods.

Through the pioneering work of two Norfolk landowners, Viscount Townshend of Rainham and Thomas Coke (later the Earl of Leicester) of Holkham, the celebrated Norfolk rotation, which became supreme in England for the next century or so, was established. Its cropping programme consisted of (a) a crop of turnips, well cultivated and folded with sheep; (b) a crop of barley or oats, undersown with ryegrass and clover; (c) the ryegrass and clover cut for hay and then grazed and (d) a crop of wheat. Much of the success of the system depended on the sheep, which, confined to hurdle pens as they ate off the turnips, greatly enriched the soil with their droppings. On Coke's estate, which only grew poor crops of rye when he took it over and was described by a neighbouring landowner as 'one blade of grass and two rabbits fighting for that', the soil was improved within twenty or thirty years and produced excellent crops of wheat. Coke, in fact, brought various changes to the Norfolk four-course rotation system, such as the inclusion of a two-year grass crop, stocking it with cattle as well as sheep, and the substitution of swedes for turnips, but those were the sort of innovations that an intelligent landowner could happily introduce once the framework was established and the general principles of crop rotation accepted.

The efficient cultivation of the turnip crop was made possible by the invention of the seed-drill by Jethro Tull (in 1701) and by his advocacy of what he called 'Horse-Hoing Husbandry'. Knowing nothing of the nutritional needs of plants, Tull thought that thorough tillage was all that was needed to produce good crops. This could be effected by the use of his horse-hoe, while the adoption of the seed-drill made possible the cultivation of the soil by the horse-hoe while the crop was actually growing. Although he did not foresee it, that was a consideration of the utmost importance in the efficient growing of turnips.

During the eighteenth century, too, improvements were made in the design of ploughs, including the introduction of cast-iron ploughshares, and experiments to produce threshing machines were begun. Many of the river valleys of England were irrigated by a system of beautifully designed water-meadows.

It is in the sphere of livestock improvement that the most celebrated advances were made in the eighteenth century. For centuries, the desirability of controlled breeding had been re-cognised by some breeders, the importation of heavy horse stallions by several monarchs being an example, but their efforts were in general nullified by widespread ignorance and indifference. There was no consistent pursuit, in generation after generation, of selected qualities.

That was the principle introduced by the great livestock improvers of this century. They made up their minds about what they wanted and deliberately worked towards it, ruthlessly culling all animals which fell short of their ideals. The best known advocate of the new technique was Robert Bakewell, a Leicestershire farmer who between about 1760 and 1795 effected an enormous improve-ment in his chosen breeds of cattle and sheep. Taking the all-purpose types of Midland England he produced a breed of Longhorn cattle designed especially to fatten economically on the excellent local pastures. His new Leicester sheep were likewise splendid grazing animals, with light frames, broad bodies, good food conversion rates and luxuriant fleeces. In achieving his targets Bakewell sacrificed other qualities in which he had little interest, such as milk production in his Longhorns, a deficiency which later gave the Shorthorns their chance and led to the eclipse of Bakewell's breed.

Bakewell was not a unique phenomenon. He worked on foundations already laid by some of his neighbours and others of his contemporaries were working along the same lines. There may be some truth in the contention that he owes his fame largely to his friendship with the great agricultural writer Arthur Young, who gave his work maximum publicity. Nevertheless, as his methods became widely known, they were adopted by other breeders all over the country, to the immense benefit of British livestock.

Such was the farming scene when King George III, thwarted in politics, turned his attention from 1760 onwards to matters agricultural.

2

ROYAL FARMING
1760-1837

The enthusiasm of King George III for his farms is perhaps best explained as an outlet for the energies of this remarkable man after his excursion into the realm of politics had been frustrated.

King George III has not been too well served by historians. His periods of insanity, or whatever the malady was, in the latter part of his long reign have been remembered to the exclusion of his undoubted earlier achievements. He is remembered, too, as the King who lost America, and his reputation as 'Farmer George' has served to perpetuate the myth that he was a somewhat bucolic nonentity. The popular misconception is far from the truth. The King was in his prime an able man, who for a time maintained the royal authority and tried to replace government by faction with a more honest form of administration.

Succeeding his grandfather, King George II, to the throne in 1760 at the age of twenty-two, he insisted on playing the then traditional role of the monarch in political and national affairs. For more than twenty years he did so with considerable success, though somewhat hampered by an autocratic approach which impelled him to entrust government to second-rate 'yes-men'. Badly served, he was saddled with much of the responsibility for the loss of the American colonies.

THE ENGLISH COUNTRY GENTLEMAN

Opposite: King George III
Mary Evans Picture Library

To leave political affairs to professional politicians, notably the rising William Pitt, and to busy himself with the farms at Windsor, to

which country residence he had recently moved, must have been a relief to the King, whose interests were always basically those of a country gentleman. All around him his contemporaries were energetically enclosing land, enlarging their estates, engaging in the new arts of livestock breeding, intensive cultivation and mechanical invention, and King George, very much a child of his age, plunged happily in. The Tory landowners were glad to welcome him. After the abortive rebellion of 1745 their lukewarm adherence to the Stuart cause had faded, and they found that they could easily identify with a monarch who, far from being an alien from Hanover, took pride in being, above all else, an English country gentleman.

His mode of living was admirably suited to the role. He had simple tastes and little time for luxury. At Windsor, probably his favourite residence, he lived in a tiny suite (a bedroom, a sitting room and a room for his servant) with a north view, so that it never saw the sun. Carpets, he said, harboured the dust; he preferred a bare floor. Every morning he rose early. After shaving, he immediately set about dealing with his correspondence and then went riding for half-an-hour or an hour. Although undeterred by rain, he had an indoor riding school built in which he could take his morning exercise in very bad weather. Breakfast was taken between eight and nine. For the rest of the day his activities were dictated by the needs of state business, but he liked nothing better than to escape to the fields of his farms.

His diet was frugal. After breakfast he ate nothing until four o'clock in the afternoon, which was then the customary hour for dinner. This was a simple three-course meal, consisting of soup, meat (usually mutton, though roast beef on Sundays) and fruit. Appropriately for a farmer of that generation, he liked turnips as a vegetable. At about seven he would join the Queen for a cup of tea, a beverage which he much preferred to wine. In those days supper was a major meal, often with an elaborate menu and certainly with much heavy drinking. King George had no interest in this. He sometimes contented himself with bread and butter and eggs or fresh fruit, of which he was fond, but he often went without supper. He liked to be in bed by eleven, then up again early next morning, and it is on record that he quoted to one of his courtiers the old country proverb, 'Six hours' sleep for a man, seven for a woman, eight for a fool.'

Like most of his contemporaries he enjoyed hunting, but preferred stags to foxes, because the hunt usually lasted longer. A splendid horseman, he thought nothing of riding ten miles in a downpour of rain and would never, if he could help it, ride in a coach. He also liked walking. Once, when fifty years old, he dismounted on a journey from Windsor to London and walked for twelve miles, just for the pleasure of it. True countrymen of every age, noting his frugality, heartiness, disregard for the English weather, love of hard work and abounding energy, would hail King George as one of themselves.

In yet another respect he displayed a countryman's values. Just as he esteemed prolificness in his cattle and sheep, so he placed a biblical value on human fecundity. When his bride, Princess Charlotte, was on her way to England for the wedding, the eager Prince, liking what he had heard about the young lady, exclaimed, 'I have now but one wish as a public man and that is that He will make her fruitful.' Later in life, on hearing that the wife of one of his courtiers was about to produce her twentieth child, he commented that he rather hoped that 'two will be produced . . . the more the better.' Queen Charlotte, in fact, was as fruitful as he could have wished, for she presented him with fifteen children.

'FARMER GEORGE'

It was not in the nature of this vigorous, well-organised man to let the grass grow under his feet. Contemporary writers have commented that he always wanted things done at once. Following his initial venture of stocking the Little Park at Windsor with cattle and sheep, he embarked on a programme of enclosing land and creating new farms wherever he had the opportunity. His operations were directed mainly at Windsor Great Park, where the scope was immense, but he also established farms at Kew, Richmond and Mortlake.

The Great Park was indeed in a deplorable state, its small arable fields scattered like islands in a waste of bog, marshes, brambles and trees, the terrain broken by meandering valleys, dry hillocks and numerous pits. With characteristic energy and thoroughness King George set about draining the marshes, levelling the little hills and valleys, filling in the pits and replanting trees in orderly array.

Once the initial work had been done, he laid out two model farms. The first and larger of these, Norfolk Farm, consisted of some 1200 acres, of which 400 were arable, 500 sheep-walk and 300 meadows. Its name connected it with the Norfolk system of farming, popularised by Viscount Townshend and much admired by King George. The second, of better soil, comprising 200 acres of arable fields and 100 acres of old pasture, was called Flemish Farm, having been planned as the replica of a model farm in Flanders.

In planning and establishing the farms King George secured the services of an able and much respected agriculturist, Nathaniel Kent of Fulham. In a career devoted at first to the diplomatic service, Kent had spent much time in the Netherlands, where he studied in depth the advanced farming methods practised by the Dutch. On his return to England he was persuaded to abandon politics for husbandry and he settled down to write a book on his studies, which, published in 1775 under the title *Hints to Gentlemen of Landed Property*, quickly ran through several editions. After the formation of the new Board of Agriculture in 1793, he was one of the first experts called upon to undertake a local survey of farming England, the county appointed to him being Norfolk. No one could have been better acquainted with

The King rewarding the industrious haymaker, *an engraving by Pollard*

44

the farming methods of these two most progressive agricultural regions – Norfolk and the Netherlands – and therefore better suited to assist the King with the projects he had in mind.

'RALPH ROBINSON'

Another contemporary with whom George became very friendly was Arthur Young who set out, while in his twenties, to explore farming England and write a series of books on his experiences. This task occupied the rest of his life, which ended in 1820. Having produced several volumes of regional travels, he founded in 1783 a periodical entitled *Annals of Agriculture and Other Useful Arts*, which he published until 1815, when his failing eyesight brought the venture to an end. The *Annals* were among the King's favourite reading matter. He enthusiastically entered into the agricultural controversies of the day, setting out his views in articles published in the *Annals* under the pseudonym 'Ralph Robinson'. To Young, whom he frequently consulted about the affairs of the royal farms, he once confided, 'I consider myself as more obliged to you than to any other man in my dominions.'

See Appendix I for a contribution made by the King to the *Annals of Agriculture* under this pseudonym in 1787, four years before his own experiments in farming got under way at Windsor. The King acquired a reputation for verbosity and saying everything three times, yet under all the prolixity is a lot of common sense. Some of the ideas he advances, such as catch-cropping turnips by sowing broadcast in standing wheat, sound extraordinarily modern – within the past few years some big farms have been doing this from the air – and the whole argument is well reasoned and showing an obvious knowledge of agriculture.

In 1794, Nathaniel Kent made a report to the King, after the enclosure and reclamation of large sections of land, entitled *Plans submitted with great deference to His Majesty on the present state and future improvements of the Great Park at Windsor* (see Appendix II). The plan was evidently entirely approved by His Majesty and Nathaniel Kent was instructed to put it into operation. Notes from his diary over the next year or two reveal that he was extremely busy with the details. His activities even extended to the gardens:–

Settled with the Gardener that two thirds of the Garden Ground now cropped with Table Vegetables shall be in proper change cropped with Potatoes, carrots and the large Drum-headed Cabbage for the use of the Farm Cattle.

And to the Deer Park :—

Accompanied the Keepers into the Park — settled with them the Limits of their respective Walks in the future, fixed the number of Deer-Pens at eight, viz, two to each Walk, and directed Mr Frost to stock them with the usual quantity of Hay. (Royal Library, *Kent's Journal of Windsor Great Park*)

It appears that even before all this activity the park, although neglected, was not entirely derelict. Nathaniel Kent engaged in a stock-taking of all the domestic animals there: these presumably included the five horses and five cows that the gamekeeper was allowed to keep in the forest, and six horses and six cows which were the perquisites of each of the four park keepers. These animals probably roamed free, under the old common system. A similar inventory, taken in October and November 1804, when the new farms were well established and at the peak of production, illustrated the success of the King's farming ventures. The stock-taking exercise was subsequently extended to the King's other farms at Richmond, the Queen's House (the future Buckingham Palace) and Kensington Gardens. Details were also recorded of the labourers working on the farms in the Great Park and of some of their emoluments.

THE KING'S SPANISH MERINOS

One of the King's most noteworthy ventures was the introduction of Merino sheep into Britain. For centuries some of the finest wool in the world had come from the Merino breed, of which Spain had a complete monopoly. Developed on the austere uplands of the Iberian peninsula, the Merinos were small animals with little carcase value, but, as a Dr Parry reported to the Board of Agriculture in 1806, they 'seem absolutely buried in wool'. Most of the ten million or so Merinos estimated to be living in Spain at the beginning of the eighteenth century were 'transhumantes', roaming in vast migratory flocks to the mountains in summer and down to the valleys in winter. These huge flocks belonged not to peasants but to the nobility, both secular and clerical, and, above all to the King. As they thus provided a valuable source of income to the Crown and courtiers, the Merinos became a strictly-guarded monopoly. The penalty for selling a single sheep outside the borders of Spain was death. No wonder the breed was coveted by every nation in Europe and that frequent attempts were made to smuggle out specimens.

The monopoly was eventually broken through gifts made by Spanish kings to fellow monarchs. In 1765 the King of Spain (Charles III) presented his cousin, the Elector of Saxony, with 300 specially selected animals from his royal flock. In 1771 the same King allowed the Empress Maria Theresa of Austria to purchase a selection, and in 1786 he granted an envoy of Louis XVI of France permission to take home a flock of 334 ewes and 2 rams.

In the meantime King George III, pursuing his new-found agricultural interests, went in the early weeks of 1789 to inspect a flock of Wiltshire Horn sheep he had installed on his land at Richmond. During the walk his equerry, Colonel Robert Greville, told him of the Merinos that had now been flourishing in the Electorate of Saxony and doing much good by improving the quality of the native sheep. The magic phrase, 'stock improvement' immediately caught the King's imagination. He wanted some Merinos, too, and he instructed Greville to explore the possibilities of obtaining them.

Greville knew where to start. He called on an old friend Sir Joseph Banks, the explorer/botanist who accompanied Captain Cook on his voyage around the world (1768–1771) and was now President of the Royal Society. At Spring Grove, near Isleworth in Middlesex, Banks had established an experimental flock of sheep which included, besides representatives of several British breeds, a Merino ram given to him by a French colleague. The ram managed to get sixteen Southdown ewes in lamb before it died prematurely.

Banks, already committed to sheep improvement experiments and coveting a replacement Merino ram, responded enthusiastically to Greville's approach, and soon the King, Banks and Greville were meeting at Windsor like three cloak-and-dagger conspirators, discussing methods of getting pure-bred Merinos out of Spain. The direct approach of soliciting a gift from the King of Spain seemed unpromising. Unlike the other royal recipients of Merinos, the English monarch was not closely related to the Spanish royal family. Nor, of course, was the impatient King George prepared to wait until the King of Spain happened to be in a generous mood.

The next alternative was to smuggle the sheep out. The most likely route seemed to be via Portugal. It was learned that each autumn a migratory flock moved from the neighbourhood of Bilbao across Spain to their winter quarters near the border with southern Portugal; also that Spanish shepherds were allowed to keep a certain number of sheep for themselves as a bonus for a successful lambing season. It was, of course, strictly forbidden to export them, but money can find a way. Plans were made to secure a small number of animals by this route.

The King was delighted with the news but was, characteristically, not content with the small consignment bargained for:–

'The King is much pleased', he wrote, 'that two Rams and four Ewes are sent for and should wish the Commission could be extended to twenty Ewes and ten Rams. . . .

'The King trusts this number from Bilbao will not stop the attempts of getting some through France as well as others through Portugal.'

All this was happening in 1787, but King George had to wait impatiently until March 1788 until the sheep arrived, and then there were only two ewes and a ram. They were taken to his farm at Kew, where the King saw them for the first time on 4 April, a date which he noted as the birthday of his Spanish flock. Throughout the following summer, a further conspiracy was hatched to obtain more Merinos via Portugal, this time from Andalusian flocks, but the Spanish agents did not prove reliable and no sheep arrived. In the summer of 1789, however, another ram and three ewes were successfully smuggled across the border of Portugal and shipped to England where they joined the others at Kew. Several other small consignments arrived along the now established contraband routes that year and more in the following years. By the time the traffic eventually ceased in 1792 the King had clandestinely acquired no fewer than seventy-three Merino ewes and fourteen rams via Lisbon.

In 1791 an event occurred which must have made him wonder whether all the intrigue and secrecy were worthwhile. The King of Spain himself granted permission for the export of four rams and thirty-six ewes from one of the best flocks in the country as a present for King George. The ship bearing the precious consignment arrived at Southampton on 14 October 1791, where an over-conscientious customs officer detained them and the ship for four weeks before the necessary formalities were completed. The sheep then travelled on hoof from Southampton to Windsor, taking five days on the journey.

By the end of the episode, the King's flock of Merinos at Kew had reached the total of 100.

Installing them on the King's farms proved, however, to be only the beginning of the venture. As time passed it became evident that the animals were not being well cared for. The serious illness of the King in 1788–89 was a contributory reason or excuse for the neglect. Mr Ramsey Robinson, superintendent of His Majesty's farms and gardens and therefore a very busy man, delegated the responsibility for the Merinos to 'Goddard the Shepherd', who not only treated them like the other sheep under his care but apparently ran the lot as a mixed flock. In consequence some doubt arose that certain progeny might not be pure but had a Wiltshire Horn or a Gloucester Nott sire.

Sir Joseph Banks, when he became aware of what was happening, went down to the farms and did his best to sort things out. For the succeeding years he worked in close co-operation with the King, now restored to health. However, instructions still had to go through Ramsey Robinson, who passed them on to his cousin, John Robinson, who was in charge of the parks and gardens at Windsor castle and who delegated responsibility to the same feckless shepherd. Sir Joseph Banks, attending the ram shearing on 18 June 1794, reported:

> The washing has been abominably ill done. I never saw anything so worthy of blame in that way.
>
> The sheep have been neglected in a very great degree they are abominably full of Ticks and much struck with the Fly. The King ordered them to be washed, sensible I hope of the necessity of ordering it sooner than was intended by the Shepherd.

The winter of 1796–97 was marked by excessive frosts, the record low temperature of 16°F being recorded in December, while the following spring was late and chilly. By shearing time in 1797, it was established that 15 out of the 37 rams stationed at Windsor had died, and 31 out of 121 ewes at Kew. In addition the lambing season was poor, with much mortality. Sir Joseph Banks urgently advised the King to remove the flock from the incompetent staff at Windsor, who had failed to appreciate that the Spanish sheep required different treatment from the traditional management of the English breeds and who tended to regard them as a bit of a nuisance. Scouting around, he found suitable alternative quarters at Oatlands Park, near Wey-bridge, the property of the Duke of York. There the Duke was running a non-breeding flock of about 300 sheep on a sheep-walk of 200–300 acres. He agreed to fence off a section of it for some of the Merinos and to provide a barn for hay storage and for winter occupation during bad weather. Most important of all, a shepherd was appointed to take full charge of the flock.

On the sandy slopes of Oatlands the Merinos flourished. Only the ewe flock had been transferred, however; the ram flock stayed at Windsor and continued to suffer. Banks, visiting Windsor in the summer of 1801, found 'them all lame and much fallen away. Their feet seemed to have been wholly neglected and the sheep themselves most certainly in a condition very disgraceful to the King's Farming, and I was the more hurt because I came immediately from Oatlands where out of 160 ewes and lambs not even one was lame.'

Towards the end of 1802, by a private arrangement between the King and the Duke of York, whose motive is not known, the ewe flock had to be removed from Oatlands Park. Their new home was Kew Gardens, from which all other sheep were removed prior to their arrival. And there they became the charge of at least a conscientious shepherd, Richard Stanford, who looked after them for the next ten years. Anyone who imagines that form-filling is a twentieth-century invention will be surprised to learn that Stanford's duties included completing a monthly return of the flock, on 'Blank papers' provided by Sir Joseph Banks, who continued to keep a watchful eye on the Spanish sheep.

Over the next few years he needed to. After relatively trouble-free years in 1803 and 1804 the flock ran into serious health problems in the winter of 1804–05. That autumn, thirty-three ram lambs had been pastured on a riverside meadow at Richmond, and before spring came fourteen were dead. The state of knowledge of animal husbandry at that time is illustrated by the catalogue of disorders to which this epidemic and other mortality is attributed. It includes 'red water', 'white waters', 'black scour', 'broken belly', 'mad staggers', 'worms in the liglets', 'flounder in the liver', 'murrin', 'dropsy', 'gripes', 'goggles', 'faggs', and the better authenticated footrot and scab. Sir Joseph Banks, puzzled by the fact that 'the young Rams only are sick while the Ewes and the old Rams are quite well', concluded eventually that the illness was connected with the young rams being pastured on grassland that was flooded by the river every spring. His description of the symptoms enables us to identify the ailment as a heavy infestation of lung worm.

When the infestation flared up again in the following autumn

Banks sent two of the worst cases to a well-known veterinary surgeon, William Moorcroft, practising in Oxford Street. Thanks to the great care taken, they survived but Mr Moorcroft rightly diagnosed that the young rams ought to be moved to drier pastures. Accordingly the entire ram flock, numbering forty-two, was moved to the grounds of the Queen's House, now Buckingham Palace. There they spent much of the winter and returned in reasonably good health to Kew in March.

Other ills that afflicted the Merinos at that period included scab, the cause of many complaints from purchasers when the flock began to have surplus animals for sale. It is obvious that the breed did not take too kindly to England's damp, chilly climate and that the shepherds, accustomed to the hardier English breeds, had little patience with these finicky animals. To add to the tribulations of the Spanish sheep, in March 1809 a mad dog got loose among the flock at Kew and caused about twenty casualties.

In the autumn of 1808 the King's Merinos received a welcome reinforcement from Spain, a country in complete turmoil. As a reaction against the occupation of their country by Napoleon's armies, the Spaniards were fighting a guerilla war, in co-operation with Sir Arthur Wellesley in Portugal. Warfare spread over most of the countryside which the sheep normally traversed in their autumn migration, and such animals as could be rescued from the marauding troops were diverted to the lowland pastures of Asturias and Galicia. At that point about 2000 of the best were selected and shipped to England, as a present from the government (Junta) of Asturias to King George. Some were distributed to Ministers of the Crown but 1581 went to join the royal flock at Richmond, Kew and Windsor, where the pastures became decidedly crowded.

In the following year, a further consignment of Merinos from one of the best Spanish flocks escaped from the French and were shipped from Cadiz as a present for the King of England, this time from the Junta of all Spain. The actual numbers are uncertain but the total was probably about 1800. Other smaller shipments followed, though the record from those confused times is unreliable. H. B. Carter, in *His Majesty's Spanish Flock*, estimates that the likely total of sheep exported to England from Spain during the Peninsular War was about 15,000, of which nearly 4000 were gifts to King George III.

The stage now seemed set for effective use to be made of this 'treasure', as contemporary writers rightly termed it, which had fallen into English hands. The far-sighted Sir Joseph Banks had a clear idea of what should be done. Throughout the war he had kept in touch with French colleagues and was aware of how the French were exploiting their share of Merinos. Imperial studs had been established which by 1809 were turning out some 1200 pure-bred Merino rams each year. These were scientifically used to upgrade the native French breeds, so that at the same date France had 5,000,000 sheep improved by Merino crossing (though the total included 800,000 imported – or looted – from Spain). A similar breeding programme, though of course on a smaller scale to start with, was what Sir Joseph visualised.

He worked out a scheme with his customary precision. A Merino Department was to be created as a government office, under the Committee of the Privy Council for Trade. It was to have an office with two rooms in the Treasury Chambers at Whitehall and was to be under the control of a superintendent to be appointed with a salary of £400 a year. Flocks of fifty ewes and ten rams each were to be offered to the best bidders and were to be controlled by managers 'chosen among Country Gentlemen skilled in Agriculture and desirous of engaging in this Patriotic pursuit.'

This excellent programme never got off the ground. It seems to have encountered both apathy and resistance in government circles, probably because of its similarity to the highly successful scheme operating in France (from which at that period nothing good could come). The immediate snag, however, was that the Merino sheep to be distributed were those that had recently arrived from Spain and were now the property of King George III. And the King could not give permission for the disposal because he was suffering one of the periods of insanity that clouded his later years.

By this time the King was not the only Merino breeder in England. The process of dispersal of the royal flock began as early as 1791 when King George decided to present a dozen rams to worthy recipients, who included Sir Joseph Banks, Arthur Young, the Society for the Improvement of British Wool (Edinburgh), and the Duke of Newcastle. While the gift was appreciated in some quarters it seems to have been somewhat embarrassing in others, for, apart from a natural English resistance to new ideas, especially those emanating from foreign parts, the poor performance of the sheep at Windsor, caused largely by mismanagement, was getting them a bad name.

Merinos were bred for their wool. They were small sheep and

never had much of a reputation for meat. By the spring of 1792 a few surplus ewes were available for slaughter and one was dressed and served for the royal dinner. Thereafter the King conscientiously ate Spanish mutton whenever it was available until, after three years, he could stand no more of it and 'desired to have no more Spanish mutton at his table'. What was less understandable was the resistance of wool merchants to buying his wool.

In the first years of the Windsor flock the ineffable Goddard, the shepherd, not only failed to wash the fleeces properly but mixed them with those of the English breeds. In 1795 the wool clips for the previous three years were despatched to some prominent wool merchants to have them assessed and valued. Five years later the King was still awaiting their report!

Faced with procrastination and lack of interest, King George, advised by Sir Joseph Banks, decided to have some of his fleeces processed and made into cloth at his own expense. This he continued to do for several years, with gratifying results. The cloth was good, and, contrary to the gloomy forecasts of the manufacturers, it wore well. In the end quality triumphed, and by 1799 home-produced Merino wool was making up to 5s. 9d. per pound, or nearly three times as much as ordinary Southdown wool.

Far from having to give away his surplus rams to sometimes reluctant recipients, (there were forty-three of them between 1791 and 1799), a procedure of which he never really approved, maintaining that people attached more value to what they paid for, the King was now able to sell as many as he had available. The going price at the turn of the century was five guineas for a ram and two guineas for a ewe. Within the next few years the breed became well distributed throughout the country, and Merinos were a frequent item in sales. In 1804, Banks, reporting on a fine young ram which was the progeny of a ewe purchased from the royal flock two years earlier by a Mr George Tollet of Tewkesbury, wrote:–

For this animal Mr Tollet has refused an offer of 200 guineas, or of 100 guineas for the next season's use of him; he also refused 30 guineas each for the sire and the dam, though old and infirm, being unwilling to part with animals that had belonged to the Royal Flock; he however sold their Ram Lamb of the last year (1803) for 30 guineas, and thus made some progress in ascertaining the value of this important breed.

These facts, which prove an amelioration in the King's Merino Sheep, are fully confirmed by the improved shape and weight of His Majesty's shearling rams for the present year (1804), and give a justifiable hope that by a due selection of Rams and Ewes, and a correct judgment in matching them, Merino Sheep will in time be produced with carcases perfectly fashionable and wool as perfectly fine. . . .

Mr Tollet thus revealed himself as a knowledgeable protagonist of the principles of livestock improvement, well appreciated by his sovereign but not yet grasped by the rank-and-file farmers.

It was in August 1804 that the first public sale of Merino sheep from the royal flock was held at Kew, in a barn near the Pagoda. Forty-four sheep, thirty of them rams and fourteen ewes, were sold, the rams averaging £19 14s., the ewes £8 15s. 6d. The top price was £44 2s. for a ram. There were eighteen purchasers, one of them buying stock for transport to Botany Bay, Australia. This was Captain John MacArthur who managed to get six of the Spanish sheep safely around the world and landed at Sydney in July 1805. Here the Merino found its eldorado. The limitless plains of Australia proved an ideal habitat and the climate promoted the production of a fine wool clip. It is not unreasonable to trace the origins of the immense Australian sheep industry back to King George III's little flock at Kew and to his pertinacity in persisting with his venture in the face of all discouragement and obstacles.

The August sale of rams and ewes from the royal flock was repeated in succeeding years up to and including 1810. Although the breed was by now sufficiently widely distributed and well known (albeit superficially) to attract some criticism, the reputation of the King's sheep remained high and the last sale was the most successful of all. Thirty-seven rams averaged £65 6s. 8d.; 70 ewes, £30 10s. 10d. Preparations began for the 1811 sale but were abandoned because of the King's now hopeless illness.

At a big dispersal sale of His Majesty's flock in March or April 1813, 2781 sheep were advertised, though observers who attended the sale stated that only about 1700 animals were brought forward. The sheep were then in a shocking condition, partly, it was alleged, because of neglect by the shepherds but partly, probably, because their winter pastures had been overcrowded. It was said that at Kew during that winter 'a man was constantly employed in wheeling away the dead carcases, to the number of 100 a day.'

Not all the Merinos were disposed of on that sad occasion. A nucleus flock was retained and flourished modestly until the death of the King in 1820, by which date it had indeed increased to between 100 and 150 breeding ewes. King George IV, in spite of his father's early and ill-advised efforts to interest him in agriculture, regarded his farming legacy with indifference. The farms were retained but presumably the flock was disposed of.

King George III's work, however, had been well done. In the very year (1811) when his illness had to be accepted as incurable and when the Regency was instituted, a group of farmers got together to form an Anglo-Merino Society. H. B. Carter, the historian of *His Majesty's Spanish Flock* aptly summarises the royal achievement:

> The inauguration of the Merino Society at the Freemason's Tavern in Great Queen Street on 4 March 1811, will serve no less to mark the day when in a sense the Royal task was done and the burden of the future was finally shouldered by the men who in one way or another would successfully foster the central idea of His Majesty's Spanish flock and conserve the germ-plasm of the stock which composed it.

Although the Society had a short life it filled a few crucial years and enabled the maintenance of a stock of Merinos which would in due course populate the new lands of the Antipodes. To claim that the scores of millions of Merinos as well as the Corriedales and Polwarths that today constitute a large portion of the wealth of Australia, New Zealand and South Africa are there because of the vision and perseverance of 'Farmer George' is not an exaggeration. The fact that the breed eventually failed to make the grade in Britain itself was due to a combination of circumstances which are still a matter of some controversy but have nothing to do with the far-sighted King.

THE KING'S OTHER STOCK

As well as Merinos the King kept large numbers of other sheep, as the chronicles of the Merinos indicate. At Kew, when the early consignments of Merinos arrived, a considerable flock of Wiltshire Horns together with some Gloucester Notts were grazing there. The riverside pastures at Richmond, where the young Spanish rams contracted such a heavy infestation of lung worm in 1804–5, were shared by some Wiltshire rams and some Merino Ryeland ram lambs. Flemish Farm, Windsor, was stocked with 200 sheep of the Cotswold breed, Norfolk Farm with 400 Ryelands which also grazed the heath and bracken land of Windsor Forest, so similar to much of their native Herefordshire. The purpose, after all, of introducing the Merinos was to cross them with British breeds in order to combine the fine wool of the Spanish sheep with the excellent mutton-producing qualities of the latter, and the Wiltshires (or the Southdowns partly derived from them) and the Ryelands seemed the most promising native breeds for crossing.

The background to the pastures at Kew and Richmond is sketched in by William James and Jacob Malcolm who prepared a *General View of the Agriculture of the County of Surrey* for the Board of Agriculture in 1794. Their description, though somewhat fulsome, is doubtless basically accurate:—

> Everything that so conspiciously marks the leading trials of the august Personage for whose recreation and amusement this concern is undertaken and here eminently displayed; the most scientific and practical agriculturalists are employed; the most improved implements are used; and everything, both as to stock and to implements, that the ingenuity of man can suggest, will here find a fair and impartial trial.

Prominent among agricultural controversies in the King's farming period was the oxen versus horses as draught animals issue. Arthur Young's reports for the Board of Agriculture are filled with the arguments advanced for and against oxen by leading farmers whom he visited, especially in the eastern counties. King George III entered the field with characteristic zest, strongly favouring oxen. On Norfolk and Flemish farms he normally kept 200 oxen for farm work, fattening them off for beef when their working days were done. But he did use some farm horses as well.

THE KING'S FARMS FAIL TO PAY

In all his many-sided farming enterprises one factor seems to have eluded King George and that was profit. The situation is comprehensively summed up by a report on the Windsor Farms, submitted by a worried Nathaniel Kent at Michaelmas 1797, when all the projected improvements had been completed.

From that time as it was His Majesty's pleasure to fix Mr Snart as check clerk upon the whole, the produce and expense of each park has been kept distinct.

The large tract of barren land that has been brought into cultivation, the number of useful experiments that have been made, and the establishment of so many oxen upon so large a scale of agricultural labour, are truly flattering, are highly deserving imitation and must have a beneficial tendency, to say nothing of their still greater importance in the presumption that they may in some measure have contributed to His Majesty's Amusement and Health which is of all things the most valuable to the community.

Still there is one wanting and that is to make them yield *a fair return of profit* and when this can be affected it will be impossible to describe the satisfaction I shall feel.

His Majesty will observe that the first point towards ascertaining the true state of the respective returns of these farms was to set a fair annual value upon each of them, which I have done. And the next thing, to charge all expenses of labour and things purchased on one side and every article of produce and sale on the other. And I must confess myself surprised and mortified that instead of a surplus each farm should be minus. It is true that last year was very unfavourable to grazing, and great loss was sustained by the flock, which it is to be hoped will not be the case in the future. But I cannot see any reason why the rents cannot be made or at least nearly so. Mr Frost is so sanguine about the Flemish Farm that he seems to think there will very soon be more than the rent produced upon it, and Milk seems to think that at least £500 a year ought to be at all events returned from the Myrtle Farm, and does not doubt of bringing it about. These are their opinions, expressed to me, but though I know that the rents should be returned and would be returned if the responsibility could be impressed upon the minds of all the different superintendents so that they might act with the same zeal as a farmer does for his own immediate interest, yet I doubt whether the result will ever be equal to what they seem confident it will. Suffice that on my part nothing shall be wanting to point out from time to time what is proper to be done to promote good and profitable husbandry and to avoid error. And by the continuance of Mr Snart's check, His Majesty will be shown how things go on and how they turn out every year. But his Majesty will I trust look no further to me for responsibility, as the greatest part of it necessarily must and ought to attach to those concerned in minutiae and executive part of the business, such as the purchase and management of the cattle, the keeping down of the expense of labour and incidental expenses, and due attention to seasons in cropping, on which the greater part of the profits of farming depend.' (Royal Library, *Kent's Journal of Windsor Great Park*)

Whether the lack of profit worried the King or whether it was ever corrected is not known, but the reasons put forward by Kent to account for it will be familiar to every farmer, and, for that matter, to every businessman. In this instance, too many intermediaries seem to have been interposed between the King and the men, like Goddard the shepherd, who eventually had to do the work. The King failed, and perhaps there was no way in which he could have succeeded, to transmit his enthusiasm to the lower echelons.

QUEEN CHARLOTTE

It is only right to mention that in his farming activities the King at least had the tacit support of his wife, Queen Charlotte. Although she did not approve of or participate in his countryman's custom of early rising, she shared his interests to the extent of being exceedingly interested in botany and gardening.

When residing at the Queen's House (Buckingham Palace) in their early married days, the Queen planted a flower garden where she grew carnations, while the King ran cows and sheep in an adjacent meadow. In another paddock a zebra and an elephant, gifts to Their Majesties, were pastured and were much admired by the London public.

Their country house in the early years was Richmond Lodge, which for Queen Charlotte had the advantage of being next door to a small botanic garden, founded in 1759. Nearby, too, was the White House, occupied by the Dowager Princess of Wales, the King's mother, who was also interested in horticulture and had created her own botanic garden. In 1781 the Queen acquired another residence in the vicinity, the Dutch house, with 69 acres of land, the whole being eventually merged into the Royal Botanic Gardens in the reign of Queen Victoria.

As the years passed, King George became more and more attached to Windsor, the scene of his main agricultural enterprises. The complaisant Queen uncomplainingly took up residence in the draughty, chilly castle but sought compensation in a new garden. Her choice fell on Frogmore, about half-a-mile south-east of the Castle, where she found a small house with an old neglected kitchen garden. The lease was purchased for her in 1790, about the time when King George was preparing schemes for the Great Park, and she immediately set about erecting greenhouses and planning flower-beds. 'Her little Paradise,' she called it. 'I am . . . of opinion that the best thing is to enjoy what I have and not to make myself uneasy about things in which no human power can direct,' she phil-osophized. So at Frogmore she and her daughters settled down to grow flowers (brought to her from all parts of the world) and study botany. In 1806 it was Queen Charlotte who acquired Shaw Farm for the Crown, which linked Frogmore with the Great Park.

THE FATE OF THE FARMS

For further accounts of the Windsor farms the reader is asked to turn to the Chapters on Windsor (Chapter 5) and the Prince Consort (Chapter 4).

On these farms the King was ostensibly the tenant, though he apparently paid no rent. During the nine or ten years of King George III's last illness the farms continued to be run by the King's manager, though it seems that for some time, probably through lack of interest on the part of anyone else, he farmed them for his own profit. On his accession King George IV took them back into his possession, doubtless to enjoy the revenues, for there is no record of his taking any practical interest in the farming activities. Managers continued to be responsible for the properties for the next thirty years, though evidently farming them at a fairly low level, until the Prince Consort took them in hand and raised them once again to the status of model farms.

KING GEORGE IV

A cursory glance at the reigns of King George IV and King William IV reveals that neither of them had any interest in agriculture. This was certainly true of King George IV, whose early experiences on his father's farms were enough to put him off farming for life. The regime that King George III set for the royal princes was, to our eyes, oppressively strict. Rising at half-past seven, the boys had to be in their classroom by eight and thereafter were kept at their studies until eight in the evening – a twelve-hour day broken only by brief intervals for meals and some longer ones for carefully supervised exercise. Even after supper they were given books to read – and they later had to give an account to their tutor of what they had read. They were allowed one hour off every other day for recreation. On Sundays they attended church and were given religious instruction. The King was also eager that they should develop a liking for farming and country life and so when they were old enough he created a little model farm for them at Kew. Here they learned to plough and sow, to harvest the corn by reap-hook or scythe, to grind the grain into flour and to make the flour into bread. Not surprisingly, they rebelled as soon as they were able.

Nevertheless, when King George IV eventually became King he took back the Windsor farms, which had passed into the hands of tenants, and farmed them on his own account. Or rather, they were farmed for him by a manager, for there is no record that he ever took much interest in them, beyond an occasional visit. On the other hand, he had plenty of other problems to cope with. Apart from the affairs of his private life, the end of the Napoleonic Wars and the transition to peacetime brought a host of economic troubles, arising from falling prices. Distress and discontent were widespread, and a series of bad harvests made things worse. King George probably valued the farms because they provided him with the background status of an English country gentleman.

KING WILLIAM IV

King William, however, *was* an English country gentleman. The third son of King George III, he was sent at the age of fourteen to join the Navy as a midshipman. After ten undistinguished years in that service, he returned to civilian life in 1789 as the Duke of Clarence. Biographers seem to consider that at that stage he would have made a competent captain but a disastrous admiral, and a royal duke could hardly be expected to remain a mere captain all his life.

William, abetted by his libertine elder brothers, sowed a liberal crop of wild oats in his youth. Like all the Hanoverians he was an ardent womaniser, drifting from one romantic affair to another, until in 1790 he met Mrs Jordan, an actress whose maiden name was Dorothy Bland. There never was a Mr Jordan, the name having been taken for convenience and respectability when in her youth she had found herself pregnant. Within a year the pair, passionately in love, had set up house together. There they lived in almost idyllic domestic bliss for the next twenty years, producing ten children and with their liaison generally accepted by both Court and country.

With two older brothers between himself and the throne, William found himself in a kind of limbo, having the status of a prince without the income or position to go with it. Mrs Jordan continued her career as an actress, even through her numerous pregnancies, not only because she enjoyed it but also because the money she earned was invaluable to the family finances. It was with some relief and satisfaction that William learned, when in 1797 he was appointed Ranger of Bushy Park near Hampton Court, that the post carried with it the use of Bushy House. The family moved in forthwith and lived there happily and unobtrusively for many years.

Attached to Bushy House was a home farm, in which William immediately became interested. Before long he was engrossed in agricultural affairs.

'As a farmer,' he wrote, 'I am well aware of the presence of the master; but at this time of year, when the harvest is going on, he ought not to be absent a minute . . . I never am out of the field the whole day.'

Congratulating an old Naval friend he said, 'I am glad to find you turned farmer. I believe officers of the navy make the best, as they are always active.'

The Prince married Princess Adelaide of Saxe-Meiningen in July 1818, some two years after the death of Mrs Jordan. He continued to live at Bushy House, though paying frequent visits to Hanover. Many of his letters written from Hanover and other German towns over the next eight years refer to affairs on the farm at Bushy, which was evidently much in his thoughts.

For example, on 14 October 1818, writing from Hanover to his steward J. W. Daniell, he returned the weekly accounts for the farm and garden that had been sent to him, expressed his satisfaction with his farm manager, Coates, who was to keep the stock within the farm enclosures, 'except during enclosures being laid up for hay,' and gave instructions about the sale of stock and the number of cart-horses to be retained. (RA Add. 44/31)

Five days later a letter expressed concern about finance (a constant source of anxiety to William). He wanted to economise at Bushy without decreasing the arable and pasture acreage. Daniell was to sell off all the wether sheep and to keep only the breeding flock. Could the number of horses be reduced if threshing were done by hand? Everything on the farm was to be kept in good repair but no alterations were to be made.

Further instructions followed thick and fast. The unlucky Daniell must have wondered whether it might not have been better to have his master fussing about at his elbow, where at least he could tactfully keep him on the right course, rather than trying to run the farm from Germany. On 14 November Daniell was told to sell the pigs; on the 16th the Prince informed Daniell how to manage the cows and instructed him to increase the breeding flock of ewes (a bit late in the season!), to keep up the fences and to plant more clumps of willows. By 16 January 1819 he was wondering whether it might not be more advantageous to give up arable farming and devote the whole farm to grass, 'but my mind is by no means made up, and I love the *plough*. . . .' Throughout his reign, the chief preoccupation of this impecunious Prince was finance, burdened as he was by debts and the need to rear, educate and launch into the world his ten children. On 12 December 1818, he hoped to be able to pay off all outstanding bills on the farm some time the following year; on 18 March 1819, he expressed satisfaction that the farm bills were less than usual. In early August he gave orders that the servants were to have only skimmed milk in future, but at the end of the month he was delighted that the harvest was abundant. Thus he vacillated, not quite sure of the course he should pursue but yet undoubtedly thoroughly interested.

Several illuminating insights into contemporary farming practices emerge from his letters. In June 1822, for instance, he gave instructions about the weekly killing of 'stall-fed deer' and the disposal of the venison. Fattening deer in stalls is no longer an agricultural enterprise, though there seems no reason why it should not be. A discourse on the relative merits of the flail and the threshing machine is a reminder that the latter was just being introduced, an innovation which was to lead to widespread riots in 1830, as farm labourers sensed a threat to their winter livelihood. The Prince noted Coates' calculation that 'The *Flail* is decidedly less expensive than the *machine*; but I have my doubts. . . .' The letters provide a useful commentary on the current weather. They confirm records that the summers 1818 to 1820 and 1825 to 1826 were hot and dry. The Prince remarked that the quality of the hay crop would have to compensate for the lack of quantity but expressed some anxiety about the turnips. He then delivered the accurate aphorism, 'However, a dry hot summer in the long run does our *Island* good.' (RA Add. 44/110)

From his accession in 1830 to his death in 1837 King William found ample occupation in the affairs of state, to the exclusion of his personal agrarian interests. He treated them with the same thoroughness, conscientiousness and attention to detail that he had evinced in dealing with the management of his farm. No one could call him brilliant but he was honest, sensible, forthright and sensitive to the moods of the nation. Compared with the disreputable King George IV he was a paragon, and he restored to the monarchy much of the popularity it had lost. To become King at last was an experience that obviously delighted him, but in retrospect he would probably have admitted that his happiest days were those middle years spent pottering around the farm at Bushy.

3

THE PRINCE CONSORT

Had King George III and the Prince Consort had the opportunity to meet, it is doubtful that they would have established an immediate rapport. King George, the hearty, down-to-earth extrovert, might well have looked askance at the artistic, introspective Albert. But closer acquaintance would have enabled them to find many common bonds. Both had the quality of quiet persistence in the face of obstacles and discouragement; both had to endure initial unpopularity which later changed to respect and even affection; and both had an abiding love for farming. King George would in particular have been eager to see what Albert was doing with his beloved farms at Windsor.

In reclaiming a large segment of Windsor Great Park in order to create Norfolk Farm, King George had been acting as a tenant of the Crown Estates, to which Government-appointed body the Park had been relinquished in exchange for a Civil List, in the settlement of 1760. His bailiff at Norfolk Farm during his years of active farming was a Mr Hatch. In the twilight years of the King's insanity, from 1810 onwards, it appears that Mr Hatch continued to farm this land as tenant on his own account. On the accession of King George IV the farm reverted to royal occupation, with a Mr Ingall as bailiff. The arrangement continued under King William IV, though neither of these two monarchs took much interest in the Windsor farms. King William IV's manager was a Mr Kendall, who continued in the post for the first years of Queen Victoria's reign.

Norfolk Farm being the royal farm that was farthest from Windsor there was a move early in Victoria's reign to take it out of cultivation, and this operation had already begun when, in 1840, the Queen married Prince Albert, who soon put a stop to it. The Prince Consort was a keen and enlightened farmer, an interest which served him well in his determination to avoid becoming embroiled in political affairs. Farming served as an escape valve for his abounding energies. Apart from an innate love for things rural and agricultural, he appreciated more clearly than most of his contemporaries that the mechanical revolution that had transformed industrial Britain would assuredly do the same for agriculture.

'Science and mechanical improvements have in these days changed the mere practice of cultivating the soil into an industrial pursuit requiring capital, machinery and industry, and skill and perseverance in the struggle of competition,' he told a farmers' meeting at York in 1845. 'This is another great change, but we must consider it a great progress, as it demands higher efforts and higher intelligence.'

In the year of his marriage he joined the Smithfield Club and exhibited cattle and pigs at its 1843 Christmas Show, a practice which he henceforth observed for the rest of his life. Queen Victoria had already become patron of the newly-formed Agricultural Society of England, to which in 1840 she granted a charter entitling the use of the prefix 'Royal'. Two years later the Prince became a Life Governor of the Society, an office in which he was considerably more than a mere figurehead, for he made a point of attending, whenever possible, not only shows and dinners but business meetings, at which he spoke frequently and with the authority that comes only from a thorough knowledge of the subject. In 1861 he ultimately accepted the Presidency of the Association.

Sir Walter Gilbey, writing in 1911, comments:

> It was his conviction of the importance of the part that machinery was to play in the agriculture of the future that led him to devote the attention he did to this department of the Society's shows. . . . Any promising novelty or invention in the shape of agricultural machinery arrested his attention at once, and if he saw reason to believe that it would prove useful, the maker was sure to receive commands to send it to one or another of the royal farms for practical trial.

In another place he asserts that 'an account of the work done on the royal farms during the twenty years of the Prince Consort's control would be a history of the agricultural improvements of all the soils in England during that period.'

A map of the Windsor estates

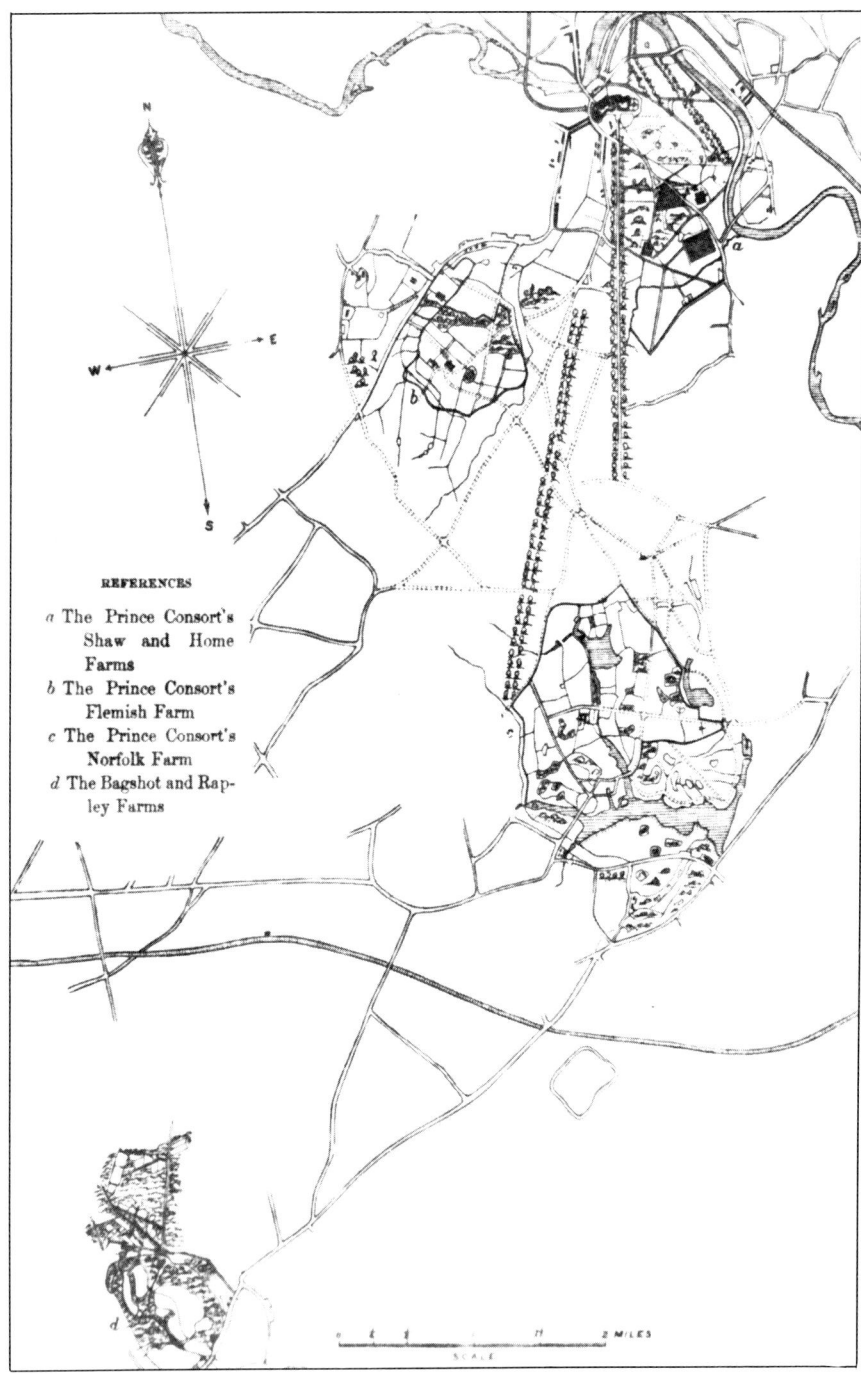

REFERENCES

a The Prince Consort's Shaw and Home Farms

b The Prince Consort's Flemish Farm

c The Prince Consort's Norfolk Farm

d The Bagshot and Rapley Farms

Soon after his marriage he was appointed Ranger of Windsor Park, an office which enabled him to take over the tenancy of Norfolk and Flemish Farms straightaway.

In 1841 he was elected an honorary member of the Highland and Agricultural Society, the oldest of Britain's national agricultural societies.

By 1843 he had animals bred on Norfolk Farm, (two Highland oxen and a pen of pigs), which were fit to be exhibited at Smithfield Show.

In 1844 he became a subscriber to the Royal Agricultural Improvement Society of Ireland and exhibited at its first annual show, winning an award for Longhorn cattle.

In 1845, the year in which Osborne was purchased, he became a vice-patron of the Royal Dublin Society, exhibited cattle at its show and won awards for his Shorthorn steer and for the best fat oxen in the Show. He also became Patron of the Royal Agricultural College at Cirencester, recently established and granted a Royal charter. Attending, as guest of honour, the Royal Agricultural Society of England's annual dinner during the Society's Show at York he endeared himself to his audience by using the phrase 'we agriculturists of England'.

In 1849 he took over the tenancy of Shaw and Home Farms at Windsor and immediately initiated improvements there. In this year, too, he began to take an interest in Devon cattle, exhibiting at Smithfield some purchased Devons which had been fattened on Norfolk Farm. He subsequently established his own herd of Devons there in 1856.

In 1850, for the first time, Shorthorn cattle which he exhibited at Smithfield are described as having been bred by himself.

By 1851 his Windsor pigs, regularly exhibited, had evidently been recognised as a distinct breed. This was the year of the Great Exhibition in the Crystal Palace, an event which materialised through the inspiration, initiative and persistence of the Prince and accorded an honoured place to agriculture. The Royal Show, held that year under the walls of Windsor Castle, exhibited only livestock, all the machinery and implement exhibits having migrated to the Crystal Palace. In the midst of all the pomp and pageantry we find the Prince taking pride in the award of a silver cup for growing the best five acres of turnips in the territory of the Royal South Buckinghamshire Agricultural Society.

In 1852–54 he was busy with the planning and construction of the homestead at Windsor Dairy Farm.

In 1855 we find him exhibiting Shorthorn, Devon and Ayrshire cattle, Windsor pigs and several breeds of poultry at a great

International Cattle Show in Paris. Never has British agriculture had a more effective and dedicated ambassador.

In 1855 when the Emperor of the French (Napoleon III) was a guest at Windsor and in 1857 when he visited Osborne, the enthusiastic Prince preached the gospel of scientific agriculture and livestock improvement to such effect that the Emperor commissioned the farm managers on the two estates to purchase for him a basic stock of Shorthorn cattle and Southdown sheep.

From 1859 onwards all of the Prince's entries in livestock classes at shows were of his own breeding. At his last Royal Show, at Leeds in 1861, he took prizes with his Hereford and Devon cattle and his heavy horses.

A survey of the Prince Consort's Windsor farms dating from about the time of his death (in 1861) depicts them as being at the height of their productivity.

NORFOLK FARM IN 1860

In the Prince's time Norfolk Farm comprised some 700 acres, but 500 acres were unenclosed pasture on the eastern side of the Great Park, this presumably the sector of rather poor land that had already been grassed down in the early years of Queen Victoria's reign. Only 200 acres were arable. The fields lay conveniently within a ring fence, extending at their south-eastern extremity to the shores of Virginia Water, and were interspersed with coppices. The farm was bisected by a stream linking the Great Lake (of about 40 acres) with Virginia Water.

The homestead and buildings, ideally situated right in the centre of the farm, were arranged around a large quadrangle. The buildings were regarded as old-fashioned: they were mostly of timber, with thatched roofs, and dated from the time of King George III. The main block, on the far side of the courtyard from the farm-house, consisted of a group of cowsheds, bull-pens and yards, with an isolated sick-bay. Around the perimeter of this block were sheds for implements and carts, a store for turnips, a boiling-house and a range of pigsties.

On one of the other sides was the great barn, picturesquely thatched and gabled, with a threshing-machine and adjacent mill-house. From a contemporary sketch it appears that the threshing-machine was driven by a rotary horse-gear fixed in the yard outside the barn. The power would be supplied by a horse or horses driven in a circle around the disc-like gear. More pig-pens and a number of poultry-houses adjoined the barn. At one end a second mill-house was situated, incorporating a horse-driven chaff-cutter.

The fourth side of the quadrangle was occupied by cottages for a shepherd and a carter, a carpenter's shop and more boxes and stalls for cattle.

Any farmer, while recognising its obsolescence, would be impressed by this thoughtfully planned and well constructed farmstead. Even in the Prince Consort's time, however, the deficiencies were recognised. 'Much labour is lost in the conveyance of food and water to the cattle,' commented one observer and compared the set-up unfavourably with that at Flemish Farm. Agriculture had become highly cost-conscious.

The farmstead was clearly designed for occupation by a herd of beef cattle. At this period the chosen breed was the Devon, a herd of which the Prince Consort had installed there in 1856. The number of cattle was just short of 100, with three prize-winning bulls as sires. It was entirely a breeding herd, with no dairy. The calves ran with their mothers on the pastures all through the summer.

The other major livestock enterprise was a flock of about 400 Hampshire Down sheep, around the needs of which the cropping of the arable land was planned. In a typical year the acreages of the main crops were as follows:– Oats 38; Beans 20; Clover 15; Mangold 39; Turnips $32\frac{1}{2}$; Wheat $57\frac{1}{2}$; Winter Barley 19. The 'turnips', one gathers, were really swedes. About a half of them, together with a half of the mangold crop, were fed to the sheep in the field, the sheep being penned there in hurdle folds. The remainder were carted off, presumably for the cattle. As for the grain, 61% was sold away from the farm.

In the time of King George III, cultivations had been carried out with twelve or thirteen horses, but the Prince Consort, with his usual enthusiasm for new inventions, had installed a steam plough which enabled the horse stock to be reduced to eight. The first steam plough had been patented in 1810, and the first practical model was put through its paces in Lancashire in 1835. Steam-engines and ploughs featured on a number of agricultural machinery stands at the Great Exhibition of 1851 as well as at Royal Shows throughout the 1850s, and it is typical that the Prince Consort should have been among the earliest to try out the new method of cultivation.

The Prince Consort was also among the early converts to the idea of supplementing farmyard manure with 'artificial' manure, as a measure for maintaining the fertility of the soil. Immense progress had been made since Jethro Tull (in 1731) had argued that the use of his seed-drill combined with horse-hoeing was all that was needed to stimulate crops to grow. The fertility was there, in the soil, and required only to be stirred up by his patented implements. Now, 120 years later, a Professor Johnson lecturing on agricultural chemistry could accurately state:—

> If, after a skilful manuring, turnips grow luxuriantly it is because the soil has been enriched with all that that crop requires. If a healthy barley crop follows the turnips, it is because the soil still contains all the food of this new plant. If clover thrive after this, it is because it requires certain kinds of nourishment which neither of the former crops has exhausted. If, again, luxuriant wheat succeeds, it is because the soil abounds still in all that the wheat crop needs – the failing vegetable and other matters of the surface being increased and renewed by the decaying roots of the preceding crop of clover. And if now turnips refuse to give again a fair return, it is because you have not added to the soil a fresh supply of that manure without which they cannot thrive. Add the manure and the same rotation of crops may again ensue.

The principles of plant nutrition and crop rotation are clearly enunciated in this lecture. The work of the soil chemists and agricultural scientists, notably Sir John Bennet Lawes who had started his classic experiments at Rothamsted in 1843, had begun to be widely accepted, and enlightened farmers and landowners, including the Prince Consort, were basing their farming operations on it.

As usual, the Prince was thorough in his application. A Lord Kinnaird had, by experiment with covered manure yards, found that 70 cubic yards of dung from such a yard were equal in value to 100 cubic yards made in the open. So, on the Home and Flemish Farms, all the farmyard manure was conveyed either to a covered yard or to a manure-house for maturing. A similar arrangement proved impossible at Norfolk Farm, so the deficiency was made good by applications of superphosphate, nitrate of soda, imported guano (from Chile), salt and soot, about £250 a year being spent on these 'artificial' fertilizers. The Prince also appreciated that the annual expenditure of £500 to £700 a year on cattle-cake and grain for livestock consumption on Norfolk Farm greatly improved the quality of the farmyard manure.

Nevertheless, Norfolk Farm was a difficult one. Much of its eastern side was of poor, light soil, which was undoubtedly one of the main reasons why Queen Victoria had been advised to have it put down to grass. It seems that the Prince made no attempt to bring these acres back into cultivation, preferring to concentrate his activities on more rewarding soil nearer home.

THE FLEMISH FARM

In the Prince Consort's time the Flemish Farm, lying a mile or so south-west of the Castle, comprised just short of 400 acres of which 190 were arable. As with Norfolk Farm, it was occupied by the Prince Consort as a tenant of the Crown Estates. Although this was one of the model farms created by King George III, it had evidently been neglected for several decades before the Prince took over, for he had to undertake a major programme of gorse and bracken clearance. While he was involved with this project, he also rearranged the fields, scrapped the old buildings, erected a new farmstead and initiated a comprehensive drainage scheme.

Recent experiments at Rothamsted and elsewhere had demonstrated the immense advantages to be derived from adequate drainage, and the soil of Flemish Farm consisted almost entirely of that heavy clay which benefits most from the operation. The Prince Consort therefore had the whole farm criss-crossed by a gridiron of drains four feet deep, at a cost of £3 an acre (exclusive of pipes and cartage).

The depth of four feet allowed a cushion of clay to remain between the pipes and the cultivated soil, a precaution thought advisable because the Prince planned to cultivate by steam power, which meant a furrow of eight or ten inches deep. The steam plough that he installed was a 12 hp Fowler's with three furrows. It worked by means of stationary engines, one on either side of the field, which drew the plough backwards and forwards across it. As Fowler had only patented his system in 1856 and had indeed not even begun experimenting until 1850, the Prince Consort must have been one of the first farmers to invest in the new device. He was evidently very pleased with it. In one autumn the steam plough ploughed 158 acres in 39½ days at a cost of six shillings per acre. It was estimated that by making an adequate allowance for interest on capital, and for wear and tear on machinery and wire ropes, (a new type of steel rope that had first been produced in 1857 was able to plough about 1000 acres before needing replacement), the cost per acre would be increased to ten or eleven shillings, but that was much cheaper than ploughing by horses. As a consequence of introducing the steam plough, the number of horses on Flemish Farm was reduced from twelve or thirteen to eight.

Flemish Farm was basically run on a four-course rotation, with some modifications. In a typical year the crops consisted of 34 acres of wheat, 15 of beans, 80 of oats and barley, $11\frac{1}{2}$ of clover and about 50 of turnips, mangolds and fallow. Sometimes beans were substituted for clover for part of the clover break, and sometimes an extra barley crop was slipped in instead of roots or fallow, a programme that was entirely feasible on this strong land. The system yielded impressive crops – 'Inferior pasture land broken up has yielded 36 to 40 bushels per acre of wheat, 60 to 80 bushels of oats and large crops of mangold wurzel, clover and beans.' Those figures are considerably in excess of the averages for England and Wales ninety years later, at the end of the Second World War.

In another respect, too, the Prince was pioneering. Even before Lawes at Rothamsted he was experimenting with top-dressing grassland with 'artificial' manures. In 1852 he set aside four one-acre plots for treatment. Of the two plots on high undrained land, one was dressed with guano at the rate of 2 cwt per acre, the other with 2 cwt per acre of nitrate of soda. Similar treatment was given to two-acre plots of low-lying meadow land. The manures were applied on 22 May and the grass cut for hay on 22 July. The results were dramatic. From untreated land the yields ranged from 8 to 9 cwt per acre; from the dressed land the yields ranged from 25 to $30\frac{3}{4}$ cwt. The applications of guano appeared to be the more effective. The report on the experiment says: 'The whole research . . . proves that our pastures no less than our arable fields are directly amenable to the influence of management. . . . Pastures need manuring, draining, weeding and may even receive tillage with advantage.' The Prince was far in advance of his time. The lessons were still being learnt or perhaps re-learnt in the 1930s and 1940s.

The livestock for which these pastures were improved and for which most of the arable crops were grown, were a superb herd of pedigree Hereford cattle. The foundations of the herd were laid by judicious purchases of high quality stock from 1855 to 1858, and by 1860 the royal herd was one of the best in the kingdom. It consisted at that time of between twenty and thirty cows, four bulls and a considerable number of home-bred young stock. Several had been successfully shown at summer shows, and prizes had also been won by fatstock at Christmas shows and sales.

The only other livestock on Flemish Farm was a herd of pedigree Berkshire pigs. The heavy soil was unsuitable for sheep farming.

The Prince Consort took a pride in the new range of farm buildings at Flemish Farm, in the design and planning of which he had had a considerable hand, though the official architect was a Mr J. R. Turnbull. In the accompanying plan the extensive central blocks of buildings are covered yards, with open yards adjacent for cows and young stock. Feeding stalls and calf-pens are also included. The third of the three blocks, farthest from the yards, comprises stables for the farm horses. Beyond the open yard to the right is a long shed for implements and carts. At right angles to this building in the foreground is a cottage, with 'bothy' accommodation for unmarried farmhands. The portable steam-engine is housed in the large building at the opposite end of the yard, with a poultry-house next door. Beyond are bull-sheds, with extensive yards just visible at the top of the picture.

The range of buildings attached to and at right angles to the covered yards is devoted to the arable crops. The projecting one at the top left-hand corner is a sheaf-barn. Next to it is a threshing-barn and next to that a straw-barn. Under the same roofs are apartments holding chaff-cutters, turnip-cutters, cisterns for liquid pig food and housing for other machinery and the engines to power it. The pigs live in a range of sties to the left of the barns. The barns and storage sheds are connected with the cattle yards and pig-pens by covered ways, so that all the livestock can be conveniently fed and serviced by the farm staff with maximum efficiency and without the need to go outdoors in bad weather.

The machinery, mostly supplied by the manufacturing firm of Clayton and Shuttleworth, was powered by one of their 8 hp fixed steam-engines. It worked a threshing-machine, winnowing machine and corn-mill, also a chaff-cutter, an oat-and bean-crusher, a cake-breaker, a root-cutter and a pulping machine made by other manufacturers. The farmstead equipment also included an interesting device for fitting a kind of container or cradle on a waggon-frame at harvest and at threshing time. When fully loaded and brought to the farmyard the container was lifted from the waggon-frame by means of a system of pulleys on a tripod, while an empty container was dropped on the frame to be sent back for the next load. Evidently it was an early Victorian prototype of modern container transport.

Other features of the buildings which may seem unexpected at this period are concrete floors to every building, a flake-proof silica whitewash for the walls, and sliding doors suspended from horizontal rods. Piped water was laid on to the stables and open yards.

The Prince was justifiably delighted with his model farmstead and, with the slightest encouragement, supplied the plans to his estate-owning friends in Britain and on the Continent.

SHAW FARM AND HOME FARM

These are the farming units nearest the Castle, in effect the Castle's back garden and home park, which at present comprise Shaw Farm and the Prince Consort's Farm. Both then and now the outlying Clay Hall Farm is included. Much of the land has been royal property for centuries, its history being briefly dealt with in Chapter 5. Shaw Farm was purchased in the middle of the seventeenth century from a Frenchman, a Monsieur de Shawe. Together with Frogmore and Clay Hall it had been occupied by Princess Augusta, the second daughter of King George III, and had been farmed on her behalf by a Mr Watkins, who continued farming it on his own account after her death in 1840. The Prince Consort took over all these contiguous farms in 1849, at an annual rental of over £1000.

Shaw Farm, with Clay Hall, then comprised 308 acres, of which 120 were arable. The Home Farm and Park consisted of 540 acres, all pastureland except for 120 acres occupied by woods, gardens, pleasure-grounds, buildings and roads. Not an ideal group of farms, especially as much of the soil was heavy clay, while the whole was said to be 'in a very wild and unequipped condition'.

The Prince proceeded to weld them into two interlocking units, each with a central farmstead. The arable land was still restricted to about 120 acres and was almost entirely at Clay Hall, on the southern sector of the farms. In the year 1858, which may be taken as a sample, 62 acres were devoted to wheat, 11 to oats, 4 to barley and vetches, 7

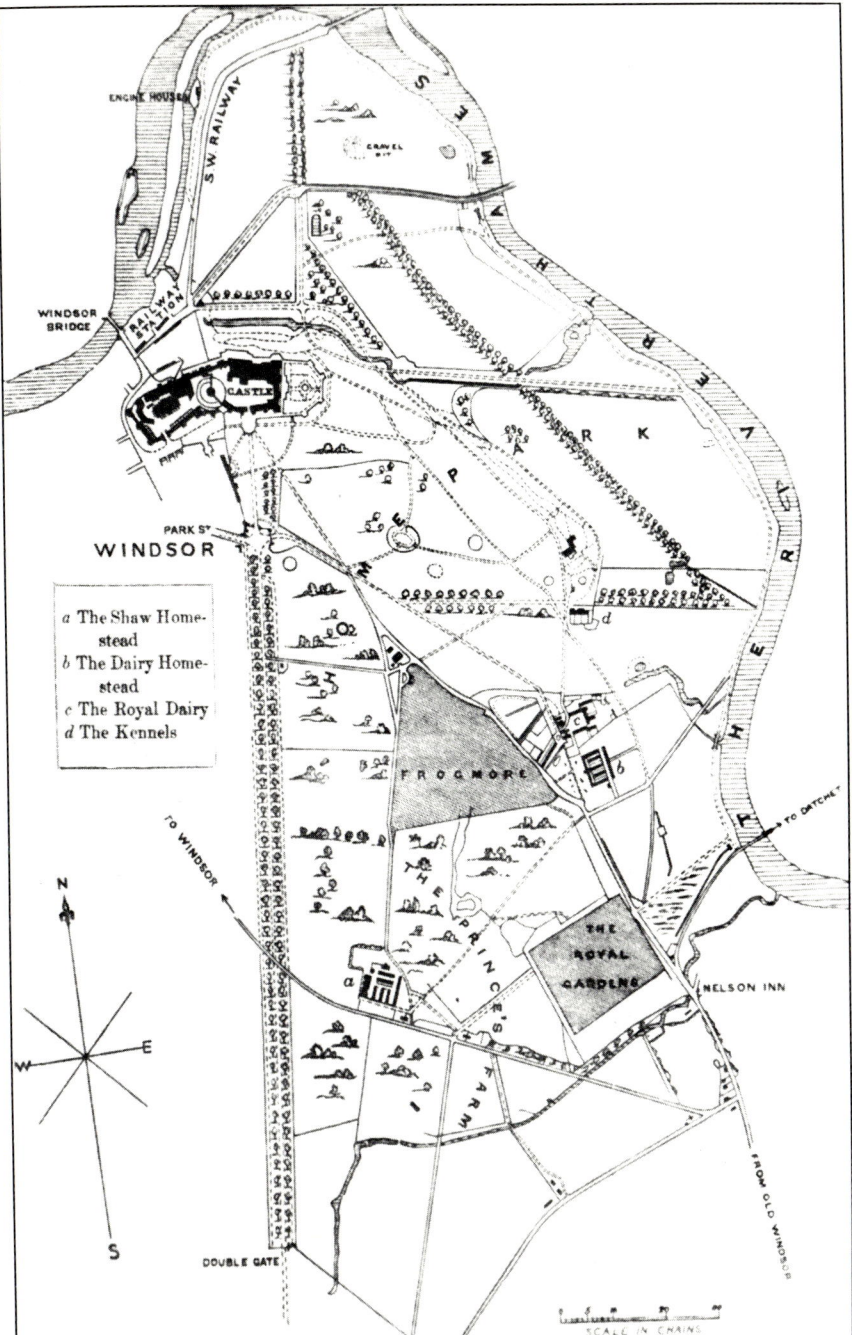

A map of Home Park including Clay Hall and Shaw farms

a The Shaw Homestead
b The Dairy Homestead
c The Royal Dairy
d The Kennels

to beans, 12 to clover and 26 to roots. On the pastureland which comprised the rest of the farm, the chief livestock enterprise was the dairy herd, mostly Dairy Shorthorns but also some cows which were referred to in contemporary records as Alderneys although they were in fact identical to Guernseys.

The Alderneys were pure-bred but this did not apply to all the Shorthorns. The policy of buying in pedigree Shorthorn bulls and cows (of the dairy type) began in 1855. Three pure-bred bulls and seven pure-bred cows were brought into the herd and a programme of grading-up from the other stock was begun. The usual strength of the herd was about 200, of which rather less than half were milking cows.

The other livestock on the farms consisted of 400 sheep, 120 pigs and about 20 horses. The sheep grazed largely on the parkland nearest the castle. The old Southdown flock had been dispersed and had been replaced by about 200 breeding ewes of the Cheviot breed, brought down annually from the North. They were crossed with Leicester rams, and the resulting progeny, together with the draft ewes, were fattened in sheds.

Two breeds of pigs were kept, one a breeding herd of ten or twelve Berkshire sows – a pork breed that has now become rare – which was kept at Shaw Farm. The other is referred to in contemporary records as 'Prince Albert's Windsor breed', which seems to have been similar to the modern Large White. Sixteen to twenty sows and their progeny were kept at the Home Farm buildings. The Prince obtained his basic breeding stock from breeders in Yorkshire and Cumberland. They were highly popular, winning many major awards at shows, and the young boars commanded high prices when sold. The Windsor pigs were a major source of revenue for the farms, bringing in up to £700 a year.

The horses were all Clydesdales, six of them brood mares. The farms also possessed one of the breed's best stallions, an upstanding horse named Briton, purchased for 250 guineas in 1855, whose colts invariably commanded high prices from £100 to £150 each.

Despite the introduction of the steam plough, these horses still found plenty of hard work to do. After the 1857 harvest, for example, twenty acres of wheat-stubble field were ploughed to the depth of twelve inches, a task which required six horses. Ploughing nine inches deep called for a team of four horses, as did subsoiling with a subsoil plough penetrating to a depth of eighteen inches. A full summer's working day for the horses was from 6 a.m. to 5 p.m., with a one-hour break from 11 to 12. Each had two bushels of corn per week and as much hay as it could eat, plus an extra ration of beans when severe effort was required.

It was on the buildings at the two farmsteads that the Prince lavished most of his attention. From the beginning of his tenure, the old dairy homestead at Frogmore had presented him with a challenge. What he found there was a set of makeshift buildings, erected at different periods and most of them in a ruinous condition. Back in the reign of Queen Anne, Sarah, Duchess of Marlborough, had had a garden at Frogmore, and the old orangery still stood and was being used as a cow-house. It was in fact the best feature of the farmstead, most of the rest of which resembled, in the opinion of one writer, 'the homesteads of the worst parts of Ireland'. Moreover, when the Thames overflowed its banks, as frequently happened, some of the houses and sheds were flooded above floor level and could not be used. The farmstead was naturally an unhealthy place for cattle, and an epidemic of pleuro-pneumonia in 1845–46 caused heavy mortality.

The Prince therefore determined to start from scratch and build an entirely new farmstead. He entrusted the design to Mr Turnbull, though it is not to be doubted that his own contributions to the eventual plans were frequent and considerable. When it was finished, he declared, he would have the best cow-house in the world, and few would have contradicted him.

It was certainly magnificent. The central feature of an imposing complex of buildings, it provided standings for sixty cows facing

A sketch of the Prince Consort's dairy homestead

77

each other in a double row, with ingenious provisions made for watering and feeding them and for draining. Parallel to the cowshed and on the far sides of the adjacent spacious yards were other ranges of buildings for housing bulls, young cattle and pigs. In the farthest range, beyond the main pigsties, were a slaughter-house, a boiling-house and a straw store. At right angles to these buildings and forming the other sides of a huge quadrangle were lines of loose boxes, hay stores, stables, cart-sheds and even an animal hospital. The whole occupied a site about 250 feet square. All the stalls and floors were concreted or covered with stone slabs, and most of the roads and passages were surfaced with asphalt. The central cow-house had a lofty roof, rising to 25 feet at the apex, and the farmstead was dominated by a tall clock-tower with a weather-vane. Exemplifying the Prince Consort's belief in the value of manure in growing crops, the buildings had an elaborate drainage system leading to a covered slurry pit where the liquid and solid manure were separated. Water-carts took the liquid fertilizer and deposited it over the fields.

Everything in which the Prince had a hand was distinguished by his thoroughness and attention to detail. Throughout the entire range of buildings, 'the door and window jambs, the ornamental coping, corbels, terminal pieces and panels in gables are executed in terra-cotta. This was done by command of the Prince Consort.' It is in the

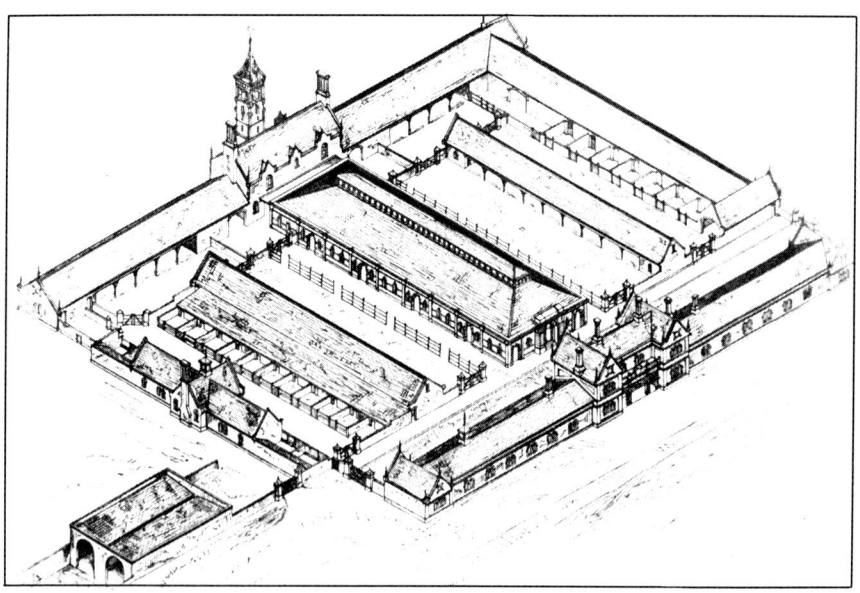

The isometrical perspective
of the Shaw homestead

design of the Royal Dairy that the Prince's architectural ingenuity and love of ornamentation found the fullest expression. It has been preserved in its entirety, exactly as he left it, so the contemporary description supplied by a writer in the year after his death is still accurate.

The floor is laid upon brick arches, with an empty space about 3 feet high below the arches. The external walls are hollow, with ventilation. The drains are of glazed tubular pipes and provided with means of efficient flushing. . . . The floor is laid with tiles of an incised pattern, with a majolica border, presenting the appearance of a Turkey carpet, and it is both beautiful to the eye and agreeable to walk upon. Below the tables and extending their whole length, are reservoirs about 2 inches deep, laid with tiles, to contain a flowing stream of cold water and provided with arrangements for filling and emptying. This arrangement preserves the coolness of the room in summer. The walls are covered with tiles of a white ground, carrying a star pattern in mauve colour, and the whole is enclosed by a border of tiles bearing a running pattern in green and white. Several bas-reliefs in majolica are also introduced on the walls, the subjects being agricultural and descriptive of the four seasons. The walls are crowned with a frieze and cornice, executed in majolica, the former of elaborate and flowing design. Medallions of the Royal Family are introduced, supported by sea-horses, alternating with shields bearing monograms, dolphins etc. The cornice is encircled by a running pattern in majolica, representing the leaves and fruit of the orange. The sloping part of the ceiling, which extends up to the roof-tie, is painted and enamelled, with a pattern of extreme beauty and delicacy. The soffit or flat part of the ceiling under the roof-tie is filled with majolica panels in the manner of coffers, a number of which are perforated to afford a passage for the air to and from the ventilator above. . . . At either end of the dairy is a fountain of majolica ware, designed by the late Mr Thomas, rising from a shell supported by a heron and bulrushes. And on the south side of the dairy is a fountain in statuary marble – a water-nymph pouring water from a jar. The tables are all of white marble, the frames and supports being tastefully decorated in colour, with Belgian and Devonshire marbles. The windows have double casements, the inner filled with stained glass, representing daisies

Opposite: The interior of the
Prince Consort's dairy   *Edward Haydon Wood*

and primroses, with a border of may-blossom. These casements open for ventilation, and there is also top ventilation by a syphon ventilator, on 'Watson's principle', which externally forms a turret, rising from the roof. There are two recesses on the south side and one on the east side, lined with tiles of an elegant pattern and fitted with ornamental racks, on which are exhibited some fine specimens of old china. The roof is supported by six ornamental pillars, on the top of which are clusters of small twisted shafts, carrying the ornamental arches in connection with the ceiling and roof; the pillars and all the splayed parts of the ceiling and mouldings are richly decorated in colour and highly enamelled. [. . .]

Mr Thomas received the commands of the Prince Consort for the various decorations, and the designs were repeatedly altered under the direction of His Royal Highness, nothing having been carried out without specimens, embodying his own suggestions, having first been submitted for his approval; and every detail, both of colour and of form, underwent a most careful revisal by him before they were finally carried into execution.

And there the Dairy still stands, though the water no longer flows beneath the marble tables, nor spouts from the fountains. More priceless china has found a home on the wall shelves, and a marble statue of Frederick the Great of Prussia incongruously surveys the scene from a pedestal. The whole is reminiscent of the Albert Memorial and is superficially more like a mausoleum than a dairy. Yet, for all the lavish ornamentation, it is strictly functional. Turn on the taps, and it could still be used. The white basins in which the milk stood for the cream to settle are still on the marble tables, with skimmers at hand to take off the cream.

The Dairy could cope with about 240 gallons of milk a day, the product of the Dairy Shorthorn and Alderney cows, which were all supplied to the Castle. Exact records were kept of the quantities produced and also of the milk yields of the cows, this probably being the earliest example of milk-recording in Britain.

The Shaw Farm buildings were less extensive and pretentious than those of Home Farm – as the two were so near to each other, there was no need to provide accommodation for large numbers of livestock. Some of the bulls and calves were housed there, including those being prepared for exhibition, and so were most of the cart-horses.

A sketch of the Prince Consort's Shaw homestead

As already mentioned, the herd of Berkshire pigs had its quarters at Shaw Farm, and a poultry department was also centred there. There were large buildings for storing corn and hay, others for carts and implements, a threshing bay with stationary threshing machines, and a range of carpenters' shops, smithies and wood-yards. An unusual feature was a sheep-shed, where about 150 Cheviot wethers were fattened every year. The sheep were confined six to a pen and fed on cut roots and cake. They were said to be housed on 'sparred floors' which would seem to be the equivalent of modern slatted floors. In view of the fact that over the past few decades numerous experiments in the indoor fattening of sheep have been made and have proved mostly unsatisfactory, it is interesting that the Shaw Farm system produced good results, the sheep thriving 'fast compared with the progress made out-of-doors'.

The Prince concerned himself with the well-being of his farm staff as well as of his animals. For the young unmarried men he provided not only good accommodation but a reading room where evening classes were held. Three times a week during the winter a schoolmaster came over from Windsor and taught them chiefly reading, writing (with an emphasis on penmanship and spelling) and arithmetic. Prizes were given at the end of term, the first being always a Bible, with an inscription recording that it was a gift from the Prince.

Queen Victoria continued Prince Albert's policies at Windsor with few changes. In particular the herds of pedigree cattle achieved new standards of excellence under able management. Throughout the latter part of her reign, individuals from the Windsor herd of Dairy Shorthorns consistently won major trophies at the leading agricultural shows. In 1882 a remarkable bull, *New Year's Gift*, was supreme champion at the Royal Show, the Royal Highland Show and the Dublin Show and was later sold for 1000 guineas.

King Edward VII, who had long cherished the ideal of making and maintaining Britain as the stock farm of the world, naturally required the Windsor herds to continue to function at the same high levels and on the same scale.

Under King George V the same principles were followed, but certain modifications had to be made. The home of the pedigree Windsor herd was Shaw Farm. The milking herd at Home Farm, which supplied the royal household with milk, butter and cream, consisted of non-pedigree Dairy Shorthorns and pedigree Jerseys. At the end of the First World War it was noticed that the Shaw Farm herd was not thriving as it should and the blame was put on cattle-sick pastures. Accordingly, 65 acres of the poorest meadows were ploughed up, cropped for five years with grain and roots and then re-seeded after liming. The policy proving satisfactory, a further 30 acres were treated in the same way when the pastures had been restored. The upheaval naturally required a temporary reduction in the numbers of cattle, and most of the older ones were sold. At the appropriate time the rebuilding of the herd was initiated, using the best blood available.

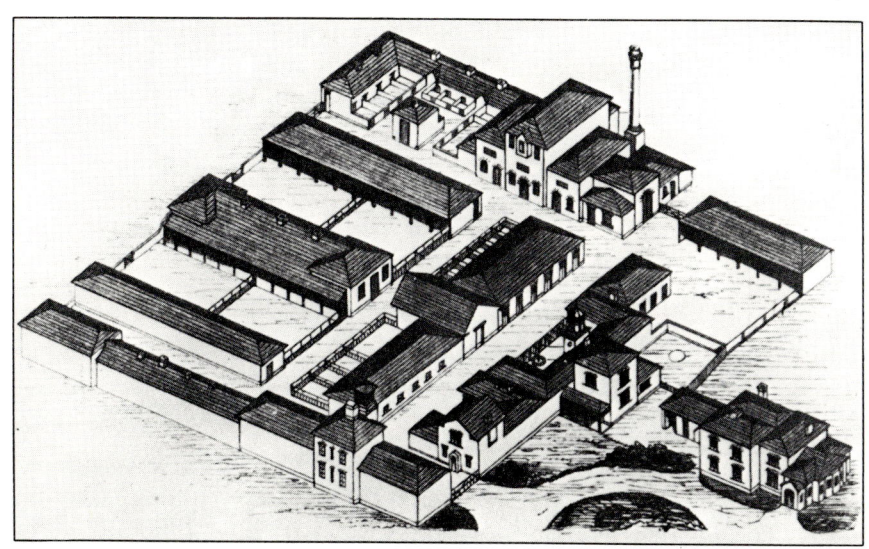

The isometrical perspective of the Shaw homestead

EAST RANGE
a   Cart and Wagon-sheds
b b Cart-horse Stables
c   Harness-room
d   Chaff and Corn-bins
e   Hay and Corn-shed
f   Drill-shed
g g Men's Living Rooms, with
     Sleeping Rooms over, and
     Clock Tower
h   Implement-shed

NORTH RANGE
i   Foreman's Cottage
j j Steward's Stable, Gig-
     house; and Hospital for
     Sick Stock
k k Poultry Department
m   Poultry Woman's
     Cottage, by the entrance
     from Her Majesty's
     Rooms to the Farm
     Offices
l l n o Blacksmith's,
     Carpenter's, and other
     Shops, Wood-yard,
     Saw-pit, &c.

WEST RANGE
A   Corn Bay
B   Hay Bay
C C Cut hay and straw
D   Corn-mixing Rooms,
     Thrashing-machine, and
     Straw-bay
E   Sheds for Corn to be
     thrashed and for Chaff
     from Machine
G   Boiler-room
H   Coal-shed
I   Artificial Manure-shed
J   Boiling-house

PIGGERY DEPARTMENT
K K Open Shed, and Sties
     with Yards for Store
     Breeding Sows
L   Slaughter-house
M   Boiler-house, with Food-
     tank

CENTRE RANGES
p q' Yard and House for
      Stallion
q p' Yards and Houses for
      Bulls
r s   Cow-house and Yard
      with Calf-pens
s'   Root-store
t u   Hemels, with Boxes on
      the farther side of the
      Gangway
v w x Yards and Sheds for
       Store Stock
y   Sheep-shed, with central
      Gangway and terminal
      Food-house at z

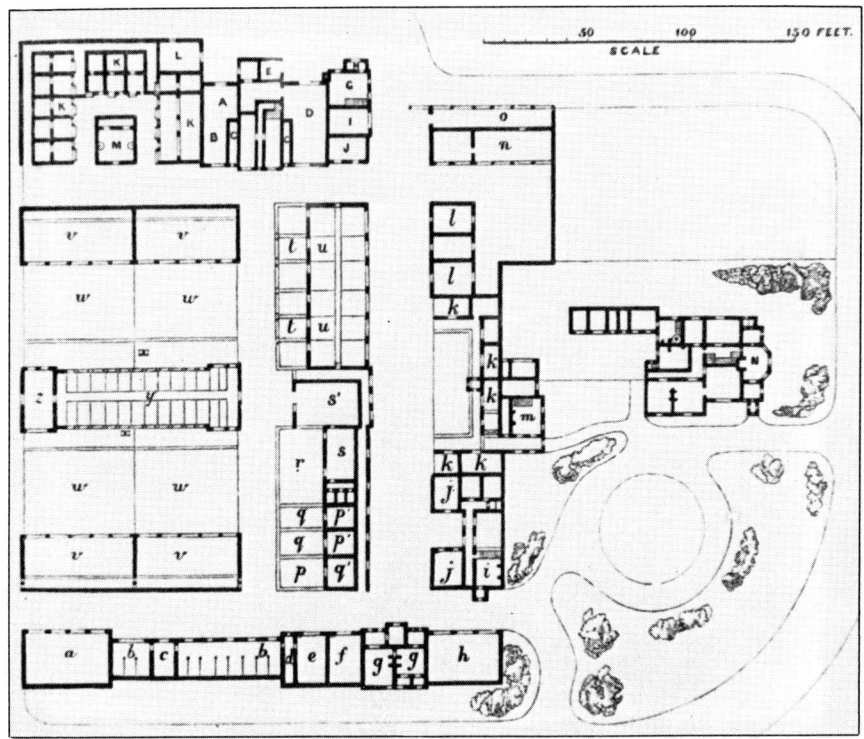

In the 1930s Shaw Farm also housed a small herd (about 30) of blue-grey bullocks and a nucleus of sows. At Home Farm the Prince Consort's dairy finally became a museum piece and a new working dairy was installed. A small herd of Devons and a larger one of Herefords were still continuing their prize-winning careers from Flemish Farm. Norfolk Farm, like so much of England at that time (the nadir of the Depression) had lapsed entirely into grassland. It was grazed by a flock of some 400 half-bred ewes, generally crossed with a Southdown ram.

BAGSHOT AND RAPLEY FARMS

Pursuing still further his agricultural interests, the energetic Prince Consort acquired the tenancies of two other farms in the Windsor district. Bagshot and Rapley Farms adjoin each other and are situated four or five miles south of Norfolk Farm and eight or nine miles from the Castle. They evidently belonged to H.M. Commissioners of Woods and Forests, and the tenancy was acquired by the Prince partly for the sporting rights and partly for the agricultural

84

possibilities. Bagshot Park, to which they were attached, had until recently been the residence of the Duke of Gloucester, lately deceased.

Opposite: A plan of the Shaw homestead and a key to the letters on the plan

The soil of the two farms, mostly peat and sand, was excellent for woods and gardens, especially favourable for the rhododendrons which still flourish there, but not so good for farming. Woods shaded many of the fields and provided cover from which pests could damage the growing crops. Game preservation had been given priority, and it was claimed that 'pheasants have fallen to a single gun at the rate of one per minute for an hour and a half together.'

The Prince, on entering his tenancy, found that Rapley had some good buildings, especially a range of piggeries, although these were dilapidated and badly in need of repair. Bagshot was poorly provided with buildings and agricultural equipment. It comprised some 160 acres, of which 100 were arable and the rest pasture; Rapley had 160 acres of arable land and 120 of pasture.

The farms were thus primarily arable. Wheat was the main cereal crop, though barley and oats were also grown. Mangolds, turnips and vetches also figured prominently in the rotation, and crops of buckwheat were sown for the pheasants. The buckwheat was allowed to ripen, dried and then stacked in the coverts, the farms being credited with its value by the game department. Rapley produced considerable quantities of potatoes though mainly coarse varieties suitable for boiling for pigs. Rapley had a two-year grass break after three years of arable crops. Bagshot used a continuous arable rotation, all the grassland being permanent.

Another crop with which the Prince experimented at Bagshot and Rapley was lupins. The seed-pods were cut off by a boy with a knife and a basket when the seed was half-ripe and the remaining stems and leaves were grazed by the sheep. The experiment seems to have been reasonably successful, as might be expected on that type of soil.

The three hundred sheep there were Hampshire Downs and Cheviots, kept primarily for the lamb crop, which was fattened on swedes and turnips. The cattle comprised about sixty stores and fattening beasts, most of them Galloways and Beef Shorthorns, the stock being purchased annually, not home-bred. Records also speak of Kyloe cattle being present at the farms. The term is generally held to refer to the Highland breed, though a picture in the Rothamsted collection shows a short-legged, pied animal resembling a Shorthorn and nothing like the modern Highlander. A small breeding herd of

Berkshire pigs was resident at Rapley. The farms were worked by
five pairs of Clydesdale horses, some of them first-class mares from
which colts were bred, by mating them with the Prince's prize
Clydesdale stallion at Shaw Farm. Most of the time there were ten or
so young Clydesdales growing up on the premises.

It seems that soon after the death of the Prince Consort these
outlying farms reverted to H.M. Commissioners of Woods and
Forests and were let to other tenants. Reading between the lines, one
gathers that they were never profitable.

OSBORNE AND BARTON

Osborne on the Isle of Wight was bought by Queen Victoria with her
private funds in May 1845, to meet the need for a secluded retreat for
her growing family. As a girl of fourteen she had spent a summer
holiday with her mother at Norris Castle nearby and treasured the
happy memories. She was delighted with Osborne, which came on to
the market at a convenient time, and it continued throughout her
long life to be a favourite residence.

Her conviction that the house would be adequate for her numerous
family proved over-optimistic. Indeed, soon after the purchase she
was advised that it would be less expensive to pull the place down
and build a new one than to try to repair it. The advice, of course, was
congenial to the Prince Consort who, in collaboration with Thomas
Cubitt, a leading London builder, set about designing a new mansion.
'It does my heart good to see how my beloved Albert enjoys it all, and
is so full of admiration of the place and of all the plans and
improvements he means to carry out,' wrote the Queen.

The Prince naturally interested himself in the estate as well as the
house. When cautious Palace officials advised against the purchase of
the property, the benefits that could be obtained by reclaiming and
farming neglected agricultural land was one of the arguments that he
advanced in its favour. Not long after the acquisition of Osborne the
Queen bought neighbouring Barton Manor. The manor-house
proved very useful for accommodating staff for whom there was no
room at Osborne. Eventually the estate comprised more than 2600
acres, much of it farmland.

Barton Manor farm comprised 820 acres, about half of it permanent
pasture, while Osborne and Alverstone extended to 1700 acres, 700
of which were arable. Not all the land was farmed by the Prince,

however, for an account of December 1853 catalogues 589 acres of
land as being let to four tenants on Osborne estate, together with a
further 280 acres let to a tenant at Alverston. In the same year, the
farmland in hand at Barton Manor is given as 604 acres, cropped as
follows:– wheat 56 acres; barley 24; oats 42; beans 4; vetches 24;
turnips 62; mangolds 4; clover and Italian rye-grass 38; meadow and
pasture 350.

An extant memorandum in the Prince Consort's handwriting,
dated 'Osborne, December 13th, 1853', (*RA PP Osborne 123*) shows
that he was then considering making changes. His grasp of affairs,
interest in farming, shrewd appraisal of character, passion for
economic efficiency and automatic assumption of authority are well
illustrated. Messrs May and Whitmarsh are castigated as a couple of
inefficient tenants. Mr Toward was the farm manager of Osborne.

I have been considering the state of the Farm down here. Barton
Farm is getting into exceedingly good order; the arable land bears
excellent crops; the Park and Grasslands require, however, a
thorough dressing to support the amount of stock which the
acreage ought to carry (about 300 sheep and 12 beasts more than at
present). The farm buildings prove excellent, but there is no
proportion between the grassland in the Park and the amount of
accommodation and machinery at the farm offices on the one hand
and the arable land on the other. The annexed memorandum
shows that the grasslands amount to 350 acres whilst the arable is
only 253 acres of which 120 or thereabouts can be in corn and only
56 in wheat. The machinery and buildings require some 500–600
acres arable to make their outlay pay.

Woodhouse (Farm) is in a miserable condition, the farm
buildings tumbling down, the land impoverished and no stock
kept upon the farm. Mr May is a poor creature. Toward assures me
that he does not buy £10 worth of manure the whole year round
and has not one bullock on the place. He keeps a few cows to make
a profit on them by the milk! He takes so little interest in
improvement that he has not had the curiosity once to look at our
new offices and machinery at Barton next door to him, although
frequently invited by Toward to do so!

Woodhouse contains 183 acres of which 133 are arable and let
at 16s. 8d. per acre. Some of the land is very fair although
impoverished; it would require to set the farm straight – new farm

buildings, a new farm house, dairy etc, a large outlay in manure and a total redirection of the fields, doing away with the quantity of crooked fences and hedges which now obstruct them.

Alverston Farm is not better. It contains 171 acres let at 12s. 5d. (inclusive of interest on draining); the Race Course belonging to it containing 138 acres is let to the same tenant at 6s. 7d. the acre, and is a perfect disgrace to the Queen as proprietor in its present neglected state, attracting much public notice and criticism, being bounded and cut by two different much frequented high roads. The tenant has done full justice to the land which he has been able to cultivate at Alverston and has buried a good deal of manure there, but it also requires a large outlay of capital to make it better, and contains some good land worth the outlay, together with a good deal of bad. Mr Whitmarsh has no capital, however, and to obtain a farmer who can give it we should have to give him the land for nothing for a long term of years. The new farm buildings just being completed are very good and would enable a fair proportion of stock to be kept. The many good roads intersecting the fields would render the carting of farmyard manure both easy and economical.

What is to be done?

It will not do to let this state of things go on much longer.

I propose to give May notice to quit, buying his goodwill, and to throw Woodhouse into Barton. Besides the advantage of getting rid of May and obtaining the eventual control over the ground, through which we shall have to extend our roads and drives, it would better the proportion of arable land for Barton, which lies all very close and convenient to the offices, increasing that to 38 acres. But it would also be a most economical arrangement, for we would save an outlay of about £3000 upon new farm buildings and a farmhouse, and the land added would be marked by an immeasurably cheaper overhead than at Barton.

The salary of Toward and the wages of Scot, of the Engineers, the Shepherd and the Chief Carter and the interest on the capital amount in the farm buildings, machinery, implements, ploughs, carts, horses etc – all those expenses would be saved upon the 184 acres of Woodhouse, which would at the utmost require 4 more horses with a man and a boy to look after them at a stable on the present spot of the Farm. As Barton pays fully 30s. an acre, and May gives us only 16s. 8d. (all heavy expenses being already charged on Barton), the financial advantage of the operation cannot be doubted.

Alverston and the Race Course will also have to be taken in hand and put to rights whatever may be done with them finally. By putting merely a foreman there at present with say £50 or £60 a year wages, under Toward's superintendence, although quite distinct from Barton we shall be able to manage it economically and will require at present to build an expensive farmer's house which with nag stable, dairy, etc, would have cost £1000. I wish to combine this with the means of training another foreman in case anything should happen to Toward. His son did not impress me, the other son is too young, but there is a remarkably clever, well-educated and well conducted young man, James Bristow, at the gardens who came from Messrs Standish's nursery, is a very good botanist and naturalist and will probably not stay with us much longer in his present subordinate situation. He might be sent to the Agricultural College in Ireland and thence to Scotland and would in 12 months' tutelage learn as much as a clodhopper would in a century. I propose to rear him for the place and to have the advantage in him, that he knows Osborne, is attached to it, knows all its beauties, plants, drains, roads and servants very thoroughly and that Toward knows him to be trustworthy and obedient.

I have spoken this whole plan over and discussed it with Toward who adheres to it and promises to make it answer. He says it would require a 12 months' notice to May and Whitmarsh, and the latter would have a right to compensation for ameliorations.

Osborne, Dec 13, 1853

It is to be presumed that the measures the Prince recommended, or rather decided upon, were duly implemented.

Other records of Barton and its associated farms are rather scarce, but it is known that the Prince kept a small herd of Jerseys there and fattened thirty or forty Galloway beasts brought in each autumn. The field work was done by several teams of Clydesdale horses.

As on his other farms he gave priority to an impressive and comprehensive new range of farm buildings. The stables provided stalls for thirteen horses, most of which were Clydesdales. The Prince Consort kept a prize-winning stallion here and bred from three or four mares each year. The cattle consisted of a bull and twelve to sixteen 'Alderney' cows (presumably Guernseys, though some reports speak of them as Jerseys). Thirty or forty Galloways were purchased each year at Barnet Fair and fattened off within eighteen months. A pig herd of eight black sows of the now unknown Sussex breed was kept, their progeny being fattened to pork weight.

The sheep stock comprised between forty and a hundred Dorset ewes, normally mated to a 'black-faced ram', and a pure-bred flock of some three hundred Southdown ewes.

By 1862 the acreage of Barton had been increased to 820, of which 420 were permanent pasture. The following acreages in that year illustrate the progress made over the previous decade:– wheat, 86 acres; barley, 44; oats 64; beans and peas 26; vetches and rape 24; potatoes 2; turnips 88; carrots and cabbages 3; mangolds 8; clover 50.

A report in 1862 declares that:

an immense improvement has been effected in the land, not only by tillage and drainage, but of course also by the purchase of artificial and other manures, and of cattle food. Less is done in this way now than in former years, when it was more needed. The produce per acre of the crops has thus been raised from four to five quarters per acre of wheat, four and a half to six quarters of barley, and from five to seven or eight quarters of oats. A few acres of Belgian carrots, for dairy cows, and of cabbages which yield most useful autumn produce, are generally grown. And five or six acres of corn stubble are sown each autumn with the Trifolium incarnatum, yielding most useful early spring food for the stables.

White mustard is also occasionally grown as a stolen or catch-crop. The Swedish turnips, of which there was last year an unusual extent, are grown either in rows sown by the Suffolk drill upon the flat, or by the sowing machine already referred to on the raised drill system adopted in Scotland; and on this plan of cultivation, as the crop then followed a filling mangold plant, there was last year several fields. The crop was remarkably full and even, not a blank being visible in the planting, and a good average size prevailing through the fields. In general, superphosphate and ashes are depended on for a crop of swedes. The dung of the boxes and yards is applied upon the clover for the wheat crop and for mangolds, cabbages and carrots. A large quantity of manure is thus provided, and, with the artificial aids already named, the farm is growing in fertility. The manure from the Royal Mews is also purchased for the farm, and this is a clear addition to the land, as all the hay and straw of the farm is consumed in the courts and buildings of the farm itself.

Alverstone Farm, which in 1862 consisted of 350 acres (50 of them permanent grass), had evidently been taken in hand soon after the Prince's memorandum had been written, for its new homestead was erected in 1855. Although the buildings included modest accommodation for cattle and horses, the 1862 report contains no mention of any livestock in residence but refers to 'large quantities of town dung, consisting of the contents of out-houses, piggeries and cow-byres, being brought from Newport, where it is purchased for 4s. 6d. per ton. The value of this dressing was very obvious on the young wheat this spring.'

Alverstone was a difficult farm with a great variety of soils, and needed much patient and good management. Clay soil in the middle of the farm proved to be excellent material for making tiles, and a thriving industry was established there, largely to provide tiles (both building and drainage) for use on the estate.

QUEEN VICTORIA AND PRINCE ALBERT AT BALMORAL

As might be expected, Queen Victoria and the Prince Consort found Balmoral very neglected agriculturally. The population of the valley was thin and widely dispersed, and little farms which hugged the river banks 'in the most wretched disorder'. It took several years of negotiation for the Prince to obtain possession of any of the holdings, Invergelder being the first one to fall in hand.

The Prince immediately set about modernising with his customary thoroughness. A new farmstead was erected with all the amenities provided at Windsor and Barton, though on a smaller and simpler scale. Every field was first sown with a green crop, then fallowed and limed and finally laid down to permanent grass. All fences were renewed, as they needed to be, to keep out the deer from the hills and forests, which, under protection, were increasing prodigiously. The new grass fields were stocked in summer with Highland sheep, destined to supply the royal household with mutton during the autumn recess. In winter they were grazed by the Queen's hill ponies.

This admirably efficient rehabilitation programme was applied primarily to the farms that the Prince was able to take in hand but he did what he could with those others, the majority, which remained in the possession of tenants. When the Queen and he took over Balmoral estate there were over sixty tenant crofters, most of them with less than twenty-five acres each and some with only ten or twelve acres. 'A croft of this size, two or three half-starved cows, a Highland pony, or it might be two, a few score sheep, all turned out to shift for themselves on the hills, constituted the wealth of most of the tenants.' The results of the Prince's activities on behalf of the crofters is summarised by John Chalmers Moreton.

> Comfortable cottages have replaced the former miserable dwellings; farm offices, according to the size of the farms have been erected; money has been advanced for the draining, trenching and improvement of waste land; new roads have been opened up and old ones repaired; fences have been repaired; and upwards of 1000 acres of unreclaimable land planted.

Quite an impressive record for less than ten years.

As on the Windsor and Osborne farms the Prince took a positive interest in education. By erecting adequate new school buildings and staffing them with well-paid teachers he made sure that none of his crofters and employers lacked good schooling. At Balmoral he established a well stocked library, accessible to everyone on the estate. It all made a deep appeal to the education-conscious Scots.

4
WINDSOR

OLD WINDSOR

The manor of Old Windsor, which is situated about two miles south-east of the present town of Windsor, belonged from an early date to Anglo-Saxon kings, who had a modest residence or hunting-lodge there. King Edward the Confessor held court at Old Windsor on more than one occasion, for a record survives of a miracle reputedly performed by him while in residence there – the restoration of sight to a man, Wulwin Spillecorn, who had been blind for seventeen years.

In January 1066, not long before his death, King Edward granted the manor of Windsor to the monastery of St Peter at Westminster. The monks' tenure of the property was however very short, for in the first year of his reign King William I, liking the look of the land, exchanged for it 'Wokendune and Feringes' in Essex. The manor attracted him as 'a place appearing proper and convenient for a royal retirement on account of the river and the nearness to the forest for hunting and many other royal conveniences'. It was William who built the first castle on the brow of the hill, finishing it before 1086. The castle was in fact one of a ring of fortresses built by William I to encircle London and so discourage any notions of rebellion in that city.

At Old Windsor the royal estate at the time of the Domesday Book comprised twenty hides (perhaps 2400 acres). In the immediate vicinity of the palace were ninety-five houses. The chief tenants were twenty-two villeins, who held land by service, and two bordars who, interestingly, held their tenancy by virtue of supplying poultry, eggs and other small produce to the Lord of the Manor. These twenty-four tenants between them occupied land sufficient for ten ploughs, which was probably about half the total acreage of the cultivated area. The estate also included forty acres of meadowland and woodland, with grazing rights (pannage) for fifty hogs, and another fenced wood, which was reserved for timber and from which the pigs were excluded.

The Castle itself was not erected on the manor of Old Windsor but on the neighbouring one of Clivore (Clewer), which had formerly belonged to King Harold. Apparently William granted the greater part of this manor ($7\frac{1}{2}$ hides) to one of his retainers, Radulfus, but retained half a hide for his own use. During the reigns of the first two Norman kings the Castle was regarded primarily as a stronghold, and royal courts and festivals were held at the palace at Old Windsor. The first reference to a court function at the Castle dates from A.D. 1110, in which year King Henry I celebrated Whitsuntide there.

THE FOREST

In early times Windsor Forest is said to have had a circumference of 120 miles and to have covered much of the counties of Berkshire and Surrey and smaller sections of Middlesex and Buckinghamshire. As late as 1813, when an Act of Parliament deforested much of Windsor Forest, the area of land thus released was around 59,000 acres and extended over the greater part of seventeen parishes. As with nearly all early forests, these boundaries included heaths, marshes and farms as well as woodland. A forest was an area to which forest law applied – a chase reserved primarily for the king's deer.

Throughout the centuries successive enclosures claimed slices of the forest. They ranged from blocks of several hundreds of acres granted by the king to some ecclesiastical foundation or important person down to peasant small-holdings formed illicitly by squatters. It was generally believed that if a man could build 'a hut of turf and have a fire lighted and pot boiled in the rudest chimney, the hut became established as a house and was wholly unassailable except by the regular processes of the law, which the forest officials frequently declined to institute'. Usually the building had to be completed between sunset and sunrise, the materials having been assembled secretly beforehand, and in some instances it was held that the squatter could claim as much land as he could fence in on the same night.

Thus, legally or by less legitimate means, the ancient forest became broken into a multitude of jigsaw pieces. The process began at an early date, for even before 1086 the king had enclosed a 'Little Park around the Castle', a holding which was enhanced in 1368 by the purchase of an adjoining tract of land, 'The Park of Hydecroft' from the Abbot of Reading, a record which indicates that an existing enclosure was involved. In the Close Rolls of the 1270s there are references to trees being felled for fencing 'the new park', a work which seems to have been completed by 1278, for in November of that year numbers of deer were fetched from Chute Forest, on the borders of Hampshire and Wiltshire, to stock the park. Before the final enclosure, the wild cattle roaming that section of the forest were rounded up and sold for slaughter. It is likely that these were feral animals. Turning cattle to graze on unenclosed heathland and woodland was common practice (which in due course led to the establishment of common rights), and there must have been many occasions when animals, unclaimed perhaps after the death of their owners, wandered off to form wild herds. But it is just possible that a small population of Aurochs, the great wild bull of primeval forests, survived into the Middle Ages.

Farm livestock in large numbers was agisted or turned out to graze in the forest in medieval times. One of the earliest records concerns a forest court held at Guildford in 1270, when it was stated that in the section of the forest known as Guildford Park, 100 cattle and 10 horses were agisted, at a penny a head, from Hocktide (the week after Easter) to the Nativity of John the Baptist (Midsummer) in 1257, and 24 plough oxen that remained there after midsummer were charged $\frac{3}{4}$d. a week. 156 pigs were also agisted, presumably in autumn to forage for acorns, a custom known as pannage, for which the king claimed every third pig. That, incidentally, is a high rate of payment, one pig in ten being a more usual ratio. From this it might appear that the king, even if not actively engaged in farming, certainly had agricultural interests in the forest.

MEDIEVAL WINDSOR

The medieval history of the Windsor estate has to be gleaned from incidental references in such documents as have happened to survive. For instance, in 1130 it appears that a William de Bochelande was farming the manor and paying rent for it. At the same time there

95

was evidently a park at Windsor, for the sum of thirty-five shillings was paid to the park-keeper. In the fourth year of King Henry II's reign the name of the farmer at Windsor (presumably the man who rented the manor) was Richard de Lucy; in the nineteenth year of the same reign, it was Osbert de Bray.

From records of the reign of King John it would seem that the manor was probably let to a tenant and not farmed on behalf of the King. The orders for provisions to be purchased for Christmas 1213, when the King kept court there, are of such dimensions that the royal household would have been expecting little from the local manor. The grocery list committed to one Reginald de Cornhill included 200 head of swine, 1000 capons, 500 lb of wax, 50 lb of white bread, 2 lb of saffron, 100 lb of good and fresh almonds, spices for seasoning, 15,000 herrings and other fish, 1000 yds of woven cloth for table napkins etc. Nor was this all. For the same festival the Sheriff of Buckinghamshire was required to provide 500 capons and 20 pigs, a citizen named Matthew Mantell provided 1000 capons and 200 pigs, while farther afield, the Sheriff of Kent had to supply 1000 salted eels. However, John Fitzburgh, who in the third year of King John's reign was paying £26 a year as rent for the 'farm' at Windsor, had to bring 500 capons and adequate supplies of wood, coal, pitchers, cups and dishes, so the royal manor presumably carried its obligations in kind as well as in cash.

As an example of the contradictory states of affairs that seem to have prevailed at Windsor in the Middle Ages, in 1224, Engelard de Cygony, the constable of the Castle, apparently farmed all the royal demesnes there, for we find him collecting rents and dues in kind and also enclosing some of the common pastures, a matter which caused the local peasantry to complain to the King. He also sold his entire stock of corn to the King (Henry III), for £64 13s. 4d. Yet in the same year we note the King giving Engelard a heap of corn in the Castle for feeding his horses.

A record of the charges on the farm at Windsor in this reign survives. They comprise 20s. 10d. to the keeper of the King's houses; 30s. 5d. to the chaplains at Windsor chapel; 30s. 5d. to the keeper of the vineyard; 7s. to 'the keepers of Windsor' (exact role unspecified). The vineyard was evidently planted on land belonging to one William de Windsor, who received 5s. a year rent for it; and Richard de Sifrewast was paid 12s. rent annually for land on which some of the King's houses were built. The monks of Bromhal, in Windsor

Forest, received 8s. 2½d. plus 40d., granted by various monarchs.

The long reign of King Henry III was a period of weak government, but things were tightened up considerably when a more vigorous King, Edward I, came to the throne. At Windsor he ordered an immediate survey of enclosures in the royal forest. Any that had been extended without permission were reduced to their original size and any unauthorised ones, made during the previous reign, reverted to the King. They were to be cultivated and sown for his benefit, as was any wasteland discovered by the commissioners making the survey. The commissioners' report, made in 1273, reveals a long list of offences and encroachments. For example.

> Geoffry de Pickeford, constable and farmer, kept a certain field unenclosed in order that the work horses of Windsor, in going towards their pastures and returning home, should not avoid it but should be taken and impounded, and so Geoffry unjustly extorted great sums of money from the whole country, levied as his dues, to the great damage and destruction of the whole country. The said Geoffry also receives ten pounds yearly for the pasture of Windsor Park, which herbage does not belong to his farm. . . .

Windsor itself was a market town, and farmers and others bringing in stock or produce had to pay a toll, ostensibly to the King, although he in fact let out the privilege to the governor of the Castle. In the reign of King Edward I, the governor was making an annual profit of £5.

When John de L'Isle was appointed constable of the Castle in the first year of King Edward III's reign, 1327, he was required to provide, from the rents, bread, wine, oil and everything else necessary for the performance of religious rites in the chapel at Windsor, and also to pay a long list of officials and servants, including 2½d. per day to 'John, the gardener of the king's garden without the Castle.'

In 1336, Parliament granted the King 'a ninth part of all the corn, wool, lambs and other profits' for the previous year. This tax produced sixteen marks from Windsor, but some of the neighbouring townships offered sundry plausible reasons for paying nothing at all. In 1359 the King called in the grants he had made of lands in the manors of Old and New Windsor and proceeded to enclose them all, pulling down or selling off any surplus houses and buildings. There is a reference to one of the King's cooks buying what was evidently a pleasant property, with a stable, granary and two barns attached to a spacious hall.

THE KING AND THE PEASANT

A delightful tale in Chaucerian verse, purporting to refer to King Edward III and to be set at Windsor, illustrates, if not the King's agricultural activities, at least his relationship with one of his agricultural subjects. Walking with only a groom as his companion in a riverside meadow in May he meets a shepherd who is full of woes, his house having been pillaged by the King's men. Not recognising the King, he pours out his complaints. The King promises him redress, saying that he is a merchant with powerful friends at court and that, in any case, the King's men owe him a lot of money. The shepherd says he is owed £4 2s. and promises his new friend 7s. for himself if he can get the debt paid. 'Come to the court tomorrow', says the King, 'and ask for me. My name is Joly Robyn. Everyman knows it well and finely.'

Adam, the shepherd, now talks freely. He relates how yesterday nine of the King's retainers came to his house, took his hens, geese and sheep, drove him into the cart-house and put his grey-haired wife out of doors. But, he says, if only he could have had some help he could have dealt with them, as he is an expert slinger.

As they walk homewards through the meadows, the King sees many rabbits outside their burrows and invites the shepherd to show his prowess with the sling by knocking over two or three. The shepherd says he is afraid to, as the warrener is 'hardy and fell' and would certainly make him pay for it, if he found out. And he would find out, because 'wood has ears, field has sight'. The shepherd gives a similar answer when the King tries to tempt him to kill some of the abundant wildfowl.

But when they arrive at the shepherd's house and sit down to a meal it is a different story. The shepherd's wife produces a meal of bread made from sifted flour and six kinds of cooked wildfowl, including a heron, curlews and a baked swan, all washed down with ample good ale. His tongue loosened by the ale and prompted by the King, the shepherd reveals that he has better meat than that. He shows the King a baked pasty containing three rabbits and some meat pies of hart and roe deer 'which were alive the day before and came thither by moonlight'.

As they continue drinking the shepherd takes the King more and more into his confidence. He has, he says, 'a littell chaumbur that was made for me'. It is an underground room, deep under the house, and it is full of venison and excellent wine.

On the way back to the fields they again pass the rabbits, and this time Adam has no compunction about slaying a couple of them with sling stones. He agrees to go to the court at Windsor the next day to collect the money due to him. They find the shepherd's dogs quietly guarding the sheep and so they part.

Next day, the shepherd puts on his best clothes and goes to Windsor Castle where the staff have been well briefed in continuing the deceit. The shepherd is invited in to drink and then to dine, which invitation he accepts reluctantly, refusing to take his hat off or to part with his staff. The charade is prolonged, to the delight of the courtiers, but in the end the shepherd is informed of the King's true identity and 'never was a man so sorry as he was then.' The last verses of the poem are missing but we may be sure the adventure ended happily for Adam.

SWANS

Reference to baked swans in the above narrative serves as a reminder of the status of the swans on the Thames at Windsor. Today there are three separate owners: (1) the Crown, (2) the Vintners' Company and (3) the Dyers' Company. Those belonging to the last two are distinguished by markings on the beak, which are made in the course of the annual 'swan-upping', each cygnet being incised with the same marking as that on its parent of the same sex. The royal marking was discontinued by Queen Alexandra, who regarded the operation as cruel. Consequently, all unmarked swans on the Thames are regarded as royal property.

WINDSOR IN TUDOR TIMES

Few records of domestic affairs at Windsor are available for the reigns of Kings Richard I, Henry IV and Henry V.

King Henry VI was only nine months old when he succeeded to the throne in September 1422, and during his long, ill-starred reign management of his estates tended to be slipshod. During his minority, the park at Windsor with its resident deer seems to have been retained as the King's private property, but all the farmland was apparently let out to tenants.

In the reign of King Henry VIII, the Windsor estates seem to have been valued primarily for the venison they produced. King Henry enjoyed hunting there and made frequent gifts of fat bucks to subjects who earned his favour. Little is recorded of farms or farming, and frequent references to consignments of fruit and vegetables brought to Windsor from other royal manors, including Richmond, Hampton Court and Greenwich, suggest that even the gardens were somewhat neglected.

WINDSOR IN STUART TIMES

In 1608–1609 King James I employed John Norden, the celebrated topographer, to make a survey with detailed plans of 'The Honor of Windsor'. Windsor Forest, Norden found, had a circumference of $77\frac{1}{2}$ miles and lay chiefly in Berkshire and Surrey but extended also into Hampshire, Oxfordshire, Buckinghamshire, Middlesex and Wiltshire (the last being accounted for by some detached parts of Wiltshire then existing near Swallowfield and Wokingham). The Forest was divided into sixteen Walks, of which three were stocked with fallow deer, twelve with red deer and one with both species. This would seem to imply that each Walk was well fenced, were it not for Norden's statement that the boundaries between them were so vague that 'not one of the keepers truilie knoweth his owne boundes'. However, within the Walks were enclosures of palings, and presumably the deer spent most of the time within these havens. The 'Greate Parke' is listed as one of these enclosures; the Little Park, adjoining the Castle, is another, its area being given as 280 acres.

The Great Park has a circuit of $10\frac{1}{4}$ miles and covered 3650 acres. An estimate of the number of deer in the park at that time was about 1800, 500 being bucks, but Norden stresses that this was only an estimate. Many of the places and landmarks mentioned by Norden can still be identified, though the task is made difficult by the fact that in his maps he did not employ a uniform scale.

Norden's survey also mentions a 'garden plott' near Windsor castle, a timber yard, a warren and various other items but says nothing of any agricultural land. It is clear that the King regarded the parks as his own property but that the farmland adjoining them had largely passed out of his control. James frequently hunted in

Windsor Park – a record of September 1617 refers specifically to 'the hunting of the wild boar' there. In 1623 the King approved an ambitious scheme for draining the Great Park 'and conveying the water which now overspreadeth divers parts', at an estimated cost of £300. The great Dutch engineer, Cornelius Vermuyden, was put in charge of the work, which was completed in 1624 having, in truly modern style, cost about twice as much as the original estimate.

In the disturbed period leading up to the Civil War large-scale disturbances occurred in Windsor Forest. Beginning in the Surrey section of the forest they soon extended into Berkshire; fences were pulled down and large numbers of deer killed. Several deer-stealers were caught and sent to Newgate Prison, but they escaped and were soon committing the same offence again. Windsor town throughout the conflict tended to side with Parliament against the King, which increased the difficulties of maintaining order in the forest.

After the execution of Charles I a committee of the House of Commons, appointed to make a survey of the royal parks, forests and other properties, determined that they should be charged with providing revenue to clear off the arrears of pay due to the army. The area of the Great Park was then found to be 3670 acres with an annual value of £1371. It was divided into four Walks and held 953 deer, as well as large numbers of rabbits. The committee earmarked 2604 trees for felling for the navy.

The same committee took note of the King's Garden, adjoining the Castle, and found it to comprise just over three acres and to have an annual value of £28. It also found a number of farmsteads or detached fields granted in times past by monarchs to individuals and now mostly in a 'ruinated' condition. Shaw Farm, already known by that name, is said to consist of 'two buttries, a milke house, three larders, a kitchen, a hall, two parlours and a chamber below staires, six chambers, three lofts and foure closetts above staires, one great barne, a stable and outhouse with a court yard and two other yards and an orchard conteineing in the whole by estimacion $3\frac{1}{2}$ acres; value per annum, £6.'

The Little Park was put up for sale and seems to have been actually sold and soon afterwards re-purchased for the use of the Lord Protector, Oliver Cromwell. A survey made for the purposes of the sale gave its acreage as $168\frac{1}{2}$ and its annual value £210 12s. 6d. The standing trees in the Little Park were valued at £220. Nearby the King's Meadowe, sold at the same time, extended over $51\frac{3}{4}$ acres and had an estimated annual value of £77 12s. 6d.

During the Commonwealth, Windsor Castle and its parks and estates was under the control of the Constable of the Castle, Sir Bulstrode Whitelock, who seems to have been a reasonably efficient custodian and to have handed back most of the property not unduly dilapidated to the King at the Restoration. In his summary of the rights and duties of his office, set down in a letter to his successor, he estimates that Windsor Forest then had a circumference of 120 miles. There is much in the document about game and timber but nothing about farmland. Some plots of land seem to have been sold off, however, during the Commonwealth, for in the years after 1660 items of payment for 'land taken into the parke' occur quite frequently in the chamberlain's accounts. Evidently King Charles II was buying back property with a view to rounding off his estate and restoring it to its former extent. One such purchase was for the specific purpose of making a tennis court.

When in 1680 the King determined to create a broad avenue, the Long Walk, linking the Great Park with the Castle, he found that all the land he needed was in private hands, and he had to pay £1242 4s. 9d. to acquire it. In 1699 an inquiry was instituted into the rents payable for land and houses on the royal estates at Windsor. The total came to just short of £800 a year, of which £542 went to the Lord Chancellor but, for some reason, £247 to the Earl of Portland.

In the same year the Windsor parishioners sent a petition to the King, William III, complaining that when purchasing land to enlarge the Little Park he had made no allowance for common and other rights attached to the land, including the right to extract gravel for road repairs. The King accepted the petition and made the parishioners a grant of £80 a year from 31 acres of the land as compensation. The arrangement was short-lived, for in Queen Anne's reign, the Queen's surveyor-general reports that he 'had directions to cause the banks and hedges on the said 31 acres to be levelled for making the more commodious way for Her Majesty with her coaches, carriages and attendants to pass there, which I accordingly did. . .'. So the Queen made alternative arrangements for compensating the tenants for their lost income from the land.

WINDSOR UNDER THE GEORGES

In 1742 a further survey of Windsor and its neighbourhood was

undertaken and a map prepared by a Mr Collier. It is concerned only
with the immediate environs including the Little Park, which is now
depicted as a park proper and not divided into small fields, as in
Norden's time (see above). The Long Avenue and other avenues were
now growing well and giving the landscape a more formal
appearance.

So we come to the reign of King George III and the wholesale
changes which that monarch effected. A survey made of the Little
Park in 1788 reflects the new interest, shared by the King, in things
agricultural. The Park is described as:–

> enclosed with a high brick wall and decorated with Clumps and
> shady walks of fine trees. That part called the Lower Park or
> Datchet and Mastrick Meadows, is a deep loamy soil on a gravelly
> bottom producing a rich Grass which fattens Cattle very speedily.
> The Upper Park, or Frogmore side, is a clay soil upon Chalk, which
> also produces good grass, but in very dry weather the higher part
> is apt to be parched.
>
> Towards the middle of the Park is the Keeper's Lodge, a
> romantic habitation under a steep bank; and along the west side of
> the Park is the Kitchen Garden, with the Gardener's House
> enclosed with high brick walls.
>
> By order of His Majesty it has been lately subdivided with neat
> railing into convenient portions by which means Cattle are
> confined to the different subdivisions at pleasure, but the railing is
> made so as to admit the Deer ranging all over the Park.

(The Keeper's Lodge is now, incidentally, the site of the dairy.)

In the same survey the following description is given of
Frogmore:–

> Frogmore Farm is a leasehold from the Crown in the tenure of R.
> Newel Esq.; that occupied by Miss Owen is a double house with
> offices, gardens, etc, for the accommodation of a genteel Family,
> with a field of rich meadow adjoining the premises.
>
> Great Frogmore is also a leasehold from the Crown in the Tenure
> of Mrs Egerton, consisting of a complete dwelling house with a
> coach house, stables and other outhouses, gardens, pleasure
> ground and Grove, a Paddock of excellent Meadow land, all within
> a ring fence and at present in complete repair.

In due course Queen Charlotte purchased the lease of Great Frogmore from Mrs Egerton and made it one of her favourite residences.

In 1791 the King appointed Prince William, son of the Duke of Gloucester, to be ranger of Windsor Park, but with agricultural schemes in mind he reserved for himself the management of the land. The Great Park then comprised 3800 acres, of which the King turned about 2000 acres into farmland, giving the two main units the names of Norfolk and Flemish Farms, on account of the Norfolk and Flemish systems of husbandry practised there. (The stock of deer in the park was, however, not reduced, remaining at approximately 3000.)

An Enclosure Act for Windsor Forest, passed by Parliament in 1817, gave the King some further large slices of land. In return for his rights in the forest and in certain manors within its boundaries His Majesty was allotted a total of 6665 acres. The expenses of the survey and award being very considerable, nearly 1900 had to be sold to meet them within the first two years after the passing of the Act, and even that was not enough. 1450 acres of the newly acquired land adjoining Windsor Great Park were incorporated in it and planted with timber for the Navy. Other large sections of the royal allotment were devoted to the Royal Military College at Sandhurst and to Ascot Racecourse. Much of the rest was planted with fir and larch. And so, in the early years of the nineteenth century, the ancient Forest of Windsor effectively ceased to exist.

In addition to these major enclosures minor ones occurred at the same period. Thus one of the two Dukes of Cumberland, who were successively rangers of the park in the second half of the eighteenth century, made a very large enclosure of wasteland in the parish of Egham. As lord of the manor, the Crown, for which he was ostensibly acting, had the right to make such an enclosure provided that sufficient common land was left for the other commoners to enjoy their established rights. On this occasion the Duke 'forgot' to allow for any compensation and the Crown had to make a substantial grant to the parish after his death. Other lands adjoining the royal property were acquired by purchase.

During the Regency the Norfolk and Flemish Farms were let out to tenants, but King George IV and King William IV took them in hand again and farmed them through the services of a bailiff. In King William's reign, too, large new orchards and kitchen gardens were laid out near Frogmore, and the lodge in the Little Park was converted to a dairy. Nearby extensive pens were made to house 'choice domestic fowl'.

PRINCE ALBERT TAKES OVER

On the accession of Queen Victoria the Commissioners of Woods advised the Queen that it was not appropriate for a public department to manage and cultivate farm lands. They paid the executors of King William IV £10,478 10s. for the farm implements, stock and crops on all the Windsor farms but proposed to cease cultivations and to lay down the land to grass. This programme had already begun when Prince Albert intervened, having been appointed to the post of Ranger of Windsor Great Park soon after his marriage. He accordingly took over all the assets of the farms at valuation from the Commissioners and proceeded to farm the lands himself, in his usual efficient manner.

At about the same time, 1843, the Crown also purchased an estate from Mr Frederick Walpole Keppel, which interlocked with the royal property near Frogmore. The new acquisition, totalling 287 acres, included Clay Hall Farm, which is still one of the farming units at Windsor.

In 1850 a new road linking Windsor with Datchet cut off a section of the Home Park, amounting to $77\frac{3}{4}$ acres, from the remainder. This detached portion was, by royal permission, used as the site of the Exhibition of the Royal Agricultural Society of England in 1851 and was afterwards made into a public park 'for the recreation of pedestrians'.

It seems, however, that the original scheme for grassing down Norfolk Farm in the Great Park was revived and partially put into execution in about 1870.

THE CASHMERE GOATS OF WINDSOR

An odd little agricultural interlude at Windsor is provided by the story of the Windsor herd of Cashmere goats. It begins in Paris in the year 1823, when someone in France conceived the idea of establishing a new industry based on Cashmere wool. Weaving Cashmere wool was quite big business in Cashmere, so why should it not be the same in Europe?

At the time when the first consignment of Cashmere goats arrived in Paris, an Essex landowner, Christopher Tower, happened to be visiting the city. For him, too, the idea caught fire and after much persuasion he managed to buy from the French importers two pairs of the coveted goats. Before long he had a thriving colony of them sharing his parkland near Brentwood with red deer.

The process of starting a weaving industry took longer than Mr Tower had expected, for even a mature billy-goat produces only about four ounces of fine Cashmere wool per year, but by 1828 he had enough for the first Cashmere shawl ever made in England from home-produced wool. It won him a gold medal from the Society of Arts. Elated, he offered a pair of goats to the King, George IV, who cheerfully accepted them.

When Queen Victoria came to the throne she found their progeny firmly established in Windsor Park. Encouraging such a project naturally appealed to the Queen and later to Prince Albert, and for the next thirty years or so they had their own 'cottage industry'. Cashmere shawls were fashionable, and helping to sort the Queen's Cashmere wool became quite a popular pastime for leisured ladies. It is said that at one time more than a thousand people were engaged in processing and manufacturing the wool.

By the 1880s the herd was showing signs of deterioration through inbreeding. Small infusions of blood from other herds established in Britain were inadequate, so in 1889 a fresh herd from India was presented to the Queen. Their appearance on arrival was startling, for, far from being clad in soft Cashmere wool, they were stark naked. On the voyage it had been discovered that they were infested with lice and fleas. The appropriate remedies were applied but unfortunately the insecticides were based on paraffin oil, which in the hot tropical sun soon took off all their hair.

However, a sufficient number survived to give the Windsor herd a new lease of life. Cashmere goats continued to live happily in the Great Park until 1936, when they were dispersed, most of them going to London Zoo. The herd there still supplies mascots for the Welch Regiment.

VEGETABLE GARDENS AT OLD WINDSOR

Reference in one of the earliest records (see p. 93) to the two bordars who in 1086 held their land on the Windsor manor by virtue of supplying the royal household, when in residence, with poultry, eggs and other small produce, serves to remind us that the king's kitchen required more than meat and bread. Most of the common vegetables including cabbages, peas, leeks, onions, parsnips, turnips, lettuce and garlic, were probably widely cultivated, even in Saxon times.

The first apparent reference to gardens at Windsor is dated 1231, when King Henry III directed payment of tithes on the royal garden there to the church at Windsor. That implies that a value was placed on the produce; the garden was not for pleasure only. Thirteen years later, in 1244, another document refers to the house of the King's gardener and to the hedge around the garden. A pleasure garden was, however, created at Windsor by command of King Henry III in 1240, and included a lawn, an oaken fence and a stone fountain. King James I of Scotland, who was imprisoned at Windsor for eighteen years, found the gardens delightful, describing them in a poem, *The King's Quair*:–

> Now was there made, fast by the tower's wall
> A garden fair, and in the corners set
> An arbour green, with wandes long and small
> Railed about, and so with trees set
> Was all the place, and hawthorn hedges knit,
> That life was none, walking there forebye
> That might within scarce any wight espy.
> So thick the boughs, and the leaves green
> Beshaded all the alleys that there were,
> And 'midst every arbour might be seen
> The sharp, green, sweet junipers
> Growing so fair, with branches here and there,
> That, as it seemed to alife without,
> The boughs spread the arbour all about,
> And on the small green twisties sat
> The little sweet nightingale, and song
> So loud and clear the ympuis consecrate
> Of love his use, now soft, now loud among
> That all the gardens and the walls rung
> Right of their song.

Another early reference to the gardens occurs in an account of the enlargement of the Castle in the reign of King Edward III. Two herb gardens are mentioned, situated apparently in quadrangles surrounded by cloisters. The herbs grown would doubtless include what would now be termed garden flowers such as violets, stocks (gillyflowers), wallflowers, lavender, cowslips and roses, all to be plucked and taken indoors to combat foul smells and to ward off illness.

By the time of King Edward IV the gardens were evidently extensive, for in September 1472, the King and a distinguished guest (Lord Gruthuyse, who had entertained him lavishly when he was in exile in the Netherlands) spent pleasant hours strolling through the gardens at Windsor until it was time for evensong. A little later, in the reign of King Henry VII, an item in the Privy Purse accounts refers to a sum of money paid, 'by the Queen's commandment to the keeper of the little garden at Windsor'.

The Tudor period saw great advances in the art of gardening, and many vegetables and flowers are mentioned in literature for the first time, though it is uncertain whether that is because they were then introduced to England or because any earlier documentary reference to them has been lost. W. Harrison, who wrote *A Description of England in Shakespeare's Youth* mentions 'radishes, carrots, melons and pompons' as examples of the crops that a poor man might expect to grow on his acre of land. Globe artichokes were also grown, and Jerusalem artichokes from 1617 onwards. Sir Walter Raleigh introduced potatoes in 1586 but they were not widely cultivated until much later.

In the reign of King Henry VIII the royal gardens certainly flourished, including those at Hampton Court, Greenwich, Windsor and Beaulieu. Consignments of vegetables and fruit were sent regularly from Hampton Court, Greenwich and Kew to Windsor Castle when the Court was residing there, which would seem to imply that supplies from the Windsor gardens were not adequate.

King William III made a number of improvements to the surroundings at Windsor. Among other projects, he enlarged the Little Park by adding several riverside meadows and had it enclosed by a new brick wall. Queen Anne gave her chief attention to the Great Park, where she loved to hunt. When her increasing weight and bulk prevented her from riding, she used to follow the chase in a specially-constructed, light, one-seater, one-horse vehicle called a calash, which according to contemporary accounts she drove furiously. To assist her headlong career through the Park, new curving roads were laid out. She also had ambitious plans for the Windsor gardens, including the construction of a new riverside pleasure garden, but its destruction by flood before it was properly finished discouraged her.

Neither King George I nor King George II lived much at Windsor, though both visited it occasionally. The principle of supplying the royal household with fruit and vegetables from all the royal gardens within reach prevailed until early in the reign of Queen Victoria. By that time, the inconvenience of obtaining provisions from so many sources had become so obvious that an official committee was appointed to report on the state of the royal gardens. It recommended that the kitchen garden at Kensington should be sold; the kitchen garden at Kew annexed to the botanic gardens; the gardens at Buckingham Palace, Cranbourne Lodge and Cumberland Lodge suppressed; and the gardens at Hampton Court let. At the same time the committee suggested that the gardens at Windsor should be extended by taking in land from the fields south of Frogmore House. An Act of Parliament containing these recommendations was passed in 1841, and in the succeeding years the new kitchen gardens at Frogmore were established at a cost of around £50,000. The first garden enclosure had an area of thirty-one acres, but as this was soon found to be inadequate it was extended by a further twenty acres. Later in the century, in the 1880s, a four-acre orchard of standard fruit trees, chiefly apple, was planted on the north side of the gardens, making the total acreage fifty-five.

Frogmore itself, deriving its name from the frogs which frequented the wet meadows there, had belonged to the Crown in Tudor times but had been sold off during the Civil War. At various times it was the property of the Duke of Northumberland, then of Sir Edward Walpole, and finally, in the reign of King George III, it was purchased by Queen Charlotte.

The Frogmore gardens still comprise approximately the same acreage, and in both vegetable and fruit production they operate on a truly impressive scale. An article in the *Gardeners' Magazine* on 6 June 1896, gives a few details of the gardens at that time:–

Here may be seen in a warm corner an acre or so each of early cauliflowers and potatoes; in another sheltered position, double the area of spring cabbages; and, outside the walls, 10 or 12 acres of potatoes; other crops being grown in proportion. For example, the asparagus beds, irrespective of those annually forced, have an aggregate length of 2219 yards, and the rows of peas that will have been sown before the end of the current season would, if placed end to end, extend upwards of five miles.

The forcing of asparagus in permanent beds forms an important

Opposite: Princess
Elizabeth and Princess
Margaret inspecting carrots
in their vegetable garden at
Windsor, 1943 *Studio
Lisa*

part of the work of the kitchen garden, and the annual supply of this delicious vegetable obtained by the aid of artificial heat must be enormous. The beds occupy a position at the north-east corner of the gardens and are placed parallel to each other, with narrow pits between them. Their length is 75 feet and their width about 6 feet. . . .

The writer of this article also supplies the total quantities of fruit sent from Frogmore to the royal household in 1895. The tally was :–

Cooking apples	400 bushels
Dessert apples	1673 dozen
Pears	1500 dozen and 20 pecks
Apricots	178 dozen and 42 pecks
Cherries	1250 lb
Plums	500 lb
Greengages	30 dozen and 36 quarts
Damsons	975 lb
Grapes	5150 lb
Peaches	520 dozen
Nectarines	220 dozen
Pineapples	239 (aggregate weight, 1600 lb)
Melons	400
Strawberries	2700 lb
Raspberries	600 lb
Currants (red & white)	2000 lb
Gooseberries	1800 lb

THE GARDENS UNDER KING GEORGE VI

In his book *The Royal Gardeners*, published in 1951, Dr W. E. Shewell-Cooper describes the Windsor Castle gardens as 'virtually a huge, well-managed allotment' or, alternatively, 'a huge horticultural factory'.

'Every day', he writes, 'a vanload of vegetables, fruit and flowers must go up to Buckingham Palace, and when the Royal Family is living at Balmoral it is usually necessary to supplement what is grown in Scotland by produce from the south. Day in and day out vegetables and flowers must be grown, cleaned and despatched.'

He gives the total acreage devoted to vegetables as twenty-four,

with about eight acres of fruit and one acre to crops under glass. Flowers grown outdoors for cutting occupy two acres.

He notes that King George VI and Queen Elizabeth always preferred vegetables to be gathered when fresh and young – marrows not more than eight inches long; runner beans when less than ten inches long; carrots pulled at the 'bunched carrots' stage; beetroot when about the size of golf-balls. The gardeners were not using any chemical fertilizers, except occasionally as a tonic, but employed vast quantities of farmyard manure from the royal farms and also compost made from vegetable waste.

King George VI was fond of the nectarberry, a hybrid fruit related to the loganberry, wine-dark in colour but sweeter than any loganberry or blackberry. Apples, pears and plums were grown in great variety, in order to extend the season of ripeness for as long as possible. Quinces and crab-apples were cultivated for fruit for jelly, and Morton thornless blackberries for making the Queen Mother's favourite blackberry-and-apple pie.

THE CONTEMPORARY GARDENS

The present gardens occupy some forty acres, of which about two acres are devoted to flowers (for cutting) and about four acres to soft fruit. In addition, there are just over two acres of glass, including two vast glasshouses of about an acre each. Sadly, all the wall fruit on the numerous tall brick walls, ideally suited to the purpose, has been dispensed with in the interests of economy. No more quinces, pears, peaches, nectarines, thornless blackberries or other delights; and an orchard of Cox's Orange Pippins has been eradicated, to be replaced by one at Sandringham. (The field where the orchard was once situated has reverted to the farm and in 1978 was bearing a crop of barley.)

Both Windsor and Buckingham Palace are, however, still supplied with vegetables, soft fruit and flowers from the Windsor gardens. The vans now go up to London three times a week, more often if necessary, for the gardens have to provide all the flowers for State visits as well as for the daily interior decorations of the two royal residences. Because the state rooms of the Palace and the Castle are so lofty, there is a demand for unusually tall pot plants, and the greenhouses produce some of the most magnificent specimens of fuchsias, begonias and other spectacular flowers to be found anywhere. Smaller pot plants, such as cyclamens, gloxinias and cinerarias, are grown in enormous quantities.

The greenhouses, gas-heated with an oil-fired reserve as an alternative when necessary, were in fact in the process of being replaced or extended in 1977/78. Their renovation was just about due, for they were last updated in 1901, having originally been erected in 1841. An extensive new range has been built and the general layout improved.

Every possible vegetable and herb is grown on a commercial scale on the outdoor plots, even such varieties as angelica and scorzonera. The royal households, of course, have priority for all produce, but a large surplus is produced and is sent to Brentford Market. The availability of adequate irrigation in every part of the gardens is a tremendous asset.

A fairly recent venture is mushroom-growing, which was started in five or six sheds in 1960. The enterprise proved so satisfactory, economically, that in 1975 the area devoted to the crop was doubled.

The production cycle is now rigidly controlled, so that a steady supply of mushrooms is ready for market every day of the year. It is one of the most up-to-date businesses of its kind anywhere but does not use the ready-made compost favoured by most mushroom growers. Instead, it is fortunate in having an adequate source of horse-manure in Windsor Barracks and the Royal Mews, twenty tons of which are delivered each week.

The mushroom project was the brain-child of Mr David Stevenson, the recently retired head gardener, a relaxed, courteous and exceptionally able Scotsman who has been at the Windsor gardens for 27 years. One of his staff who retired a few years ago can remember the time when 149 men were employed in the garden; now the staff is down to about 25. The attractive gardener's house which he once occupied ('designed for a household with two servants') is now divided into offices and flats, and he lives in a pleasant new bungalow a courtyard away. The new head gardener is Mr Anthony Wilkie.

When the Queen is at Windsor, she frequently visits the gardens and takes a great interest in what goes on. Prince Philip is also interested, but the really keen gardener in the Royal Family is the Queen Mother, who is a horticulturist in the tradition of Queen Charlotte.

THE VINEYARDS OF WINDSOR

Within the past ten or twenty years the cultivation of grapes in England has become so widespread (there are now more than a thousand acres of English vineyards) that it is no longer a novelty. Earlier in the present century the number of commercial vineyards, confined to the Home Counties, could be counted on the fingers of one hand. But the myth that grapes will not grow outdoors in England has been effectively dispelled, and indeed a perusal of past records would at any time have shown that the idea was fallacious.

Grapes grown for wine were an English crop for many centuries from Roman times onwards. The practice of cultivating vineyards, however, fell into disuse in the Middle Ages, when a temporary deterioration of the climate coincided with the sovereignty of English kings over the splendid wine-growing province of Aquitaine. For several hundred years Bordeaux was an English port, sending huge shipments of wine to England, and English vine-growers, harassed by cool, rainy summers, could not compete.

It should be no surprise, therefore, to find early mentions of vineyards at Windsor. One of the first occurs in the reign of King Henry II, when mention is made of a vineyard in the Castle ditch, and from 1155 onwards the payment of the 'vintager' and the cost of gathering the grapes are regular annual charges in the accounts. When in 1466 King Edward IV took his guest, the Lord Gruthuyse, Lieutenant-General of Holland, walking one evening in 'The Vineyard of Pleasure' at Windsor, the vines were producing some thirty tons of wine a year.

Two hundred years later the vineyard was beginning to be split up, for in 1699 we read that Mr Philip Lovegrove, a local gardener, was allowed to plant a new garden in a section of the Castle ditch which included a vineyard. The permission seems to have been given in the hope that Mr Lovegrove's activities would help to abate a nuisance, for evidently the former gardens, now very much neglected, had become a dumping-ground for refuse. Encroachment had also become common, and among the buildings erected on the site of the old vineyard was Burford House, built for Nell Gwyn and afterwards acquired by Queen Anne. By the end of the eighteenth century all traces of the Windsor vineyards had completely disappeared.

NORFOLK FARM IN WARTIME

When the ploughing-up campaign, designed to return old grassland to cultivation, was being pressed with great urgency in the early years of the Second World War, King George VI, eager as always to set an example to his subjects, decided that the section of the Great Park which had once constituted Norfolk Farm should be reclaimed for food production. A necessary preliminary was the disposal of a vast herd of deer roaming the Park. One day in 1941 they were rounded up and driven into a stockade to be slaughtered, with the exception of a small breeding stock.

The land thus made available for cultivation amounted to about 2000 acres, 1400 of them arable and the rest rough grazing. Reclamation was a formidable task, as the area had been untouched for nearly seventy years. Much of it was growing coarse grass, much of it bushes and bracken, and there were many medium-sized trees to be uprooted. Nor was the soil an easy one to cultivate as it was mostly heavy clay with sandy caps on the hilltops.

The crop rotation adopted was very similar to the original Norfolk four-course, except for modifications that were necessary in order to meet the wartime need for cereals. Either three or four successive arable crops were taken, usually wheat, oats, beans and then either oats or barley undersown with grass, followed by a grass ley for four years. After a rest of seventy years the soil was capable of supplying nutrients for four consecutive crops, after which a further four years under grass, heavily stocked with animals, enabled it to replenish its reserves. The beans were a crop not widely grown in Britain, either then or now, but the clay soil evidently suited them well. In an average year the farm grew about 300 acres of wheat, 200 acres of oats, 200 acres of barley, and 100 acres of beans.

Under the system of alternate husbandry, publicised by Professor Sir R. G. Stapledon in the 1930s and now given the opportunity to demonstrate its excellence, grass was considered a crop worthy of attention equal to that given to other crops. Plant-breeding programmes, notably at Aberystwyth, had produced new varieties of familiar grasses, such as rye-grass, cocksfoot, timothy and meadow fescue, as well as improved varieties of clover, and these were blended into mixtures forming highly productive leys. The mixture used most extensively at Windsor consisted primarily of S23 rye-grass and S100 white clover, designed to give three cuts of grass for silage plus several weeks of grazing annually.

To utilise the grass a herd of about thirty Friesian cows was installed. The best available stock was naturally purchased from some of the leading herds in the country and rewarded their purchasers by producing an average of 12.5 lb of milk at 3.4% butterfat annually over the next six years. All the calves born were scientifically reared, the heifers being kept for herd replacements, the surplus males castrated and either fattened on grass for marketing at three years old or sold as stores at two years. In addition, more Friesian steer calves were bought so that at any one time the farm was supporting about two hundred young beef cattle of various ages.

Besides these main enterprises, Norfolk Farm also ran a herd of Wessex Saddleback pigs, based on forty or fifty sows. The rations for these, as for the milking cows, were made up largely from home-grown cereals. In this connection a wartime crop on the farm was linseed, of which some twenty acres were grown.

THE OTHER WINDSOR FARMS IN WARTIME

Unlike Norfolk Farm, the other royal farms at Windsor retained their agricultural status throughout the late nineteenth and early twentieth centuries. At the outbreak of war they constituted a unit of 650 acres, most of it comprising the present Prince Consort and Shaw Farms. They were run as a typical mixed farm of the period, with a diversity of stock and crops.

The crop rotation was adaptable but usually consisted of three years of cereal crops, chiefly wheat and barley, followed by three years of grass leys (mostly a ryegrass and clover mixture), with potatoes and kale interspersed as required. The Prince Consort's herd of Beef Shorthorns had been transferred to Sandringham, but Queen Victoria's Jersey herd remained, and a herd of pedigree Ayrshires had been acquired. There were no sheep but a considerable flock of poultry and a small herd of Large White pigs.

A survey in 1953, when the farms were reverting to a peace-time economy, shows 230 acres of cereal crops including 44 acres of winter wheat, 41 of spring wheat, 98 of spring barley and 47 of winter oats. The cereal varieties listed will be of interest to farmers, especially to an older generation which remembers them, for all are now obsolete. The winter wheat was of the variety *Hybrid 46*, the spring wheat of the old favourite, *Atle*, the winter oats of *S172*, and the spring barley of *Plumage Archer, Carlsberg* and *Earl,* this last having produced an exceptional malting sample in the previous harvest. The farms had acquired an eight-foot combine-harvester and had installed an oil-fired in-sack grain-drier with a capacity of fifty sacks at a time.

Winter feeding for the dairy herd was based on silage, of which 250 tons were made in 1952, and kale, with a ration of home-produced oats, though some hay was also made. The Ayrshire herd of some forty cows, established in 1951, produced an average of 8239 lb at 3.8% butterfat.

The Jersey herd, of nearly forty cows, (with about thirty followers), were kept primarily for their rich milk, averaging a butterfat content of about 5%. Some of the milk was made into butter and some bottled to supply the royal household. In autumn and early winter the two herds strip-grazed kale until the crop was finished, rationing being by means of an electric fence that was moved daily.

In common with many other mixed farms of the 1950s the royal farms at Windsor kept a commercial flock of poultry in straw yards. The popular Light Sussex/Rhode Island Red cross was favoured, and the flock of a thousand achieved an egg yield of over 60%. Considerable numbers of cockerels were also fattened, and these were caponised.

THE PRESENT DAY FARMS

About 500 acres of land at Windsor can at present be classified as farmland. The main farming units are Shaw Farm, 120 acres; Prince Consort Farm, 210 acres; and Clay Hall Farm, 170 acres. In addition, the horse paddocks are grazed by sheep and cattle, and part of the golf course is cut for hay.

THE SOIL AND TERRAIN

From a farming point of view, the Windsor farms are difficult units. Hemmed in on almost every side by built-up areas, parkland and paddocks they are almost suburban. Numerous tall trees enhance the scenery though not the agricultural potential, and macadamised roads are rather more numerous than a farmer would prefer.

Although so near the Thames, much of the soil is not the rich alluvium so often associated with riparian farms. The flat fields near the river have from 12 to 24 inches of coarse sandy loam over beds of gravel. In winter they can be very wet, as the water rises through the gravel. In summer, when the rainfall (26 inches per year) is usually deficient, they dry out very rapidly and in most years can be very unproductive between mid-June and mid-August. On the higher ground further away from the river, the soils improve to a pleasant, easily-worked loam. Here too, however, the water table in winter is extremely high, making it necessary to remove stock by late October. There are also approximately 170 acres of medium clay which can be much more productive than the other soils in a dry summer. In the 1950s and 1960s, much of this land was devoted to continuous cereal-growing, with the result that by 1970 the crop yields were very poor. In 1971 this area was tile-drained and grassed down.

Soil fertility has improved since a policy of ploughing in as much farmyard manure as possible has been adopted. This valuable commodity was formerly sold off to local gardeners. Even now cereal crops average only about 26–27 cwt per acre, at a time when farmers on better-favoured land tend to regard anything less than 35–40 cwt as unsatisfactory.

The droughts of 1974, 1975 and the worst on record, 1976, are still vividly remembered. Production of all crops was severely reduced, no second cuts of grass could be taken for silage, and the maize crops faltered and died off early. The Windsor lands do best in a showery summer and a dry winter.

ADMINISTRATIVE COMPLEXITY

To the topographical and soil difficulties of the farms one might add administrative problems. Responsibility for the various properties is divided between the Privy Purse, the Crown Estates and the Department of the Environment.

Shaw Farm and Clay Hall Farm belong to the Crown Estates, who are responsible for the maintenance of roads and buildings. For these farms the Queen pays rent in the normal way. On the Prince Consort Farm the buildings and other features form an appurtenance of the Castle and are therefore maintained by the Department of the Environment. No rent is paid for this farm, which is, in effect, a back garden to the Castle. As with all the royal farms, the Windsor farms are nowadays budgeted on the basis of being self-supporting.

ARABLE CROPS

In view of their low yields, it is as well that cereals are not the main product at Windsor. The acreage devoted to them fluctuates, dependent upon the numbers of livestock, the quantities of winter foodstuff in stock and the rotational demands of the farm. In 1977 the total crop consisted of 80 acres of spring barley, in 1978 there were 35 acres of winter barley, and 65 acres of spring barley. The grain is destined for feeding to the farm livestock, supplementing other rations which are all home-grown as far as possible.

The basis of the winter rations for the cattle herds is about 2000 tons of silage. Ideally, two-thirds of it is grass silage, the rest maize silage, 60 or 70 acres of maize being grown each year. In addition 150 to 200 tons of hay are made. Fortunately the grazing season can be extended and adequate crops of grass ensured on the pastures near the Thames by the operation of an irrigation system using water from the river. The Wright Rain unit employed is capable of applying one inch of rain to 2 acres every three hours. It concentrates chiefly on 40 acres of grassland grazed by the Jersey cows, irrigating them about once a fortnight.

The animals for whom all this fodder is conserved are primarily the two herds of pedigree cattle, one of Jerseys, the other of Ayrshires.

THE WINDSOR HERD OF JERSEYS

Of all her farm animals, the Jerseys are the Queen's pride and joy. Hints that they should be replaced by higher-yielding Friesians meet with definite Royal disapproval. The only concession to the demands of economic viability has been that exhibiting at shows has been abandoned for the past few years. It was argued that to have a big proportion of the herd calving at the right season for summer shows meant that maximum milk production tended to coincide with the lowest prices.

Nevertheless, it must have been a difficult decision, for the herd had a remarkable record in the show ring over a long period of years. The Queen was proud of its achievements and particularly of the fact that nearly all of the major prizewinners were home-bred. Details of the Queen's Jersey herd are contained in Appendix III on page 243 Data such as these, although conceivably dust-dry to many of her subjects, are far from being so to Her Majesty. When, at the age of six,

Princess Elizabeth had a school curriculum prepared for her by her governess Miss Crawford, Queen Mary, to whom it was submitted, considered that it ought to allow more time for history, geography and Bible reading. 'Her Majesty felt that genealogies, historical and dynastic, were very interesting to children and, for these children, really important.'

The Queen was right. Most children go through a phase when they are fascinated by lists, catalogues and pedigrees, and if their imagination is captured at the critical stage they may retain that interest for life. Queen Elizabeth II is one of those fortunate persons. Her knowledge of her family history is unsurpassed, and the interest in human pedigrees has been extended to those of her favourite animals. Her love for her horses is well-known. Her knowledge of their breeding is encyclopedic. By her desk she keeps books of racehorse pedigrees. And it is only to be expected that she would have a similar interest in the breeding of the splendid herd of Jersey cattle inherited from her great-great-grandmother, Queen Victoria.

Since 1971, fifty animals from the Windsor herd of Jerseys have been exported to establish or reinforce notable herds overseas. Oman, which is in the process of establishing a modern dairy industry of its own, has been the chief customer, purchasing four

Jersey cattle from the
Queen's herd at Windsor
Edward Haydon Wood

bulls and fourteen heifers. Of the other exports, eight heifers and a bull have gone to Brazil; six heifers and a bull to Libya; four heifers and a bull to Turkey; three heifers to France; one bull to Greece; two heifers to New Zealand; two bulls to Kenya; one bull to U.S.A.; and two bulls to Iran.

THE WINDSOR HERD OF AYRSHIRES

The Ayrshire herd was founded in 1951 in the last year of the reign of King George VI. The foundation animals were purchased mainly from the Clarendon herd, and throughout its early years a succession of Clarendon-bred sires was used. In the 1960s the breeding policy was to use the Bull of the Day from the Reading Artificial Insemination Centre, with the occasional hiring of a 'laid-off' bull from the Milk Marketing Board. The herd remained fairly closed until the early 1970s when considerable expansion occurred. It now numbers about 150 cows with their followers, a total of some 260 animals.

In the 1970s, numerous nominated sires have been used as well as young bulls hired from breeders. An excellent young bull, Townhead Worthy Line, purchased in 1974, is leaving his mark on the herd as his daughters come in to milk.

Approximately 30% of the herd is inseminated with a beef bull. The Continental exotic breeds have been used with mixed results. The Charolais was the most successful until the 1976/77 calving season when some fairly disastrous calving problems resulted. The beef sires now used are Murray Grey for cows and Aberdeen Angus for heifers. Of the remaining 70% of the herd, the policy is to breed 50% to proven sires and 20% to young bulls (on progeny test), using natural service. The lactation statistics for 1974–1976 are as follows:–

Ayrshires	No. Cows	No. Heifers	Average Cows (lb)	Yield Heifers (lb)	% B.F.	Calving Index
1977–78	87	33	12441	12025	3–91	372

MILKING ARRANGEMENTS

The Prince Consort's cowshed, where seventy cows stood head to head, was used by the Jersey herd until 1973. Then an 8:8 Gascoigne Rotary Tandem milking parlour was installed. With semi-automatic feeding, the parlour enables fifty cows per hour to be milked at a very comfortable rate for both man and cow.

As for the Ayrshires, since the herd was started in 1953, three different types of milking parlour, each of the latest design when installed, have been used. From 1951 to 1968 a 6:8 abreast parlour served; from 1968 to 1977 a 5:10 herringbone parlour took over; and in 1977 a 14:14 low-line herringbone parlour, equipped with automatic cluster removal, was installed. This latest parlour makes it possible for the expanded herd, now 160 cows, to be milked in two and a half hours in the morning and two hours in the afternoon.

THE PIG HERD

From 1968 to the end of 1977 the Windsor farms were engaged in producing gilts (young sows) for the firm BOCM. At first, this involved crossing Wessex sows with Landrace and Large White boars; then in 1971 the policy changed and Large White sows were crossed with Landrace boars. From January 1st 1978 the herd became purely a commercial pig unit, breeding its own replacements.

Between 1 April 1972, and 31 March 1978, the average number of sows in the herd increased from 50 to 64.4, and the number of pigs sold, from 1078 to 1436. In the year ending 31 March 1978, the number of litters born per sow was 2.12, the average number of pigs per litter was 11.3, and the average number of pigs reared per sow per year was 22. The pigs were sold at an average weight of 176 lb.

MACHINERY AND EQUIPMENT

The power units at the farm at the time of my visit in May 1978 were seven Ford tractors, from the giant Ford 8100 to the little Dexta, two of them equipped with foreloaders. There was a complete range of cultivation equipment, including a Ransome four-furrow reversible plough. Also a Vicon 30-cwt fertilizer-distributor, a Chafers 450-gallon sprayer and a Howard farmyard manure spreader. For haymaking, silage-making and harvesting, the farms had a New Holland combine-harvester and baler, a Claas Jaguar-60 forage-harvester with maize attachment, a Fahr mower, a hay-tedder and a swath-turner. Hay was dried in a barn by a drying unit with underfloor air ducts.

An important part of the equipment of this drought-harassed farm

is a Wright Rain irrigation unit, capable of applying an inch of rain to two acres every three hours. It is employed principally to irrigate the grazing pastures at intervals of between ten and fourteen days.

BUILDINGS AND HOUSES

Ample buildings and houses are maintained to enable all the present staff and livestock to be housed in total comfort. The nucleus of the farmstead is the group of buildings erected by the Prince Consort in 1852–1858, which have changed very little exteriorly from the original design. Additions have been made in the form of two covered yards, and a new rotary milking parlour has been installed at one end of the Victorian cowshed. A large forage barn has been built to replace existing storage space destroyed by fire at Shaw Farm. Other recent additions are a pig-fattening house for two hundred pigs (1958) and two large sow-yards (1968, 1973). A large 'midden', once the only means of making high-quality manure for fertilizing the fields, is still maintained.

ROYAL VICTORIAN DAIRY

The original dairy, although now unused, remains as an historic monument to the most hygienic manner (cost was no object) of handling milk and milk products in the nineteenth century before the days of refrigeration, at a time when bovine T.B. was widespread.

SHAW FARM

The original farm steading designed by Mr G. H. Dean, was built by Prince Consort in 1853 but has now almost totally been demolished and rebuilt to suit modern farming requirements. The major renovation work took place during Her Majesty Queen Elizabeth II's Jubilee Year. The only remains of the original steading are the farm manager or land steward's house and two herdsmen's cottages including the Old Clock Cottage.

Clay Hall Farm buildings consist of an old wooden building originally built and used as a quarantine cowshed for T.B. eradication. It is now used for machinery storage.

In 1973 a large forage barn was erected to store a thousand tons of silage, hay and straw, and also to house young dairy stock.

Clay Hall Farm also used to provide seven cottages, but these were given up in exchange for four new cottages built in the Home Park in 1974.

THE STAFF

The Farm manager at Windsor was, until May 1979, Mr Robin Reeks, who was appointed in 1971. A young Dorset-born graduate of Reading, he had previously served the Milk Marketing Board as a Low Cost Production officer and before that as manager of an intensive arable and livestock farm in Norfolk. His predecessor at Windsor was Mr A. V. Pelly, M.V.O. who held the post for exactly twenty years.

Over the past twenty-seven years the royal farms, including Windsor, have been advised by two consultants, namely Mr Frank Sykes (1951–1971) and Mr Brian Loxton of A.K.C. Ltd (1971 to present date). The other staff comprises:–

Head herdsman of the Ayrshire herd, Dennis O'Hagan, aged 63, who has been at the Home Park farm since 1950, working for twenty years with the Jerseys, Shorthorns and pigs.

Head tractor-driver, Eric Moores, aged 51, who was born in county

The Prince Consort's dairy
Edward Haydon Wood

Angus on the estate of Lord Airlie (father of the Hon. Angus Ogilvy), and who started work at Windsor in 1952.

Head herdsman of the Jersey herd, Alan Cowdrey, aged 48, who had previously been herdsman with Lord Faringdon's famous Buscot herd and who took charge of Her Majesty's Windsor herd in 1957.

Head pigman, Dennis Juffs, aged 52.

Shepherd and tractor driver, Eddie Feswick, aged 30, whose father is head gamekeeper in Windsor Great park.

Assistant herdsman with the Jersey herd, Tony Burton aged 26.

Assistant herdsman with the Ayrshire herd, Roy Warwick, aged 42, who will be head herdsman when Dennis O'Hagan retires shortly. With his three brothers and father he was a tenant farmer on the Chamberlain Estate near Winchester until 1971, when he became head herdsman of a new dairy herd of the same estate. He took up his appointment at Windsor in November 1977.

The 'dairymaid' at the Prince Consort's Dairy, of which she is the custodian, is Mrs June Williams. She lives with her husband in the adjoining cottage and is responsible for bottling milk and making cream and cream cheese for the Palace and Castle.

The milk is delivered to Buckingham Palace three times a week by Mr Williams in bottles stamped with the cypher 'E.R.II' surmounted by a crown and bearing the inscription 'Royal Dairy Farm, Windsor' and capped with green and gold aluminium foil bearing the same cypher and the inscription 'Untreated Milk produced on Royal Farms, Windsor'. Cream and cheese is supplied as required, the cream cheese being packed in special little cartons.

THE GREAT PARK AND ITS FARMS

As noted in Chapter 1 (page 30), the Crown surrendered most of its land revenues in 1760 in return for a fixed annual allowance known as the Civil List. The properties in question, which are administered by the Crown Estate Commissioners, include most of the Windsor estates. Shaw Farm and Clay Hall Farm are both rented by the Queen from the Crown Estate Commissioners, though Prince Consort Farm is regarded as an extension of the Castle grounds.

The state of the agricultural land in Windsor Great Park is somewhat different. That is also administered by the Crown Estate

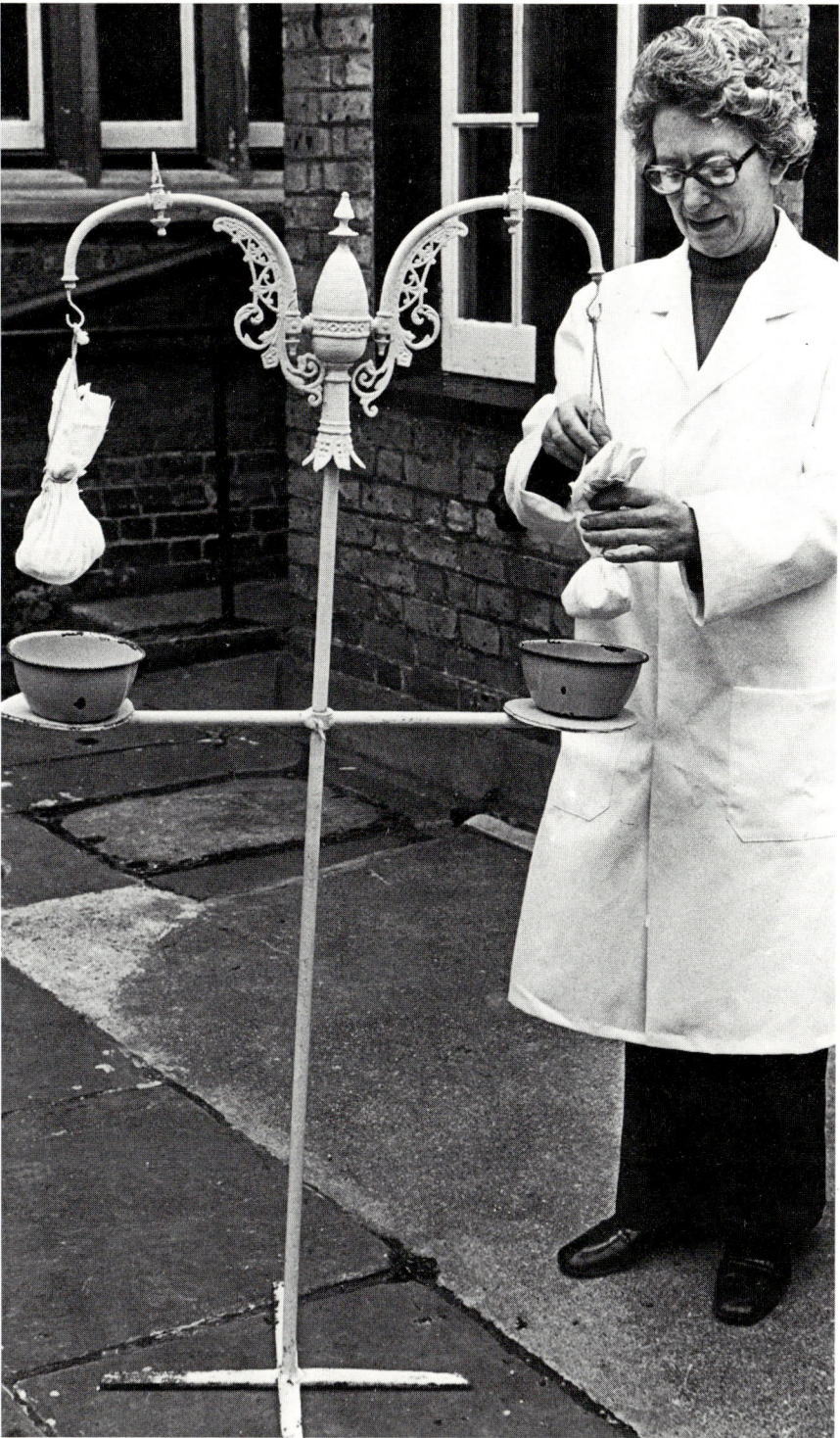

Mrs June Williams, the dairymaid at the Prince Consort's dairy, preparing special cream cheeses for the Queen, using the equipment installed in the Prince Consort's time   *Edward Haydon Wood*

Commissioners but is farmed by them as a commercial enterprise. On the other hand, the Royal Family has a direct interest in it because Prince Philip holds the office of Ranger of Windsor Great Park. It has become customary for a member of the Royal Family to assume this office, recent holders having been:–

Prince Consort	1861
Queen Victoria	1861–1867
Prince Christian	1867–1917
(son-in-law of	
Queen Victoria)	
King George V	1917–1936
King George VI	1936–1952
Duke of Edinburgh	1952–to date

With the Duke of Edinburgh the post is no sinecure. He takes a lively interest in what goes on and particularly in the latest development, the plan to take about seven hundred acres of land out of cultivation and restore them to their former status of a deer-park.

It seems a sensible move. The land can be productive in an emergency, as has been demonstrated, but it is basically poor farmland. Not only is heavy clay the predominant soil, causing drainage problems, but many of the fields are studded with trees, creating difficulties for the modern machinery. If in the future it is urgently needed again it will be all the better for an enforced rest from cultivation, as it was in 1941. It will be a great amenity for the public to have a well-stocked deer-park within easy reach, and for some, as for members of the Royal Family, it will probably be a welcome revival of a remembered landscape.

The introduction of the first batch of red deer from Balmoral in February 1979, made a considerable inroad into the farm acreage. 700 acres subtracted from the 1312 which were then under cultivation reduced the effective farm acreage to about 600. Changes in the farming pattern were obviously necessary. Everything is always in a state of transition, and this applies particularly to the farms in Windsor Great Park in the late 1970s.

A survey of the farming activities before the deer returned reveals that about 400 acres were devoted to cereals (approximately half to winter wheat and half to spring barley), the rest being grassland. The grass was fed, either as hay or grazing, to four hundred Hereford Friesian cows and their progeny, which constituted the main farm

enterprise. Some of these cows were mated with South Devon bulls, others with Sussex bulls, and in 1977 for the first time, with a Charolais bull. All the calves from this autumn-calving herd were kept and fattened, becoming ready for market at the age of about eighteen months. In addition to the recognised farmland, the herd had the run of a variable acreage of parkland, of which some 200 acres a year were usually cut for hay. In winter the parkland also provided grazing for eight or nine hundred sheep, generally agisted from Romney Marsh.

Some of the red deer recently released in Windsor Great Park   Edward Haydon Wood

The future, at the time of writing, is still uncertain but the truncated farm will be basically a beef-producing enterprise. Its boundaries will be very similar to those of the original Norfolk farm and it may well be run on the old Norfolk four-course rotation, with four years of arable crops followed by four years of grass. One possibility is that the basic cattle stock will be commercial Irish blue-grey heifers, mated for their first calf with an Aberdeen Angus bull and for subsequent calves with a Charolais bull. A small pedigree herd of a British breed may also be kept. Everything, however, is still at the conjectural stage.

To make the farm a more viable economic unit it is now being run, for management purposes, in conjunction with the Queen's own

129

farms (Shaw Farm, Prince Consort Farm and Clay Hall Farm) at Windsor. The two units are naturally being costed separately, but an integrated management structure allows labour and machinery to be used more economically. The overall management continues to rest on Mr Roland Wiseman, who has been Deputy Ranger of the Park since 1973. Under him a new farm manager, Mr D. Menzies, who has experience on major estates both in England and Scotland, took charge of the Great Park farm in October 1978, extending his control to the other Windsor farms in April 1979.

The horse ploughing championships at Windsor, 1978 *Nicholas Meyjes*, and *opposite, Windsor, Slough & Eton Express*

5

SANDRINGHAM

When one day in the fifth century AD a party of rough, tough Anglo-Saxons from across the North Sea came to north-western Norfolk and decided to settle there, they found Roman British villagers still in residence. We know this because the name of one of their settlements, Dersingham, combines both Celtic and Anglo-Saxon words. It means 'the dwelling by the water meadow'. Dersingham was evidently one of the most desirable sites in those parts.

Sandringham comes into existence later. It first appears in history as 'Sant Dersingham', or 'Sand Dersingham'. As the population of Dersingham grew, some of the younger families moved out to the higher, poorer land in the vicinity. To be accurate, the soil is not sand but a thin loam overlying chalk, but it is light enough to be regarded as sand by contrast with the lush wet meadows of Dersingham.

ROYALTY'S PREDECESSORS

In the seventeenth century, the manor of Sandringham belonged to the family of Hoste. At some time in the second half of the eighteenth century, the last heiress of that family married one Cornish Henley, who pulled down the old Tudor mansion and replaced it by a typical but unpretentious Georgian house. His son sold the estate, which thereafter changed hands several times before coming into the possession of Charles Spencer Cowper in 1843.

Cowper was addicted to architectural improvements. To him, Henley's house lacked character, an omission he sought to repair by adding a number of imposing features, including a conservatory which, now a billiard room, is the only part of the old house still

surviving. He made use to some extent of the local building material, carstone, a rather soft dark brown stone quarried at Snettisham, a few miles from Sandringham. It is the only stone found in the neighbourhood and can be seen, used in small thin slabs, in many of the local churches and houses.

KING EDWARD VII AT SANDRINGHAM

In 1862, having completed his renovations, Charles Spencer Cowper made up his mind to sell Sandringham and to move to France. His decision coincided with a search Queen Victoria was making for a country house for her eldest son, Albert-Edward, Prince of Wales. In the previous year the Prince, then aged nineteen, had entered Trinity College, Cambridge, and his parents had decided that, although his main home would be at Marlborough House in London, he needed a country retreat where he could relax and enjoy the life of a country gentleman.

The Prince Consort's sudden death in December 1861 did nothing to alter these plans. Instead, Queen Victoria characteristically insisted that, as they had been approved by Albert, they must be implemented. In February the purchase was finalised, and by September the last of the Cowper possessions had been removed and the Prince had taken over.

It was an eventful year for Prince Albert-Edward. He acquired not only a country house of his own, but also a fiancée. In that autumn he embarked on a European tour which included Belgium, where he became engaged to Princess Alexandra of Denmark, whom he had first met in the previous year. Returning to England in November, he stayed at Sandringham for the first time a few weeks later. Then in the following March he was married at Windsor and came to Sandringham to set up his new home.

There followed a period of extensive rebuilding. At first the plan was for a new wing and new guest lodges and outbuildings, and several of the houses, including Park House and The Bachelor's Cottage (later York Cottage), were built. Increasing demands, however, both by the Prince's growing family and for accommodation of numerous guests, soon made the original concept obsolete. The Prince decided that the only course was to pull down the old house and rebuild. Plans prepared by the architect A. J. Humbert were approved in 1867 and the work was completed in 1870. At the same time, the grounds were extensively landscaped, a formidable undertaking involving the filling-in of an ornamental lake and the construction of two new ones.

A royal country estate naturally had to have a farm and the Prince enthusiastically set about providing a completely new set of farm buildings, of which he was very proud. An unusual feature of the farmyard was a gasometer, from which the house and estate were supplied with gas. No trace of it now remains.

When the ambitious schemes were at last completed, certain deficiencies were still apparent. There was, for instance, no room large enough to be used as a ballroom. So in 1881–1884 this was remedied and further extensions made. There was a disastrous fire in 1891 which damaged twenty-six rooms and necessitated substantial repairs. The opportunity was taken to provide yet more bedrooms and to effect other alterations.

During his long years as Prince of Wales, Edward VII spent much of his time at Sandringham, which was one of his favourite residences. Queen Victoria, however, in spite of her determination to purchase the place, visited it only twice.

King Edward VII's prime interest in farming was in stock-breeding. He continued the practice begun by his father at the other royal farms, of establishing flocks and herds of the best stock obtainable and exhibiting animals in the competition classes of leading agricultural shows. His choice of cattle breeds at Sandringham could pass for masterly diplomacy, for his Shorthorns represented the preponderant breed of England, his Highland herd the most characteristic breed of Scotland and his Dexter-Kerries the typical cattle of Ireland. How Wales came to be omitted is not recorded.

His tact even extended to the establishment of two separate Shorthorn herds, in deference to the somewhat rancorous division then existing between the 'Bates' strain of Shorthorns, which concentrated on milking qualities, and the 'Booth' strain, which was primarily concerned with meat production. The herds were kept distinct for many years, until time healed the differences between the two camps. The Sandringham herds were then merged. Prize-winning bulls and cows were purchased from time to time from the best herds of the time, and in 1896 a bull named Gael, which won first prize at the Royal Show at Leicester, was sold for export for the then fantastic figure of one thousand guineas.

The Highlanders were not a regular breeding herd but were maintained by annual importations from Scotland. When fattened, they were frequently exhibited at Christmas fatstock shows, including Smithfield.

The Dexter-Kerry herd was founded in 1887, at the express command of the Prince of Wales, with imports from Ireland and for many years exhibited award-winning entries at breed and fatstock shows. Dexter and a few Jersey cows supplied milk and cream to the royal household at Sandringham.

An early stock-breeding venture on the estate was the establishment of a flock of Southdown sheep in 1866. It became one of the leading flocks in the breed for many years, scoring numerous show successes and developing a sizeable export trade.

Sir Walter Gilbey in his book *The Royal Family and Farming* (1911) writes:

King Edward always took a close interest in the livestock at Sandringham, keeping himself fully informed concerning the progress of studs, herds and flocks. When in residence he never failed to take his place at the ring-side on the occasion of a sale. Success as an exhibitor, whether with horses, cattle or sheep, always gratified him and when he made his inspection of the exhibits at any show he would display the discrimination of a practical farmer in his comments upon the prize-winners and, it often happened, upon animals which had been passed over by the judges.

As Prince of Wales, King Edward became a Life Governor of the Royal Agricultural Society in 1864 and was elected President in 1868–69, 1878–79, 1885–86, 1889–90 and 1900–01. The office was no sinecure. He often attended Council meetings and took part in discussions.

In his time, the British Empire came to high noon, and King Edward was much concerned with the improvement of agriculture and stock-breeding in the colonies and dominions. Any well-devised scheme for exporting good bulls, stallions or rams to the English-speaking countries overseas had his approval. He himself sent Shires from Sandringham to tour the autumn shows in Canada in the early 1890s. His Sandringham Shire Horse stud, established in 1881, became world-famous. Champion after champion came from this stable and the annual Sandringham Shire sales attracted buyers from all parts of the kingdom. He also founded at Sandringham a Hackney Horse stud, which flourished from 1887 until 1901 and won many honours in the show ring.

In spite of King Edward's undoubted interest in agriculture and in stock-breeding in particular, however, there were limits to his dedication, those limits being most sharply defined in relation to sport. In her biography *Queen Alexandra*, Georgina Battiscombe writes:

> It was whispered that the Prince cared little for his tenants' comfort or the condition of their crops in comparison with the well-being of the pheasants and partridges in which the estate abounded. At Sandringham the game was preserved with a strictness which gave rise to talk even in a generation when landlords as a whole were fanatical on the subject of game-preservation, a strictness which made the Prince unpopular with some of his tenants.

Sir Walter Gilbey mentions, in passing, that 'at one time Queen

Alexandra had a farm of her own, on which every animal and every bird was pure white, and in this establishment she took close personal interest'. Unfortunately no records of this enterprise seem to have survived.

KING GEORGE V AT SANDRINGHAM

Sandringham's great fire occurred in November 1891, when the house was being prepared for the Prince of Wales's fiftieth birthday celebrations. On the Prince's insistence the party went on, under a temporary roof of timber and tarpaulins, but the place had been thoroughly drenched in putting out the fire and had not properly dried out. The trying conditions had perhaps something to do with Prince George falling ill with typhoid almost immediately afterwards and with Prince Albert-Victor, the Duke of Clarence, contracting influenza. Prince George (later King George V) was rushed off to more salubrious quarters in Marlborough House, but the Duke of Clarence, heir to the throne, died at Sandringham, aged just twenty-eight and having just become engaged to Princess May of Teck.

Eighteen months later Prince George, by then Duke of York, married Princess May, his late brother's fiancée. The Prince of Wales gave them York Cottage as their country house, and there they spent their honeymoon. Prince George, a conventional man, continued throughout his life to have a great affection for York Cottage and returned there whenever possible. All his children, except King Edward VIII, were born there. On the death of King Edward VII, Sandringham House was left to Queen Alexandra, and King George and his family continued to occupy York Cottage, now a little enlarged, until the death of Queen Alexandra in 1925. It was somewhat cramped for the growing family but the King, surfeited with palaces, loved it.

One can gather that Queen Mary, then Duchess of York, was not at first so enamoured of the place. York Cottage was not a particularly inspiring home. In his *George V, His Life and Reign*, Sir Harold Nicolson calls it,

a glum little villa, encompassed by thickets of laurel and rhododendron, shadowed by huge Wellingtonias and separated by an abrupt rim of lawn from a pond, at the edge of which a leaden pelican gazes in dejection upon the water lilies and bamboos. The local brown stone in which the house was constructed is concealed by rough-cast which in its turn is enlivened by very imitation Tudor beams. The rooms inside, with their fumed oak surrounds, their white overmantels framing oval mirrors, their Doulton tiles and stained glass fan-lights, are indistinguishable from those of any Surbiton or Upper Norwood home. The Duke's own sitting-room, its north window blocked by heavy shrubberies, was rendered even darker by the red cloth covering which saddened the walls. Against this dismal monochrome (which was comprised of the cloth used in those days for the trousers of the French Army) hung excellent reproductions of some of the more popular pictures acquired by the Chantrey Bequest.

His lugubrious account seems, for me, somewhat exaggerated. The present-day York House, though admittedly undistinguished, is a pleasant enough grey and brown stone building in charming surroundings.

The atmosphere when the Duke of York took his bride home was somewhat stifling. The Royal Family at that time was, says Sir Harold Nicolson,

a family little given to intellectual pursuits, without much in the way of artistic tastes or taste, a family not easily to be converted to any other manner of life than that which they had found all-sufficing in an age wherein privilege vigorously survived.

The Duchess was intellectually on a higher plane, she was already well educated and constantly seeking to increase her store of knowledge in many fields beyond the range of the Princess of Wales and Princess Victoria. She was full of initiative, of intellectual curiosity, of energy, which needed outlets and wider horizons. Their recreations were not hers. . . .

Yet she had to adapt herself to a way of life which involved 'the daily call to follow the shooters, to watch the killing, however faultless, to take always a cheerful, appreciative part in man-made, man-valued amusements'.

[Moreover] 'she was living in a small house on an estate which drew its inspiration wholly from the Prince and Princess, whereon every smallest happening or alteration was ordered and taken note of by the Prince. The very arrangement of her rooms, the planting of her small garden, were matters which required reference to Sandringham House, and the smallest innovations would be regarded with distrust. There was so much she might usefully have done on the estate. Her ideas might have influenced a score of local institutions and increased the well-being of the neighbourhood. But such matters were the prerogative of the Princess, whose charm and kindliness often made up for her lack of system and order. . .'.

No such reflections disturbed her husband. Once he had adopted a routine he liked to stick to it. The Sandringham he knew suited him very well and he saw no reason to make any changes. Sir John W. Wheeler-Bennett (*King George VI, His Life and Reign*) comments,

> It was at York Cottage, however, that he lived in complete happiness for 33 years, from the date of his marriage until he took possession of Sandringham House in January 1926 after the death of Queen Alexandra. Here five of his six children were born, and here he cherished so dearly that Sandringham way of life, the love of which was inherited by his second son, 'dear old Sandringham' he called it, 'the place I love better than anywhere else in the world'.

A man of intensely conservative tastes, King George continued to run Sandringham much as in the time of his father. He maintained the splendid Shire stud in which King Edward has taken a pride, his horses winning competitive trophies on numerous occasions. From 1910 till his death in 1936 he was Patron of the Shire Horse Society. Writes Mr Keith Chivers, in his monumental monograph on *The Shire Horse*, 'The King was always at home among Shire men, because he was one himself. . .'

William Burkitt, writing in the *Transactions of the Highland and Agricultural Society of Scotland* in 1931, mentions that at that date about twenty Shire mares were still being kept, though for everyday work on the farms and not for showing. The Dexter-Kerry herd had been replaced by Lincoln Red Shorthorns in 1915, probably because of the wartime demand for large dual-purpose cattle. They were kept on the maritime pastures at Wolferton and were said to be remarkable both for their size and their milk production.

A herd of the then popular dual-purpose Red Polls had also been acquired. The herd of Highland cattle had dwindled to about six animals but were of the highest quality, for the King liked to exhibit some of the breed every year at Smithfield Show and he won numerous trophies with them there. The Shorthorns were still in residence but had sunk to non-pedigree status, the cows being crossed with an Aberdeen-Angus bull to produce beef-type calves for fattening. At the home farm, a herd of twenty-one Jersey cows supplied the royal household with milk, butter, cream and cream cheeses, the Shorthorn cows making up any deficiencies.

Sandringham at that time supported, in addition to the cattle and horses, pure-bred stocks of sheep and pigs. The sheep were a Southdown flock, established in 1870, and in the early 1930s consisting of 300 breeding ewes and their followers. Every year the flock sent representatives to Smithfield where they secured many trophies, and exports were made to many countries overseas. Some 400 purely commercial feeding sheep, mostly Suffolk crosses or pure Suffolks, were also kept. The pig herds were of two pork-producing breeds, Middle Whites and Berkshires. Both were maintained at show standard and the Berkshires won the breed cup at Smithfield Show in 1929.

Of the arable crops, William Burkitt mentions barley and about twenty acres of sugar beet, the latter being an innovation, for sugar beet was not cultivated in England to any extent until after the First World War. He states that 'the old East Anglian custom of letting the harvest still obtains', by which one gathers that local farm workers contracted to harvest the grain for a fixed sum. As the harvest 'may be completed in a fortnight or may drag on to five or six weeks', according to the climate, they took a bit of a gamble, but at Sandringham they earned a good deal above the national average wage (then about 30s. a week), for it is recorded that 'of recent years each man has received £11 for the harvest', which, even under the most adverse circumstances, would give him £2 a week.

The King took a patriarchal interest in the estate employees, both working and pensioned, and provided them with housing well in advance of the contemporary average. He also, to minimise the temptations of the demon alcohol, closed down the public houses in the five parishes of Sandringham, replacing them with village clubs. 'These clubs are spacious and comfortable and are equipped with good billiard rooms. The sale of beer is permitted, but no other intoxicants. In addition, there are parish rooms for Women's Institute meetings, concerts, dances and other events.'

King George V, like his father, was particularly interested in the sporting amenities of Sandringham and greatly enjoyed the pheasant shoots, indulged in by frequent house-parties. Here again, though, he was conservative to the point of rigidity. King Edward VII's main criterion on shooting days was the size of the bag; he had little interest in the quality of the sport. Plantations designed to make pheasants rise and fly high and fast were therefore interdicted as tending to reduce the numbers killed. In King Edward's time such an attitude was fashionable; by the time King George V came to the throne it was changing dramatically, but not at Sandringham. 'His Majesty was a great traditionalist', writes Aubrey Buxton in *The King in His Country*, and was disinclined to reform the Sandringham drill in the coverts.' It was left to King George VI to modernise the shooting arrangements on the estate.

KING EDWARD VIII AT SANDRINGHAM

The clocks at Sandringham were, in the reign of King George V, always kept half-an-hour fast, and events in the royal household were recorded with the 'S.T.' affixed to the time, the initials standing not for 'Summer Time' but 'Sandringham Time'. Thus the King wrote in his diary for 14 December 1895, 'a little boy was born, weighing nearly eight pounds at 3.40 a.m. S.T.' The baby was the future King George VI. One of the first acts of King Edward VIII after his accession on 20 January 1936, was to abolish 'Sandringham Time'.

For some years Edward, as Prince of Wales, had been out of sympathy with the old-fashioned ideas which motivated his father and of which the 'Sandringham Time' tradition was typical:

> I was, after all, the first King of the 20th Century who had not spent at least half his life under the strict authority of Queen Victoria. My father was already halfway through his lifespan when his grandmother died, and by the gravity of his temperament it was to her, rather than to the livelier example of his own father, that he looked for a model of the Sovereign's deportment. His court retained a Victorian flavour to the end, and I had come to look upon it as at least sexagenarian in composition and outlook.

For him, Sandringham epitomized 'the private war with the 20th century' which King George V had waged and which 'had ended in the almost complete repulse of the latter'. It was here that he determined to begin his onslaught on what he regarded as outdated ideas and obsolete practices. The Norfolk estate was, in his opinion, a white elephant, making unacceptable demands on the Privy Purse. In the very first month of his reign he sent his brother, the Duke of York, down to Sandringham to study the matter of economics.

The future King George VI took with him on this commission an experienced landowner, his friend the Earl of Radnor, and between them they produced a comprehensive and eminently practical survey with recommendations many of which he himself was to put into effect when he became King.

There was little time for King Edward to implement many of them before the Abdication crisis was upon him.

KING GEORGE VI AT SANDRINGHAM

It was the misfortune of King George VI not only to succeed to a throne which he had never wanted but also to spend most of his reign in the throes and aftermath of a devastating war. His natural predilection for a quiet life in rural surroundings had therefore to be sacrificed to the needs of the nation, a sacrifice made with complete self-negation and outstanding success.

From 1940 to 1945 Sandringham was occupied hardly at all by the Royal Family. The King was, however, keenly interested in what went on there and made it his business to implement by degrees many of the recommendations that he and Lord Radnor had made in their report to King Edward VIII. He was determined, too, that the royal farms should set an example of achieving maximum food production in wartime.

Accordingly, it was on his initiative that 450 acres of marshland at Wolferton were reclaimed for the plough. Neighbours were inspired to follow his example, till eventually some 1400 acres of unproductive coastal marshes were brought into a high state of cultivation. Along the old sea-bank, now well inland, he caused extensive plantations of the Yellow Acre variety of plum to be planted, partly as windbreaks and partly to supply plums for canning. He also started a programme of commercial fruit-growing on the estate. Ten acres of the fifty acres of dessert apples which he planned were planted before his death, as also were nine acres of the projected fourteen acres of blackcurrants.

In his time, the old Norfolk four-course rotation, as established by

Coke of Holkham 200 years earlier, was fairly strictly adhered to on the arable land, with sugar beet substituting for turnips and swedes, and potatoes and peas fitted in as additional crops. Yields of up to thirty-six cwt of wheat and twelve tons of sugar beet per acre, excellent for those times, are mentioned in contemporary records. The farms being heavily stocked with livestock, it was policy to manure every arable field either with a heavy dressing of farmyard manure or else by folding sheep once every four years.

In the years immediately after the war, the Sandringham farms were supporting at least 1600 head of livestock, including over 400 cattle. The leading herd consisted of about 200 Red Polls, of the best lines obtainable, which had been founded by King George V in 1914. The herd had, in fact, been split into two in 1949, one based on the Wolferton Farm and the other on Appleton. All were fully attested and recorded for milk yields and butter fat content of the milk. The 1952 records show that for that year the Appleton herd, the larger of

King George VI inspecting the harvest at Sandringham *Fox Photos*

143

the two, averaged 900 gallons of milk at nearly 4% butterfat. The Sandringham Red Polls were familiar in the major show rings of the country, providing the Royal Show champion (a cow named Royal Frolic) in 1950 and 1951 and the Royal Show reserve champion (another cow, Royal Gladiolus) in 1951. Many young bulls and heifers from the Sandringham herds were exported to breeders in Australia, South Africa, U.S.A., Canada and Kenya.

The other dairy herd at Sandringham comprised thirty-five Jersey cows, with the prime function of providing the royal household with milk when in residence. Butter and cheese were also made from their milk.

Of the beef cattle, about forty were Galloway cows and heifers, mated with a Beef Shorthorn bull, for the production of young fat cattle weighing 9–10 cwt at the age of about two and a half years. For most of the time they were pastured on the remaining marshes at Wolferton. The calves were born outdoors and came inside (into straw yards) only in the severest weather.

A second beef herd of Beef Shorthorns was introduced to Sandringham from Windsor soon after the war and in the early 1950s numbered some fifty animals. These were reared and fattened at a somewhat higher level than the Galloways and were ready for market a little earlier.

The sheep, in variable numbers, were a mixed lot, the basic stock being Scottish half-bred ewes mated with a Suffolk ram. The resultant young ewes were in turn mated with either an Oxford Down or Hampshire Down ram, to produce large, heavy, quick-maturing lambs which did well either on swedes, kale and sugar beet tops or on pasture. The lambing average in the early 1950s was 150 ($1\frac{1}{2}$ lambs per ewe).

At that time the farms, still run in the tradition of mixed farming with as wide a diversity of enterprise as possible, were producing both pigs and poultry. Of pigs Sandringham had herds of Essex and Wessex Saddlebacks, with some Large Whites x Large Blacks introduced as an innovation. The poultry were Rhode Island Reds kept for laying and occupying straw yards in winter.

As with other progressive British farms, Sandringham was in the process of becoming fully mechanised. The Shire stud of King George V had gone but for much of his reign King George VI kept a fine stud of Suffolk Punches at Sandringham. A brief note by Captain Fellowes in April 1947 says, 'We are gradually getting out of the horses, and I think the day will come when we should be entirely mechanised. All the big farmers round here are going that way.' In the early 1950s the farms possessed ten tractors, of which three were crawlers, but a reduced stock of Suffolk horses were still doing much of the farm work.

It was at Sandringham that the King was born, was christened and confirmed, and it was at Sandringham that, on 6 February 1952, he died. In less eventful times and under different circumstances he would undoubtedly have been happy to have spent his life there, for as Sir John Wheeler-Bennett says in his biography of King George VI,

> he was essentially a country gentleman, taking a meticulous concern in the day-to-day details of his estates, the welfare of his tenants and the upkeep of his properties. Indeed, he wore himself out with his care for detail. No addition could be made to a cottage at either Sandringham or Balmoral, no new tenant taken on, no employee discharged, no tree cut down, without the King's approval, the decision being submitted to him personally, even if he was in London. In this correspondence he replied invariably in his own hand.

A royal party in the fields at harvest time *Fox Photos*

THE FLAX FACTORY

Since about the middle of the nineteenth century flax-growing in the British Isles has been confined to Northern Ireland, except in time of war. There it has traditionally been a peasant industry, using manual methods of growing and processing. Even the great linen factories of Northern Ireland and Scotland relied heavily on imported flax, chiefly from Belgium and Russia. Moreover, fresh supplies of seed had to be imported each year from the same sources.

This state of affairs naturally left the country extremely vulnerable in wartime, when the demand for flax products, such as sail-cloth, linen, thread and twine, naturally increased. The factories were caught out badly in 1917 when, following the devastation of Belgium by the battlefields of the First World War, the supply of Russian flax was cut off by the Russian Revolution. In something approaching panic, seed of doubtful quality was collected from miscellaneous sources, mills were constructed, and some 10,000 acres of flax were sown. Much failed through lack of knowledge of the needs of the crop, and by the time the first harvest was ready the war had ended. Thereafter, interest evaporated, and by 1930 all the new mills had been abandoned. Flax-growing again sank almost to the level of a neglected peasant industry.

It was in 1931 that the royal farms at Sandringham became involved in flax-growing. At the invitation of the King (George V) three acres of the improved seed were sown and produced a crop of about two tons an acre. After having been hand-pulled, the crop was shipped off to Northern Ireland, processed and later made into linen for the Royal Family.

The King was encouraged and gave permission for a further trial of 100 acres, in 1933. Again the results were entirely satisfactory, so much so that a group of Irish and Scottish manufacturers agreed to finance a small experimental mill in East Anglia, to be run by a non-profit-making company, Norfolk Flax Ltd. The King immediately agreed to lease seventy acres of land at West Newton to the company for fifty years. Other landowners brought the total for the first year's operations, 1934, to 170 acres, and a residential headquarters was set up at Flitcham Abbey, nearby.

From 1934 to 1938 between 200 and 250 acres of flax were grown each year in East Anglia. Botanical and mechanical research was carried on effectively at Flitcham, and two other flax-growing schemes were started, one in England and one in Scotland. A question of closing the establishment arose in 1938, but after lengthy efforts to obtain official support, the scheme was eventually saved by the direct intervention of King George VI. As a result of his interest, the Government took over the organisation in Norfolk and set up His Majesty's Norfolk Flax Establishment, under the control of the Admiralty, who, of course, were directly interested in its products.

With the invasion of the Netherlands, Belgium and France in 1940 our supplies of flax from the Continent were again cut off, but thanks largely to Norfolk Flax and the royal encouragement given to it, a reasonably adequate supply of good seed was available. Meantime some prototype modern machinery had been obtained from Belgium and now served as models for a series of new factories. Before the end of the war, seventeen factories were operating and 66,000 acres of flax were being grown annually in Britain, in addition to 125,000 acres in Northern Ireland and 30,000 acres in Eire.

The rundown at the end of the war was slower than after the 1914–18 war, but the end was the same. At first it was decided to fix the peace-time production of flax at 16,000 acres, but the acreage declined still further and flax-growing once again became a peasant industry, confined largely to Northern Ireland. As between the wars, Britain again relied on supplies from Belgium and Holland, though Norfolk was still engaged in producing high-quality seed. The Norfolk Flax establishment was sadly but inevitably closed in 1956. But it had served its purpose well, and much of the credit for its achievements must go to two farseeing and persistent monarchs, King George V and King George VI.

THE MODERN ESTATE AND FARMS

Since the original purchase of Sandringham, the estate has expanded. It now comprises around 20,100 acres (8,100 hectares) and includes the villages of Wolferton, West Newton, Appleton, Flitcham, Anmer and Shernbourne.

3200 acres are farmed by the estate.
11,890 acres are let to tenant farmers.
450 acres are let to smallholders.
117 acres are devoted to fruit.
243 acres are devoted to the thoroughbred stud.

1950 acres are woodland.

470 acres are parkland around Sandringham House.

1780 acres are devoted to the Sandringham Country Park.

The estate lies some nine miles north-east of Kings Lynn, by the A.149 road from Kings Lynn to Hunstanton.

THE QUEEN'S STAFF AT SANDRINGHAM

The estate is managed on thoroughly professional lines. Mr Julian Loyd, the estate agent, is a Cambridge graduate, having read estate management at Magdalene College in 1950–53. Joining the firm of Savills, he served first at Wimborne, then at Norwich where he became a partner in the Norwich branch. He took over as agent at Sandringham in 1964, on the retirement of Sir William Fellowes. A tall man of military bearing, he earlier served with the Coldstream Guards until invalided out in 1945. He has a son and two daughters.

Following a wise professional principle, the Sandringham staff are mostly recruited locally. Mr Roger Mutimer, who has been farm manager since 1956, was previously managing farms in the neighbouring county of Lincolnshire for King's College, Cambridge. His talk is of crops and cattle, of markets, machinery and the weather. He too has three children, all now grown up. Like the estate, the farms are a commercial enterprise. They have to pay their way and, from the point of view of the estate, Mr Mutimer is treated exactly like a tenant farmer.

Mr Mutimer's assistants are Ronnie Frohawk, who is responsible for the arable side of the farming, and Tony Bidewell, who is livestock foreman. Ronnie Frohawk, assisted by under-foreman Roy Howling controls eighteen regular workers on the farm, plus a few students, a lorry driver and two rabbit-catchers. Tony Bidewell has two assistants. In addition, three full-time engineers are employed in the estate workshop, spending most of their time keeping farm and estate machinery and vehicles in good order. Over the past twenty-five years, the farming staff has been reduced from forty to twenty-seven, in keeping with the lower labour requirements of modern mechanised farming, while the acreage in hand has increased from 1800 to 3300 acres, but the reduction has been effected entirely by retirement and natural wastage.

Fruit-growing is a specialist enterprise under the control of Mr

R. W. Kemp, who from 1939–72 was County Horticultural Adviser in Norfolk. Since his retirement in 1972, he has been looking after the fruit on a part-time basis, coming out several times a week from his home in Norwich. Forestry is managed by Mr W. A. Proctor, who came to the estate from the Forestry Commission.

In all, the estate has 110 employees, including keepers and the building staff, as well as those engaged on the farms and in the woodlands.

As in all well-run estates, working at Sandringham tends to be a family affair. Many of the men come from families who have lived and worked on the estate for generations. It is usual for them to come straight from school and to work there until retirement, when they receive a pension based on their years of service. In their old age they are well looked after and often remain in the cottages they have occupied all their lives; if that is impossible, they are offered comparable alternatives. Quite recently the estate has built a number of bungalows especially for the widows of workers.

THE CROPS

The arable land comprises two farms, one at Appleton of 1800 acres, the other at Wolferton of 1200 acres. Appleton has a thin loamy soil over chalk and has one outstanding speciality – it is ideally suited to growing malting barley. Wolferton's soil is rather richer, much of it being silt and clay. The farm concentrates on producing wheat.

Fields are large and the hedges which form their boundaries are low and well-trimmed. In a recent year the acreage of the various crops were: barley 900; mustard (*for seed*) 120; kale 30; wheat 700; onions 30; sugar beet 360; potatoes 70; oats 20; herbage seeds 130; maize for silage 50. Onions, maize for silage and sugar beet are comparatively new crops.

Mr Mutimer is enthusiastic about his maize which, introduced in the early 1970s, produces a heavier crop of cattle food than any other. The potatoes are all first or second earlies and are grown with the aid of irrigation. Maincrop varieties have been discontinued because of a clash with other crops at harvest. The entire cropping programme is planned to make the most economical use of labour and machinery and to provide a more or less continuous operation from June to December. The onions were introduced a few years ago to fill a gap at the end of August in the harvesting schedule.

Grass seed crops, mostly rye-grass, are grown on some of the poorer and remoter fields.

As a technical detail for farmers, the main varieties of cereals used are as follows: Winter Barley, *Maris Otter*; Spring Barley, *Tern*; Winter Wheat, *Atou, Flanders, Maris Huntsman*; Spring Wheat *Sappo*.

THE FARM LIVESTOCK

For many years a pedigree herd of Red Poll cattle was the pride of Sandringham. The Red Polls, however, a dual-purpose breed with a not very high milk yield, did not pay their way, and so in 1959 they had to go.

Sandringham now has no milking herd. Its main livestock enterprise is beef production, based on three fifty-cow herds of blue-grey cattle and two of Hereford x Friesians. The blue-greys are a numerous and well-known cross, the progeny of a White Shorthorn bull and Galloway cows. Of the five herds, each is mated with a bull of a different breed and the results compared. In fact, bulls of five breeds are in use at the moment, namely Hereford, Lincoln Red, South Devon and two breeds introduced from Europe in recent years, Simmental and Charolais. Originally Hereford bulls only were used, but it was found that the Hereford breed were gradually becoming smaller in size and producing a smaller calf. Of the four breeds being put through their paces at present, the Hereford is used on heifers and the Simmental produces the quickest mature animals at the best

Young beef cattle   *Farmers Weekly*

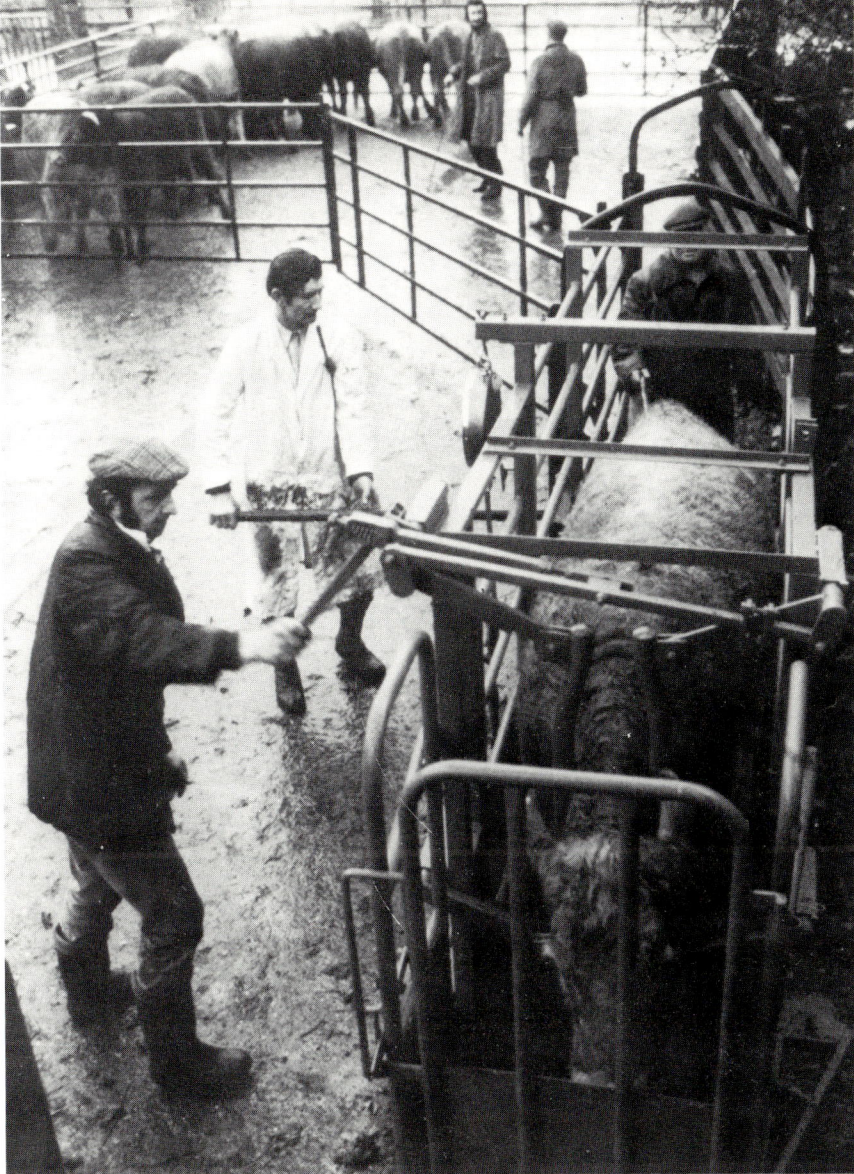

price, whereas the Charolais provides the heaviest cattle, maturing rather later after a second winter in the fattening yard.

The calves are born outdoors in February and March and remain with their mothers for 200 days, which means until the following November. They are weighed at birth and at weaning. In November they move to yards, where they have a winter ration of maize silage, sugar beet pulp, barley straw and 5 lb per day of concentrates.

Meanwhile, the cows stay outdoors, living on a ration of hay, grass silage and sugar beet tops.

The next summer sees the young stock out on the pastures again, ending up on the salt marshes by the sea at Wolferton. From October onwards the cattle become ready for market, a stage reached when they weigh $9\frac{1}{2}$ cwt. The peak marketing period is from February to April, when nearly every week sees a load of about twenty fat cattle shipped to King's Lynn market.

In all, some 591 acres of grassland are devoted to the 800 cattle. About 120 acres are cut for grass silage and a further 120 acres for hay. Five years is the usual period for a temporary ley. Unlike many farms, Sandringham does not rely on perennial rye-grass but prefers a mixture of cocksfoot, white clover and meadow fescue. Cocksfoot is widely regarded as a rather coarse grass, but it suits the light Sandringham soil well. Being deep-rooted, it stands summer droughts and produces good bulky cuts of hay.

Cattle are now the only livestock kept on the Sandringham farms. The last flock of sheep consisted of 500 Border Leicester x Cheviot ewes, but the land tends to be somewhat acid for sheep and, when the shepherd died in 1952, the flock was dispersed. The pig herd has also been disposed of, and there are no poultry.

Until the early 1950s, Sandringham possessed a magnificent stud of Suffolk Punch horses, but in the end they had to give way to modern power units.

THE MACHINERY AND BUILDINGS

Instead of giant muscular horses, tractors now do the land work at Sandringham. The basic power force consists of twenty-two wheeled tractors, three crawlers and two lorries, reinforced at busy times by additional vehicles from other departments. The crawlers are needed for the silt of Wolferton in winter when the soil is as slippery as a cake of soap.

After cultivations drilling is undertaken, while the seventy acres of early potatoes are often planted by the end of February or early March, using a four-row planter. The farms have two types of potato-harvester, one of which delivers the crop neatly parcelled in half-cwt paper bags, which are then sold straight from the field. No potatoes are stored, but in recent years about two hundred tons of the best onions have been kept through the winter in a refrigerated store to take advantage of the high prices in late spring.

Grain harvesting is by five combines which, working together, make short work of even the largest field. Grass is cut for silage by a forage harvester, and new equipment has had to be introduced for the maize harvest. Most of the straw from the grain crops is baled and used for litter for the cattle. Less than 10% of the arable stubbles are burned after harvest and then primarily as a cleaning operation.

Sandringham has been a pioneer in farm irrigation, installing its first irrigation system in the late 1950s. Some years ago, a rotary sprinkler, capable of watering twelve acres a day, was purchased, primarily for boosting the yields of sugar beet and potatoes, which are often twice as heavy as those from unirrigated crops. Recently, a reel-type irrigator has been added to the irrigation equipment on the farm, also capable of covering twelve acres a day. In all, some 1000 acres of the farms can be irrigated, a tremendous advantage in this normally dry corner of the country.

Another crop which benefits immensely from the irrigation system is blackcurrants, which are sprinkled on cold mornings as frost protection. The film of ice which forms on the plants prevents the temperature around the tender buds from falling further and so prevents frost damage.

Sandringham's combine armada *Farmers Weekly*

153

The farms are fortunate in having their own ample water supplies for irrigation, both from a deep bore in the chalk and from the little river Babingley which runs along the southern edge of the estate.

The other water problem, drainage, is taken care of by miles of pipes through the Wolferton silt and clay as well as by forcing a subsoiler to a depth of twenty inches or more through the arable land once every two years.

THE ORCHARDS AND FRUIT PLANTATIONS

Fruit production at Sandringham is specialised, consisting of forty-eight acres of blackcurrants and sixty-four acres of apples. Blackcurrants are a traditional crop in parts of Norfolk and they have had their place on the Sandringham farms for many years. All are grown on contract for processing into blackcurrant juice (by the Ribena firm).

The Prince of Wales wittily summarised the blackcurrant situation in proposing the toast at the 1977 Annual Dinner and Dance of The Farmers Club. He said – 'Our coal production figures may have been exceeded, the tonnage of our shipping may have been overtaken, but there remains one area where we still reign supreme – blackcurrants. It is a little known fact that Britain still leads the world in the production of blackcurrants. We are still, believe it or not, self-sufficient in blackcurrants. There are no imports to disturb our trade figures in this particular soft fruit field, no foreign price rises to threaten our blackcurrant market. The wind still blows through 10,000 acres of British blackcurrants, and quite a lot of them, if I may say, ladies and gentlemen, reside at Sandringham. Very few people know all this, but perhaps they will ponder on this rare glory as they sip their next Ribena.'

The apples are all of dessert varieties and mostly Cox's Orange Pippins. The public, descending on the orchards at a rate of about 3000 a day in September and early October, clear the lot under a 'pick your own' arrangement. This popular idea was first tried in 1972 and proved so successful that it has now become standard practice.

Both the apples and currants are grown in large blocks on the Appleton farm. It is not good orchard soil and the twenty-five-year-old trees are small for their age, but good husbandry keeps them bearing well.

THE RECLAIMED LAND

Wolferton has a muddy foreshore by The Wash and owes some of its silty acres to ancient reclamation schemes.

In 1965 it was decided to reclaim a further 710 acres of saltings. Of the amphibious territory scheduled for the operation, 120 acres were owned by the Queen, 240 were rented by the estate from the Crown Commissioners and 350 were let to a neighbour. The estate has subsequently bought the 240 acres it was renting and so now has a 360-acre block of new land which it farms. The reclamation involved the construction by the Crown Commissioners of a new sea wall and a network of drainage dykes. Subsequently, the estate filled in the tortuous old creeks, cut interception dykes, laid tile drains throughout the area and constructed access roads – the total cost of the work required to bring the area into arable cultivation amounted to about £32 per acre enclosed. The scheme began in 1965 and the first harvest from a small acreage of the reclaimed land was taken in 1967.

Dykes divide the land into five compartments or enclosures and the rule is to proceed slowly and cautiously. Cultivations are at first very shallow, not more than four inches deep in order not to bring salt from the subsoil to the surface. Fertilizer and spray chemicals are sometimes applied from the air to prevent damage to the somewhat delicate soil structure.

Wheat is the main crop produced so far, with yields up to 54 cwt per acre, but sugar beet, potatoes, onions and mustard have also been grown in the new fields.

THE FORESTS

Sandringham has 1900 acres of woodland, though that total includes 136 acres of plantable scrub land and 79 acres of unplantable land, which reduces the area of the fully-stocked forests to 1683 acres.

In the time of King Edward VII, the woods totalled only about 692 acres and were devoted primarily to game and amenities. Occasional inroads were made for timber for estate use. At some time in the nineteenth century, rhododendrons and other shrubs were introduced, a development heartily deprecated by modern foresters. They provide unwelcome cover for deer (of which a large herd of fallow flourishes on the estate) and rabbits.

Scientific management of the woodlands on commercial lines

began in 1954, when, of the 1168 acres then existing, only 568 acres were classed as productive, with a further 600 acres partly so. Most of the trees were very old, only 49 acres of hardwoods being less than eighty years old and only 239 acres of conifers less than fifty years. Since then considerable new plantings have been made – 864 acres from 1955 to 1977. The woodlands are of three main types:

1. Mostly hardwoods on the rather heavy lands of Wolferton, where fen peats overlie silt and sand.
2. Mixed conifer and hardwood woods on the sandy heaths, many of which have poor acid soil.
3. Beech, oak and mixed hardwood and some conifer plantations on the chalk.

The climate is not ideal for forestry, the freely draining soils suffering severely in drought, while early and late frosts often occur.

The estate is exposed to gales from the south, west, north and east and has an average rainfall of about twenty-four inches. The woodlands do, however, contain some remarkably fine specimens of both hardwoods and conifers.

The woods are now expertly managed, with systematic thinning and planting to meet the needs of the estate and the dictates of good forestry. A foreman and seven other men are permanently employed, besides which most thinning and felling is done by contractors.

Equipment includes four tractors, a digger, an eight-ton lorry and numerous saws, trailers and other gear. There is, of course, also a well-equipped sawmill.

THE ROYAL FAMILY AT SANDRINGHAM

Sandringham is for the Royal Family a conveniently accessible retreat, where they can relax in brief intervals in the round of official engagements. As a rule, many of them come down just after Christmas and stay until about 5 February, their longest period of residence.

The Queen likes to spend a long weekend here towards the end of April and will pay other weekend visits as opportunity offers. Prince Philip enjoys several long shooting weekends in early October and mid-November. The Prince of Wales and Princess Anne sometimes join in.

The Queen Mother makes a point of being at Sandringham for the King's Lynn Festival at the end of July and for the Sandringham

Cottage Horticultural Society's Show, which is held in the Park on the last Wednesday of July. The Society has its centenary in 1980. The Queen Mother is president of the Sandringham Women's Institute and attends its meetings whenever possible.

The Queen and Prince Philip at Sandringham
Farmers Weekly

For family parties and for the more official occasions, Sandringham House is used, but for weekends taken at short notice and when few or no guests are invited or when Sandringham House is open to the public, the Queen has a more modest retreat at Wood Farm. A few hundred yards down a gravelly lane and half hidden by trees, it is a pleasant red brick and flint building, once the home of the local doctor. Here the Queen and/or Prince Philip or other members of the family can relax with a minimum of fuss and formality. Mrs Hazel, wife of Jack Hazel, one of the farm tractor-drivers who lives in the cottage next door, pops in and 'does' for the royal party.

When Sandringham is out of sight, however, it is not out of mind. Mr Loyd has to submit monthly reports, which are carefully scrutinised and digested. Twice a year he attends a general management meeting with Prince Philip and Palace officials. Ideas for innovations have to be discussed with the Queen and Prince Philip,

157

and the Prince frequently brings back his own suggestions, based on what he has seen on his extensive travels.

Wolferton Station, the former terminus for royal trains, is now closed and the station buildings have been transformed into two houses. Royal parties now arrive by car or air.

As soon as possible after arrival the Queen is at the paddocks renewing friendship with her beloved horses. After that, an inspection of the farm is an early priority. The Prince is particularly interested in comparative trials involving the various cattle breeds.

THE PUBLIC

Since 1968 when the Country Park was established, large parts of the Sandringham estate have been accessible to the public. The Country Park itself with sundry adjacent lands comprises 530 acres and offers facilities for picnics, rambles and nature study. The focal point of the Park, just across the road from the House and gardens, has a tea house, souvenir shop, car park and lavatories in a spacious woodland setting, but the miles of forest provide ample opportunities for lovers of rural solitude to get away from the crowds. Through the centre winds an asphalted drive, flanked on either side by grassy lawns which have replaced solid thickets of rhododendrons, bulldozed in the interests of landscaping in 1972.

There is no charge for visitors to the Country Park, but a small one is made for access to the House and grounds, which are open at varying dates and times throughout the summer. In 1977 (Jubilee Year), the first year that the House was open, nearly 300,000 visited it, and many more must have enjoyed the amenities of the Country Park.

In the House visitors see the most important of the ground floor rooms including the main drawing-room, the smaller drawing-room, the saloon, the long corridor and the dining-room. The former coach-houses have been transformed into the Sandringham Museum, first opened to the public in 1973. The exhibits include a splendid collection of vintage cars once used by Royalty.

In addition to the general public, special parties from such organisations as the National Farmers Union, Young Farmers' Clubs and Stockmen's Clubs are given conducted tours or farm walks from time to time. In 1977 the Caravan Club held its annual rally in the Park.

RECENT MAJOR ALTERATIONS TO THE HOUSE

In 1975 by far the largest alterations to Sandringham House since the rebuilding after the fire of 1891 were put in hand. To lighten the burden on the staff, much reduced in numbers since Edwardian times, ninety-one rooms were demolished, though the work was done so skilfully that their absence is noticeable only to those who were familiar with the House before. The opportunity was taken to effect a number of other urgent repairs, to the stonework, roof, the central heating system, and electric wiring. For the two years while the renovations were in progress the Royal Family continued to visit Sandringham but stayed at Wood Farm.

SPORT AND WILDLIFE

Although Prince Philip and Prince Charles greatly enjoy the shooting at Sandringham, all the pheasants on the estate are wild. No artificial rearing is done. The farms carry a good stock of partridges, many of them red-legged. Hares have been increasing in numbers in recent years, as have rabbits. The woods conceal a lot of fallow deer and a few red deer, but no roe deer have yet been seen.

Norfolk has for many years been one of the few areas of Britain which still hold a stock of indigenous red squirrels, but within the last few years grey squirrels have been seen at Sandringham, an invasion which may herald the doom of the red species.

The shores of The Wash attract large numbers of duck and waders. When the new reclamation scheme was put into operation, Prince Philip insisted that forty-five acres should be kept in their original condition as a wildfowl reserve. He has had a shepherd's hut with viewing window perched on the old sea-wall, giving him a panoramic view of the salt marsh. Prince Philip's position as President of the World Wildlife Fund is no sinecure; he is keenly interested in natural history and seldom misses the opportunity of a few hours' bird-watching when at Sandringham.

Unfortunately the wildfowl reserve has run into a snag. The draining of the adjacent fields has caused the salt marsh to start drying up, too, and it is now rapidly becoming grassland, although recently two scrapes have been made on the Reserve and these are kept flooded by two windmills pumping water from adjacent dykes. That, of course, does not mean that it is losing its interest but that its fauna is changing to match the changing conditions. There are still creeks haunted by wading birds, and on a recent late April visit I saw many 'grass-widower' shelducks (or sheldrakes) and a migrating male pintail.

THE GARDENS

An extensive range of glasshouses, devoted partly to flowers and partly to fruit, was built by King Edward VII with the money earned by his celebrated Derby winner, *Persimmon*. Attached to them were more than seventeen acres of walled gardens, engaged in producing fruit, vegetables and flowers for the Royal Family when in residence. The precinct walls were covered with trained fruit trees, chiefly pears and apples, some of them of unusual varieties.

Those golden days are now past. Flowers are, of course, supplied to the House when the Family comes down for the Christmas visit. Early every morning during that period, two men replenish the flower decorations, water the pot plants and undertake whatever renovations are necessary. Apart from that, the gardens are now a thoroughly commercial enterprise. The main crops are carnations, roses and pot plants, which are sold to the summer visitors. Raspberries growing in the old walled gardens are also sold on a 'Pick Your Own' basis, but the old fruit trees against the walls are now out of production and are due to be pulled up.

THE ROYAL STUDS

For some 200 years the headquarters of the Royal Studs were based at Hampton Court. King Edward VII, when Prince of Wales, started the stud farms at Sandringham and Wolferton in the late 1870s, and these studs soon began to play a major role in the royal breeding enterprise.

The Sandringham Stud, covering some 150 acres, is situated immediately to the east of Sandringham House, on either side of the Anmer Road. The smaller, Wolferton Stud, comprising 100 acres, is on the lower ground about two miles to the north-west of Sandringham. Both studs have large, well-sheltered paddocks, screened from the wind by belts of trees or boarded fencing. Boxes are practically all of carr-stone construction in common with most other buildings on the estate.

The first really important racehorses to be bred at Sandringham were three brothers, *Persimmon* (1893), winner of the St. Leger, The Eclipse Stakes, The Derby, and the Ascot Gold Cup; *Diamond Jubilee* (1897) winner of The Triple Crown, and *Florizel* (1891). *Persimmon* retired to stud at Sandringham, where he was highly successful until his premature death through an accident in 1908. His statue by Adrian Jones stands in front of the stud, and is a prominent landmark. *Diamond Jubilee* retired to stud at Wolferton until his sale to South America a few years later.

In the 1920s the highly successful stallion, *Friar Marcus*, stood at Wolferton. The best horses bred at Sandringham and Wolferton during the 1920s and 1930s were *Scuttle*, who won The 1000 Guineas, *Weather Vane*, winner of The Royal Hunt Cup, and *Limelight*, winner of The Hardwicke Stakes in 1933. *Limelight* retired to stud at Wolferton but was only moderately successful.

The years immediately following the Second World War saw the start of a tremendous resurgence in the fortunes of the Royal Studs with the victory of *Hypericum* in The 1000 Guineas of 1946. This was followed by a flood of high-class winners in the 1950s, the most notable of which was *Aureole*, second in The Derby in Coronation Year. He later established himself as the champion racehorse of Europe by winning the King George and Queen Elizabeth Stakes. *Aureole* retired to stud at Wolferton in 1954. In the next twenty years he was twice champion sire, and his offspring won well over £1,000,000.

Another high-class royal winner of this period was *Doutelle*, who retired to stud at Sandringham, where he showed great promise with the successes of his first runners. His death, following an accident in 1963, was a major disaster for the Royal Studs.

The 1960s were a comparatively lean period, highlighted by the victory of *Canisbay* in The Eclipse Stakes of 1965.

The 1970s have so far proved as successful as the 1950s, with four classic victories by *Highclere* and *Dunfermline* and a steady stream of other winners.

In 1976 the Royal Studs stopped using Hampton Court, and under the present system, Sandringham has become the headquarters for the twenty or so brood-mares belonging to the Queen and for the five brood-mares belonging to Queen Elizabeth the Queen Mother. In addition, Sandringham housed the 1978 English and Irish Derby Winner, *Shirley Heights*, and his forty-five visiting mares, who came to him in the first half of the year. *Shirley Heights* replaces The Irish

Derby and St Leger winner *Ribero*, who stood there since 1970, and has since been sold to Japan, and *Canisbay*, who was sold to Italy in 1974.

Aureole was succeeded at Wolferton by the St Leger winner, *Bustino*, in 1976. *Bustino* will always be remembered for his epic and record-breaking duel with *Grundy* in his last race at Ascot. So Sandringham and Wolferton each house highly successful young stallions, whose services are much in demand from breeders all over the world.

During the first six months of the year the two stud farms are devoted to the care of the visiting mares. The forty-five or so mares to each stallion arrive during January and February, and all have normally left by August. The visiting mares which are in foal usually arrive a month or more before their foals are due. Covering starts on 15 February and continues until the end of July, but most mares are dealt with in this respect by the end of May.

Bustino, whose fee is now £5000, has proved extremely fertile, with over 90% of his mares tested in foal in each of his first three

Some of the Queen's brood-mares at the Royal Stud
Jarrold, Norwich

seasons. His first runners raced in 1978. Naturally great hopes are held of *Shirley Heights*, whose fee is £8000.

The second half of each year is devoted to the weaning of mares belonging to the Queen and the Queen Mother. The mares, on their return from the various stallions which they have been visiting, are normally kept at Sandringham where the stud has a separate annex for them, with its own range of boxes and paddocks. Weaning is carried out in August and September when the foals are between four and six months old. In late October or early November the foals are sent to Polhampton, some ten miles south of Newbury in Berkshire, where they are kept until they go into training some ten or eleven months later.

The Royal Stud at present possesses what is perhaps one of the best selections of brood-mares in Great Britain, though it is a small stud compared with the large international organisations with which it is in competition. The Queen has an intense personal interest in the stud and her horses and an encyclopedic knowledge of all aspects of thoroughbred breeding. Beyond any reasonable doubt the Queen will continue to be one of Britain's most successful racehorse breeders.

6

BALMORAL

The first documentary mention of Balmoral is in the late fifteenth century, when the estate and the adjacent one of Abergeldie were acquired by the Gordon family. Abergeldie is still held by the Gordons, but in the seventeenth century Balmoral passed to the Farquharson family and later to the Earls of Fife, both of which families still possess considerable estates in the district. Early in the nineteenth century the Gordon family returned to Balmoral, as leaseholders from the Earl of Fife, and around the year 1830 Sir Robert Gordon largely rebuilt the old castle. A painting of the castle in 1848 by W. Wyld shows a pleasant, turreted building in an attractive setting but very much smaller than the present castle.

QUEEN VICTORIA ACQUIRES BALMORAL

It so happened that when Sir Robert Gordon died in 1847, Queen Victoria and Prince Albert were thinking about acquiring a Highland property. Five years earlier, in 1842, the Queen had paid her first visit to Scotland. From her capital Edinburgh she made a short expedition to Taymouth Castle where the royal party stayed as guests of the Marquis of Breadalbane. Having been greatly impressed by the beauty of the Highlands, they returned on two subsequent occasions in the next few years, one of them being spent in sailing around the western isles in the Royal Yacht. The Queen and the Prince loved the scenery but were discouraged by the rain.

The son of Sir James Clark, the Queen's physician, had also been holidaying in the Highlands, as guest of Sir Robert Gordon at

Balmoral, and sending home enthusiastic reports to his father. Above all, he said, it did not rain every day on Deeside. The air was dry and bracing. Sir James impressed on the Queen that it was just what she needed.

View of Balmoral Castle from the south-east
Pilgrim Press by courtesy of Balmoral estate

So, in February 1848, after intensive enquiries and negotiations, the Queen and the Prince bought the lease (which had a further twenty-seven years to run) without ever seeing the property. They paid their first visit to it on 8 September of the same year and were pleased with their bargain. In her diary for that day the Queen wrote: 'It was so calm and so solitary, it did one good as one gazed around; and the pure mountain air was most refreshing. All seemed to breathe freedom and peace, and to make one forget the world and its sad turmoils.' And in a letter to her uncle, King Leopold of the Belgians, she declared, '. . . the scenery all around is the finest almost I have seen anywhere . . . we are certainly in the finest part of the Highlands and quite in the heart of them, and the soil and climate are the driest I almost saw anywhere. You can walk for ever . . . and then the wildness, the solitariness of everything is so delightful, so refreshing, the people are so good and so simple. . . .'

In fact, so delighted were they with their Highland home that soon they were negotiating for its purchase, which was finally completed on 22 June 1852. Meantime the neighbouring property of Birkhall had been bought for the Prince of Wales, then still a small boy, and a long lease had been taken on Abergeldie.

QUEEN VICTORIA AND PRINCE ALBERT AT BALMORAL

The Queen found walking over her new estate exhilarating. 'I seldom walk less than four hours a day, and when I come in I feel as if I want to go out again,' she wrote. Prince Albert enjoyed the shooting, which occupied most mornings when the family paid their autumn visits to Balmoral. In the afternoons they went out walking or driving. 'The Queen often goes about alone,' wrote a guest, 'walks into the cottages, sits down and chats with the old women.' Expeditions were made to Loch Muick, near the far end of the estate, deep in the mountains and about six miles from the Castle. Here the family enjoyed the fishing and boating, and after a time they built a mountain shelter on the shores of the lake where they sometimes spent the night. It was an informal, free-and-easy life, and the Queen and Prince loved it.

Before long the Prince initiated other building schemes, including cottages, servants' quarters, stables, workshops and a ballroom. He also began a programme of afforestation, planting extensive plantations of firs and pines along the valley. By 1852 it was realised that the house itself was not large enough for the rapidly growing family, so the present castle was planned. Work on it started almost immediately and was virtually completed by 1855. The Prince then turned his attention to the garden and the grounds, 'which no one understands as well as he does,' wrote the Queen. The task kept him busy until 1859, and then it was the turn of the farms.

At Invergelder, the home farm of the estate, he had a set of new buildings constructed. The new model dairy at Windsor had greatly pleased him, and he determined to make another like it at Balmoral. At this juncture he fell ill with typhoid and died tragically after an illness of three weeks. Characteristically, the bereaved Queen insisted that his wishes should be carried out, so over the next two years the dairy was completed and a new water supply constructed to service it.

Apart from cairns erected on hill-tops on important family occasions, little further building work was done at Balmoral for the remainder of the Queen's reign, but Deeside remained her favourite country seat, where she spent as much time as possible, often as much as three months in autumn, with a spring visit as well whenever it could be arranged. She always left it, 'that loved and blessed land' as she described it, with regret.

In or about the year 1881 Queen Victoria visited the great cattle-breeder, William M'Combie, of Tillyfour, Aberdeenshire, and inspected his famous herd of Aberdeen-Angus. M'Combie was doing for the black cattle of north-eastern Scotland what Bakewell, Colling and other breeders had achieved with English cattle a hundred years earlier. Impressed, the Queen determined to help the promotion of Scottish cattle-breeding and went back to Balmoral to establish her own herd of Aberdeen-Angus at Abergeldie Mains. The herd flourished throughout the rest of her reign and through those of her two successors, winning many prizes at agricultural shows and sending out beasts which commended the highest prices at fatstock markets. William Burkitt, writing in 1931, found the herd then consisting of twenty-five cows and heifers, a stock bull and about twenty-five young cattle. Some twenty animals were regularly fattened for the Christmas sales.

The other Balmoral farm, Invergelder, was then mainly arable but also carried a small herd of fourteen Ayrshire cows, averaging just over 1000 gallons of milk a year. Their function was to supply the royal household with milk during August, September and October, for which reason they were a summer-calving herd. Grassland adjoining the arable farm was in process of being improved to extend the very limited grazing area.

Although Birkhall had been his property since the age of seven, King Edward VII spent little time on Deeside, seldom more than a few weeks each autumn. King George V and King George VI normally stayed for a couple of months when paying their autumn visits, both of them having a great affection for Balmoral. Of the sporting facilities, King George V preferred deer-stalking and did little grouse-shooting, but King George VI, one of the best shots in the world, thoroughly enjoyed driving the grouse, which increased considerably during his reign, due to judicious heather-burning and other good management.

THE PRESENT ESTATE

The Balmoral and Birkhall estates together now comprise 42,770 acres, to which should be added a grouse moor of some 6700 acres

eight miles or so to the north, which was acquired by the Queen in 1977. The northern boundary is the river Dee, and the estate is shaped like a great irregular rectangle, some twelve miles deep and fourteen or sixteen miles broad. However, the Abergeldie estate, still owned by the Gordon family, is interposed like a wedge between Balmoral and Birkhall, though the sporting rights are rented by Balmoral.

The estate embraces some of the most spectacular scenery in the Highlands, including the great crescent-shaped scarp of Lochnagar which rises to a height of 3786 feet and has a mantle of snow for the greater part of the year. Much of the estate consists of mountain and moorland. There are immense, heather-clad moors, mountain slopes and tumbled scree, extensive bogs and numerous glens. About 6200 acres are woodland, of which 2200 acres are leased to the Forestry Commission. 1000 acres are a vestige of the ancient Caledonian Forest, its age-old pines saved from destruction by the express intervention of Queen Victoria.

In this wild countryside the farms are very much a minor feature, occupying only 380 acres. These are riverside fields and pastures, one group of them near Balmoral Castle and another by the little river Muick at Birkhall. They are quite small, averaging about seven acres per field. In addition, far to the south about ninety acres of virgin pasture land in a glen at Moulzie affords excellent summer grazing on which the cattle do well, though it has never experienced re-seeding or treatment by fertilizer.

THE BALMORAL FARMS

From its completion in 1861 till the spring of 1965 the Prince Consort's dairy dealt with the milk of the Balmoral herd of Ayrshires. At that point, the herd, which consisted of some twenty-six milking cows, was dispersed. In the following autumn it was decided to build up a herd of commercial beef cattle, and the breed chosen was the Luing, which had been established less than twenty years earlier by the Cadzow brothers on the island of Luing, in Argyllshire. The nucleus of the new herd was purchased early in 1966.

At that time the only farmland in hand was Invergelder Farm, consisting of 96 acres of arable land, together with a couple of fields and some rough grazing at Birkhall.

However, between 1966 and 1971, several rented farms and crofts

Opposite: The Queen climbing the heather hills near Balmoral *Central Press Photos*

fell vacant and were taken in hand, so that by 1972 the total farmland amounted to 380 acres of arable and 196 acres of rough grazing.

As most of the farmland was near Birkhall the balance of the farming activities now moved to the eastern sector of the estate, and the farm grieve was accordingly installed in the Dalliefour farmhouse.

When the farms in hand consisted of only Invergelder, Alltcailleach and Toldhu the Luing herd was based on Invergelder. These hardy cattle outwintered, but the erection of a covered silo incorporating a feed shed in some woodland near Invergelder enabled the herd to be increased to sixty-five cows and calves, which was held to be the maximum capacity of the farms. With the acquisition in 1970 of the important farm of Dalliefour, however, it was possible to increase the total number of breeding cows to one hundred. The farm grieve has the key breeding animals, including the bulls and the replacement heifers, under his personal supervision at Dalliefour.

The function of the Luing herd is to produce and rear beef calves, which are sold when weaned, usually in the markets of Oban and Stirling. Several experiments have been undertaken to determine the best crosses to produce calves of the right type, but none has proved entirely successful.

In 1973 a bull of the recently introduced Blonde d'Aquitaine breed from south-western France was bought from Sandringham, and this proved the most successful crossing breed yet. Balmoral now has four Blonde d'Aquitaine bulls – big, handsome and very quiet animals. The calves they sire are large and active. One Luing bull is kept for breeding pure replacements of the Luing herd, running in winter with about twenty-five pure-bred cows and heifers.

After the acquisition of Knock Farm in November 1971, it was decided to base a herd of Galloway cattle there, with the aim of breeding blue-grey heifers for sale to Sandringham; a foundation stock of twenty-five Galloway cows and heifers and one Whitebred Shorthorn bull was bought in December of that year. Within a year the Galloway herd doubled, and then a further nineteen Galloway cows were transferred from Sandringham. To accommodate this increased number, the Luing herd was reduced in the autumn of 1973 to eighty breeding cows and one of the Luing stock bulls was transferred to Sandringham. A first consignment of Balmoral-bred blue-grey heifers was sent to Sandringham in 1973/74, but for various reasons this Sandringham/Balmoral beef unit project has been abandoned. The Galloways are now being crossed with Blonde d'Aquitaine bulls, with excellent results.

With both Luing and Galloway herds a change has recently been made to autumn calvings. The calves thus produced stay on the farm for a year and are sold in the following autumn as yearlings; they then graze on for the rest of the year and are housed for the winter. In spite of the size of the Blonde d'Aquitaine bulls, no difficult calvings have been experienced with either Luing or Galloway cows. Of 106 calvings from Blonde sires in 1977/1978 only two needed assistance, and one was a case of twins; the other was a malpresentation.

In addition to these main cattle enterprises Balmoral has, appropriately, a small and well-established herd of Highland cattle – the technical term is a Highland 'fold' – established in 1955. The present herd consists of one splendid Highland bull, 'Tearlach of Camerory', twenty-seven cows, six bulling heifers and a number of calves.

The cattle enterprises at Balmoral are entirely commercial, the stock being sold in the normal markets, but two steers are slaughtered each year for household use.

The small flock of Soay sheep is, however, kept solely to provide

A highland bull   *Ralph Whitlock*

171

tender mutton for the royal table. Royalty does evidently not subscribe to the sentiments in 'The War Song of Dinas Vawr', as versified by Thomas Peacock and learned by generations of schoolboys:

> The mountain sheep are sweeter,
> But the valley sheep are fatter;
> We therefore deemed it meeter
> To carry off the latter. . . .

Soay sheep derive their name from the island of Soay, one of the St Kilda archipelago, where they lived in a feral state from time immemorial. They represent, in fact, a prehistoric breed or type once widely distributed throughout much of Europe and thought to have had their main origin in the wild moufflon of Corsica and Sardinia. Their survival in the St Kilda group was doubtless due to the remoteness of the islands.

When the last human inhabitants were evacuated in 1930, 107 sheep were brought from Soay to the main island, Hirta, where they have flourished. The flock there now probably numbers between 1000 and 1500 sheep. The transfer drew attention to the existence of this primitive breed, with the result that breeding stock were exported to several parks and farms in mainland Britain. A survey made in 1974 by the Rare Breeds Survival Trust recorded about 650 breeding ewes in Britain, excluding those on St Kilda. In addition, flocks have been established in Canada, Belgium and Germany.

It would seem appropriate to be able to record that the Balmoral flock of Soays were derived direct from St Kilda, but in fact it was presented from a flock in southern England and has not been on the estate for many years. They are treated almost as wild animals, out of necessity, for they are extremely difficult to round up, even with dogs. They have the run of a fair-sized pasture in summer and are brought into a shed in winter and fed, to prevent casualties from starvation, but they never become as tame as most breeds of sheep. At the time of my visit in May 1978, there were probably twenty-six ewes in the flock, but nobody was quite sure. Twenty-eight lambs had been born that spring, but twelve had died, probably the victims of foxes.

The arable land of Balmoral, totalling 380 acres, is devoted almost entirely to growing winter feed for the livestock. On the ploughland a conventional rotation between arable and leys is followed, but there is some permanent grass in addition to the 196 acres of rough grazing. Barley and turnips (both swedes and what the Scots call 'neeps') are grown, and about two hundred tons of grass silage are made annually, as well as much hay.

In addition to the cattle and sheep, fourteen stalking ponies have to be provided for. Most of these are Highland and Fell ponies, but there are several Haflinger ponies as well. Two Haflinger mares were presented to the Queen by the President of Austria in 1969 and these versatile ponies are used for riding and driving, together with the Highland and Fell ponies, as well as for carrying stags off the hill.

THE QUEEN'S STAFF

From 1965 to 1979 the resident factor at Balmoral has been Colonel William G. McHardy, MVO, MBE, MC, who had previously seen service with the Seaforth Highlanders and latterly with the Queen's Own Highlanders. He retired in July 1979.

The farm grieve at Dalliefour is Mr Robbie Anderson, and the rest of the staff consists of three stockmen – Mr Eddie Esson at Invergelder, Mr Jock Ross at Toldhu and Mr Willie Sim at Sterinbeg. All are trusted employees of many years' service.

ROYALTY AT BALMORAL

The Royal Family normally spends the period mid-August to mid-October at Balmoral, enjoying a late summer recess. They also try to pay another visit, for a long week-end, in May or June. The Queen, as always, has several hours of work to attend to every morning, even on holiday, but greatly enjoys walking, riding and the free-and-easy atmosphere of Balmoral. The Duke of Edinburgh, too, looks forward to his autumn months in Scotland and usually manages to pay other short visits as well. Birkhall is the Queen Mother's domain, where she spends much time casting for salmon in the Dee.

One of the great attractions of Balmoral is its game. The estate holds approximately 2500 red deer, of which around 150 stags and 275 hinds are culled annually, to maintain a healthy stock. The technique now adopted is stalking, not driving or hunting, and the Queen herself is an expert and an experienced shot. The estate also includes Delnadamph, a first-rate grouse moor of 6700 acres which was recently bought by the Queen. Some black grouse and

capercailzie are also resident on the estate, and there are ptarmigan on the high mountains.

On the Balmoral farms the Duke of Edinburgh takes a keen interest in the cattle and likes to be kept informed about events. As with the other royal farms and estates, a detailed monthly report is sent to the Queen.

THE GARDENS

Lying so far north and at an altitude of approximately 1000 feet, Balmoral is not an ideal locality for gardening. Dr Shewell-Cooper mentions that twelve degrees of frost have been recorded as early as 12 August! However, there is compensation in the length of the summer days and the rapidity of plant growth during summer months. Tender vegetables, such as summer beans and marrows, are not cultivated here, but most brassicas and root crops do very well, as does lettuce. The crop with which Balmoral excels is raspberries; the canes grow very tall and produce abundant crops of fruit. Strawberries, of suitable varieties, are almost as prolific. The gardens

Opposite: The game larders at Balmoral   *Pilgrim Press by courtesy of Balmoral estate*

The Royal Family on holiday at Balmoral, 1957   *Central Press Photos*

can also usually provide sufficient flowers for indoor decorations when the Royal Family is in residence.

Queen Elizabeth the Queen Mother has a delightful garden, with herbaceous borders, vegetable plots and fruit trees, by the river Muick at Birkhall.

BALMORAL AND THE PUBLIC

Balmoral Castle Gardens were the first to be opened to the public, in 1931, under Scotland's Gardens Scheme, which was formed to collect money to maintain the District Nursing Service. Since then the number of days on which the public may enter the grounds has been gradually increased until by 1968 the grounds were open on weekdays from 10 a.m. to 5 p.m. from 1 May to 31 July. Much of the money collected is donated to a wide range of charities, with by far the largest proportion going to the District Nursing Service. In response to public demand a small stall for the sale of postcards and surplus garden produce was started in 1966, and in the following year a guidebook and a small selection of souvenirs were on sale. Two years later a refreshment room was opened in the staff recreation room in the stable block.

During the summer the number of visitors to the Loch Muick area has gradually increased, and in 1976 Aberdeenshire County Council decided to provide a new car park for seventy cars at the head of the public road near the Spittal of Glenmuick. At the same time the estate office was receiving a lot of requests from a wide range of individuals and organisations seeking permission for walks, hikes and tours over the moorland around Loch Muick. For every request received, there were at least ten 'visitors' who did not seek permission. To try to provide some control over this ever-increasing invasion, a Ranger/Naturalist has been appointed, to work directly under the factor. The present Ranger succeeded to the post in 1973, and although his work is concerned mainly with public access to the estate at Glenmuick he also keeps an eye on other areas.

An agreement has now been made with the Scottish Wildlife Trust whereby the general area around Loch Muick and the Dubh Loch and around the summit of Lochnagar has been declared a reserve. The sporting activities and forestry of the estate are in no way affected, nor is the ownership of the ground, but the Scottish Wildlife Trust has been active in developing the area as a nature reserve. An information centre has been established at Spittal of Glenmuick, staffed by members of the Trust as well as by the official Ranger at busy times. Work is proceeding in order to provide clear directions on the paths which the public are welcome to use, and members of the Aberdeen branch of the Trust have started a detailed survey of the plant, animal and freshwater life of the reserve.

For several decades the steep cliff face of Lochnagar has been popular with mountaineers and climbers, particularly in winter, when the mountain is normally covered by snow and ice. Climbers approach it either from the public road to the Spittal of Glenmuick where, after leaving their cars or motorcycles, they walk past Alltnaguibhsaich to the foot of the Lochnagar face, or, leaving their vehicles at Easter Balmoral village, they walk up Glen Gelder. On Sundays during winter there may be more than fifty climbers tackling various sections of the cliff face.

In response to a request from Lord Hunt, then Rector of Aberdeen University, the bothy at Alltnaguibhsaich Lodge was leased to the Larig Club (the Aberdeen University Mountaineering Club) in 1967 to be used as a base for mountaineers from the Club. At the same time the stable behind the Gelder Shiel was fitted with wooden double-tier bunks, as shelter for mountaineers in severe weather. To try to help climbers in distress, and particularly to provide essential information to the various mountain rescue teams, all climbers and hill walkers in winter are asked to complete a simple form which is available at the Spittal of Glenmuich and at Easter Balmoral. Unfortunately, many of the climbers and hill walkers ignore this request, and it has been found that self-professed experts are the worst offenders. In 1969 two university students died while climbing on Lochnagar, and in 1972 an experienced climber, who left his three companions on the descent from the summit, was found dead three days later in deep snow.

THE FORESTS OF BALMORAL

The greater part of Balmoral estate is technically deer forest, but the term applies to extensive areas of mountain and moorland, much of it heather-clad. There are, however, substantial areas devoted to commercial forestry, with the emphasis naturally on high-quality conifers. An afforestation scheme was first initiated by the Prince

Consort, and a number of the plantations for which he was responsible have since been felled, on reaching maturity, and replaced by new ones. The young trees for planting are reared in the estate's forest nursery, by the side of the South Deeside road.

The forested area at Balmoral includes fragments of the ancient Caledonian Forest which once covered the greater part of Scotland. They are distinguished by magnificent old Scots pines underlaid by a carpet of needles which have never been disturbed. These venerable woodlands are renewed by natural regeneration. They were originally saved from destruction more than a hundred years ago by the personal intervention of Queen Victoria.

THE WILDLIFE OF BALMORAL

That Lochnagar, Loch Muick and their environs should be designated a nature reserve is entirely justified. No comparable area of Scotland is richer in wild life. In addition to the numerous red deer, which may be seen almost any day, grazing the mountain pastures like herds of dun cattle, roe deer have also become plentiful. The hills harbour large numbers of blue or mountain hares and many rabbits and foxes. They are also among the last refuges of the savage wild cat. There are some otters and stoats, and the woodlands are the home of a population of red squirrels.

In summer the high, snow-clad peaks are shared with the ptarmigan by the now rare dotterel and the snow bunting. Both golden eagles and peregrine falcons (several pairs) nest there. Red grouse are abundant nesting at an altitude of up to 3000 feet, and a smaller number of black grouse are resident in the conifer woodlands. The big, turkey-like capercailzie are much at home in the remnants of the old Caledonian pine forests.

THE CASTLE OF MEY AND LONGOE FARM

The Castle of Mey on the northern coast of Caithness, the most northerly corner of mainland Britain, is popularly supposed to be a wild, lonely and somewhat desolate spot, but attached to it, in fact, is a pleasant little farm of about 120 acres, Longoe Farm.

As might be expected of a farm so far north, (it is in approximately the same latitude as the port of Churchill on Hudson's Bay, and only a couple of degrees south of Cape Farewell in Greenland), its main enterprise is stock-raising. It has a herd of pedigree Aberdeen-Angus cattle, consisting of twenty-five breeding cows and their followers, and also seven commercial suckler cows. The sheep are pedigree North Country Cheviots, the breeding flock being in the process of building up to one hundred ewes. Pedigree bulls and tups (rams) are reared for sale at eighteen to twenty-four months, the other surplus stock being sold as stores at local markets in Thurso.

The farm grows hay, turnips, kale and barley. The hay, turnips and kale are produced entirely for winter feed for the livestock. Such barley as achieves malting grade is sold for that purpose, while the remainder is stored in a wet grain silo, also for feed.

The farm has the normal machinery and equipment for cultivations and haymaking, but the combining of the barley is done under contract.

The Queen Mother with her prize-winning entry in the North country Cheviot sheep section at the Royal Highland Show in 1977
Douglas Low

179

The farm staff is small, consisting of a farm manager, Mr Donald McCarthy, who is responsible to the factor, Mr M. R. M. Leslie, and a stockman/tractorman, Mr John Ross.

Queen Elizabeth the Queen Mother takes a keen interest in all the farming activities and especially the stock. When residing at the Castle, which is usually in May and October, she enjoys walking round the fields and seeing the animals, and all the year round she is kept fully informed of events on the farm. She has successfully shown stock at both the local Caithness County Show and the Royal Highland Agricultural Society's Show in Edinburgh. In 1977 and 1978 a North Country Cheviot ram, owned jointly with Mr W. N. Clyne, a neighbour at Moss Farm, was male and overall breed champion at the Royal Highland Show, and in 1977 was reserve supreme sheep champion there. In 1978 Her Majesty also showed a tup lamb which was first in its class at the Royal Highland. The Caithness Show has the finest and largest exhibition of North Country sheep in Britain, the classes having up to three times the number of entries found at the Highland Show. The tup which won at the Highland was not exhibited on the advice of the co-owner, as it does not do to keep sheep in Show condition for so long; however, Her Majesty achieved the following results:

The prize-winning North country Cheviot ram
Douglas Low

Dinmont (Shearling) Tup Class	4th out of 33
Tup Lamb Class	4th out of 24 (Class winner at the Highland)
Ewe in milk Class	2nd out of 7

The other show successes were won by another Dinmont tup which went to shows in the south in company with other sheep from Caithness, looked after by one shepherd representing all the owners.

Royal Show	2nd in his class and Reserve Male in the North Country Cheviot section.
Great Yorkshire	1st in his class and Male Champion.

In 1976 and 1977 the Longoe Farm stock bull, Cannon Ball of Peebles, won the supreme beef championship at the Caithness County Show and in 1978 a son of his won the trophy for the best bull bred in the county at the same show. He also sired the two-year-old heifer who was reserve for the best Aberdeen-Angus bred in the county. The supreme trophy for the best animal of either sex bred in the county was a Longoe cow sired by the previous stock bull, Janric Eric of Buchaam. In 1977, a heifer from the herd was awarded the reserve female prize at the same show for the Aberdeen-Angus breed.

As with all the royal farms, Longoe is run in accordance with good husbandry practice and is required to pay its way. It makes no pretence of being a show farm and is not open to the public, though the Castle gardens are, on two days in July and one in August, under Scotland's Garden Scheme.

Her Majesty is the Patron of the Aberdeen-Angus Cattle Society and is an Honorary Life Member of the Royal Agricultural Society.

7
GATCOMBE

GATCOMBE BEFORE ROYALTY

An old prehistoric ridgeway winds over the high Cotswold plateau above the village of Avening to one of the Gatcombe fields. Gatcombe appears in more recent history in about 1720, when the present house was built by Edward Shepperd, a wealthy clothier and flock master. Farming at the time of the livestock breeding revolution, he acquired at least some of his wealth by crossing his Ryeland sheep with the newly introduced Spanish Merinos, which produced a vastly improved fleece.

In 1814 his son sold the house and estate to David Ricardo, M.P., a political economist who employed the architect Basevi to do a good deal of work on it. Since his time the house has remained virtually unaltered, even the handsome conservatory being much as it was when erected in 1829.

In the intervening period the property has changed hands a number of times, the latest owner before it passed to Princess Anne and Captain Mark Phillips in 1976 being Lord Butler, who as Mr R. A. Butler had a distinguished political career in the 1950s and 1960s, occupying at various times the offices of Deputy Prime Minister, Foreign Secretary, Chairman of the Conservative Party, and many others.

GATCOMBE BECOMES A ROYAL FARM

It was at Michaelmas 1976 that Princess Anne and Captain Mark Phillips started farming at Gatcombe. A typical small Cotswold estate of 733 acres, it is situated in the triangle of country between Nailsworth, Minchinhampton and the village of Avening.

Opposite: Gatcombe
Manor   *Edward Haydon
Wood*

In November 1977, the Queen bought 530-acre Aston Farm in the neighbouring parish of Cherington about a mile and a half from Gatcombe, and is leasing it to her daughter and son-in-law at a normal economic rent.

Captain Phillips left the Army on 1 April 1978, and immediately began to devote all his time, or as much of it as possible, to running the two farms.

GATCOMBE AND ASTON

The topographical pattern of the southern Cotswolds, where Gatcombe and Aston are situated, is a fairly high plateau (at an elevation of 500–600 feet) intersected by deep, smooth-sided valleys. The plateau is relatively level, lending itself to arable cultivation. The valleys on the other hand are narrow, mostly sinuous, and with such steep slopes that in most places ploughing is impossible. Many of them are half-filled with tall, broad-leaved trees, the combination adding greatly to the scenic attraction of the landscape, though not to its farming potential.

Aston Farm   *Edward Haydon Wood*

Gatcombe Manor sits at the head of such a combe, enjoying a

delightful view southward down a funnel-like glen lined with towering beeches. Other tall trees shield it from the north, east and west. The house itself is not as large as has frequently been reported; Captain Phillips makes the total number of rooms no more than thirty-two, including lavatories and large cupboards! It settles itself so snugly against the cliff wall behind it that there is no room for a back garden.

Aston Farm, the house still occupied by Mrs Vaisey Davis, widow of the late owner, has a more spacious site on the plateau. Here the glens, less well wooded than at Gatcombe, support a growth of rough downland herbage, with much thorn scrub and an occasional pond.

The soil of both farms is limestone brash, reasonably productive though not the best of soils and inclined to be stony.

The total acreage of the two farms is 1263 acres, of which 250 acres are woodland, Gatcombe Wood occupying 180 acres. Of the remainder, 675 acres is the probable maximum of ploughland, the balance being accounted for by permanent grass and rough grazing on the steep banks. At the time of my visit (May 1978), 553 acres were under the plough. The soil has proved especially suitable for winter barley, of which as large an acreage as possible is sown each year.

The livestock enterprise at both Gatcombe and Aston consists of breeding beef calves for sale as stores. The Gatcombe herd which was there when the farm was bought comprised between seventy and ninety beef type cows for single-suckling. Their breeding was described to me by Captain Phillips as 'Heinz 57 – a really mixed lot!' The Aston cattle are somewhat more homogenous, being primarily Shorthorns in the process of being graded up by Charolais bulls. Many of the young cattle are now of good Charolais type, closely resembling their sires. The herds are still being sorted out. It is intended to keep a total of about 120 beef cows, some Hereford x Friesian, some Blue-greys and about thirty of the up-grading Charolais cows. Charolais bulls will be used on the commercial stock, but the grading-up cows will be inseminated by the best Charolais sires available through the A.I. service.

The programme is intended to make the commercial cattle an autumn-calving herd, which means that the calves will remain with their dams all the winter. They will then be just the right age to take full advantage of the spring and summer grass during the following year. In the autumn they will be sold in local markets as yearling stores. The Charolais will be calved in the spring.

For the winter keep for the cows much hay is made (at the time of my visit there was enough in stock, in a big Dutch barn, to support the herd for a whole winter), but no silage. Immediately after harvest stubble turnips are sown by direct drilling on land cleared of winter barley. These fields are strip-grazed by the cattle, to the great benefit of the spring corn which follows. Stubble turnips supplemented by barley straw and vitamin blocks keep the cows going throughout the autumn until January, thus effecting a considerable saving of hay.

Five Ford tractors constitute the main power units of the farms. In general, minimal cultivations are favoured, which means as little ploughing and as much direct drilling as possible. As the acreage

Charolais cattle at Gatcombe *Edward Haydon Wood*

under cultivation has been increased, a Laverda combine-harvester has been purchased to assist the old Ransome Cavalier combine in the harvesting operations. Gatcombe farmstead has storage capacity for about 600 tons of grain, provided partly by a bin with an under-floor cold air drier and partly by ducts through which cold air is circulated by a Lister blower. Storage at Aston can take up to 400 tons but consists of a range of about ten square bins which are difficult to fill and empty, and the grain has to be dried in advance. Adapting this store to modern requirements is one of the major problems confronting the new farmers.

In reply to a natural query about the family riding horses I learned that they occupy a very minor role on the farm. There are about ten of them, of which more than six are seldom in residence. In fact they spend most of their time on pastures some miles away, on the banks of the Severn.

ROYALTY AT GATCOMBE

Visiting Gatcombe was for me a nostalgic as well as a delightful experience. I had the feeling that this is where I came in just over forty years ago. Here were this young couple, recently married as my wife and I had been in 1939, undertaking the herculean task of reclaiming and taming a formidable acreage of recalcitrant land. I cannot describe the farms as derelict or neglected, as ours were in the 1930s, but Gatcombe had been just 'ticking over' for some years, while Aston, though evidently once quite progressive, bore the evidence of having been the property of a man over ninety years old.

Mark Phillips brings to the challenge the energy and enthusiasm of youth. Country bred and with a farming background (his father once had a small farm not many miles away), he has an instinctive appreciation of country ways, but, bearing in mind the fact that he had left the Army and become a full time farmer less than two months before my visit, the extent and depth of his agricultural knowledge are surprising and impressive.

This is no hobby farm – it has to be commercially viable. Interest has to be paid on invested capital. Aston Farm is rented from the Queen at an economic rent. Above all, the conversion of the two farms into a sound and profitable unit involves a tremendous amount of hard work, and here are a young married couple buckling down to it. 'Tractor driving? We all do our bit when needs must,' Captain

The unusual pyramid tower which stands in the grounds of Gatcombe Park *Edward Haydon Wood*

Phillips told me. Does Princess Anne take a turn? She does when she has time – at harrowing, haymaking, harvesting and the other seasonal operations – happy, hardworking and carefree in jeans.

In October 1978, Captain Phillips began a year's course at the Royal Agricultural College in Cirencester, an important part of his training for his new career, but one which further curtails the time available for the day-to-day work of the farm. And of course, the couple are to some extent handicapped by the time which has to be spent on official engagements. That naturally affects Princess Anne rather more than her husband, but there are occasions when he has to accompany her on tours, sometimes for weeks at a time. Fortunately the type of farming chosen is one which fits in with such a programme. As long as the farmer is around at seed-time, haymaking and harvest he can afford occasional absences during other seasons.

One gets the impression that Princess Anne and Captain Phillips are being left by both families to work out their own farming destiny. The Queen, having helped her daughter to get established in her own household, looks in occasionally to see how things are going. The young couple will have the satisfaction of winning success by their own efforts. Both sets of parents are now only occasional visitors.

FARM STAFF

The farm staff at Gatcombe and Aston could hardly be smaller. It consists of a working manager, Mr Geoff Stevens; a tractor driver, Mr Chris Excell; a stockman, Mr Jack Russell; and a woodman, Mr Eric Hanchett, who looks after the kitchen garden as well as being responsible for more than 250 acres of woods.

Those are all, except that at busy times Captain Phillips occasionally enlists the aid of students from the Royal Agricultural College in Cirencester, some eight miles away.

GATCOMBE AND THE PUBLIC

Unlike Sandringham, Balmoral and Windsor, Gatcombe is not open to the public. There is, in fact, nothing for the public to see, not even gardens to be opened once or twice a year for the District Nursing Association. The farm is not and is not intended to be a showpiece. If ever it achieves that status, it will be as a result of a long uphill struggle, perhaps ten years or more. Meantime all those who wish Princess Anne and Captain Phillips well, will follow the example of their parents and leave them to get on with the good work.

SPORT, WILDLIFE AND CONSERVATION

Gatcombe is no sporting estate. It would lend itself to pheasant-shooting, the tall trees fringing the grassy combe being near ideal for producing a towering target, but no pheasants are reared and there are probably not more than a dozen or two wild birds in the woods. One reason for scarcity is the abundance of foxes, which take heavy toll of all ground-nesting birds. And keeping foxes under control is a frustrating task, for at the first sound or sniff of hounds the foxes make a bee-line for the dustbins and suburban gardens of the

190

neighbouring small towns. As a result, the local hunt limits its thankless activities here to one meet a year.

There are no deer in the woods, perhaps because the fawns, too, fall victims to foxes, but plenty of rabbits and wood pigeons and a fair population of badgers.

On some of the virgin downland slopes in the combes of Aston Farm, several rare downland orchids flourish, their well-being watched over by the local natural history society.

PLANS FOR THE FUTURE

Princess Anne and Captain Phillips naturally have the future much in mind. Everything they do at Gatcombe will effect some improvement. Now at the beginning of their farming career, the immediate problems and day-to-day routine have to be foremost in their minds, but the longer-term programme is already shaping itself.

As a commercial farm, financial considerations have to be paramount – the figures quoted to me by Captain Phillips speak for themselves. Beef cattle return a gross margin per acre of £25, cereal growing a gross margin of £125. Therefore the policy must be to grow cereals on every possible acre, leaving the cattle to earn their living from the unploughable slopes of grassland. A flock of sheep is a distinctly possible acquisition for the future, especially as they can act as scavengers behind cattle, grazing on what the larger animals leave. However, at present the fencing is not good enough for sheep, and sheep fencing is expensive and straying sheep a nuisance to everyone. In time, a house cow may also be kept, but there are no plans for installing a dairy.

A small flock of poultry keeps the house supplied with eggs.

8

BARNWELL

Across the lawn from Barnwell Manor stand the impressive ruins of the Castle. The walls, with rounded turrets at the corners, still tower twenty feet or more high but are merely a shell, now enclosing a tennis court. The stone stairways in the turrets have crumbled to form a scree of tumbled masonry at the foot and intriguing tunnels lead nowhere, but in spring the ruins glow with thickets of golden-bronze wallflowers and purple aubrietia.

The Castle was built in 1264 by one Reginald le Moine, whose family had occupied the estate since 1091. Before that, the lands had belonged first to the ancient bishopric of Dorchester-on-Thames, then to the Benedictine Abbey of Ramsey. At the end of the thirteenth century they reverted to the Abbots of Ramsey, who occasionally resided there but more often installed a steward to look after their extensive estates in the district. Towards the end of the Middle Ages the manor was badly neglected and seems at one time to have been occupied by peasant squatters.

At the time of the Dissolution in 1536, King Henry VIII granted the Castle and estate to Edward Montagu, his Lord Chief Justice, but the Castle was too ruinous to be used as a dwelling. Instead, Montagu built Boughton House for himself, nine miles away, and for a time Barnwell was regarded as an outlying part of that estate.

In 1568 Edward Montagu, son of the Lord Chief Justice, developed Barnwell as the nucleus of an estate, building the present manor-house with outbuildings, and laying out the gardens with the Old Castle as a background landscape feature. The third Edward Montagu, created Lord Montagu of Boughton in 1621, held the estate during the Civil War when he used the old Castle as an arsenal.

Barnwell Manor *Sport & General*

The beginning of the eighteenth century saw the Castle in a further stage of dereliction and being frequently used as a quarry for building stone. During the course of the century the Montagu family and the Dukes of Buccleuch, who were living at Boughton House, united by marriage, maintained the unity of the two estates.

In 1910 the Barnwell estate was sold by the Earl of Dalkeith, the father of H.R.H. Princess Alice, Duchess of Gloucester, but part of it was purchased in 1938 by H.R.H. the Duke of Gloucester.

THE BARNWELL ESTATE

The estate in 1938 comprised a little over 2000 acres, of which about 500 acres were in hand, constituting a home farm. The land around the Manor, as with most of the property, had been inefficiently farmed, and the buildings, fences and ditches were in a deplorable state. At the Manor itself there were no farm buildings except an attractive stone barn. The two adjacent areas of parkland in hand were initially grazed by ponies and hunters only. The first arrivals of farm livestock, during the early weeks of the war, were a flock of

Romney Marsh sheep, 'evacuated' from Kent. As most of the fences were not stockproof they did not stay long.

When Prince William was expected, a suggestion was made that it might be advisable for Their Royal Highnesses to have their own tuberculin-tested cows. This idea was taken up and, as His Royal Highness did not want horned cattle with the horses, three Red Polls were purchased from Delapré, Northampton. A dairy girl was appointed to take charge of them but unfortunately proved less than satisfactory and found it convenient to disappear when a heifer calved. It was left to the agent to milk a frightened animal before the eyes of interested grooms and others, waiting for him to be kicked out of the loose box!

The next dairy girl was much more satisfactory and, being attractive too, soon became the bride of a local farmer. Before leaving, however, she was joined by an experienced general farm worker. When one of the Red Polls reacted to the tuberculin test it was decided to replace them with Guernseys, a herd of which was started by the purchase of two cows in Reading. These two were followed up with further purchases from Reading and from private sources.

Whenever the opportunity occurred, more land was taken in hand and the herd increased, until all the available boxes at the stables were full of cattle. The Guernsey bull, dispossessed of his pen, was often to be seen grazing on the lawn by the side of the Castle.

Staffing presented great difficulties at this time, particularly as there were no cottages available, and most sadly, the employee mentioned above was killed by a flying bomb. He was eventually replaced by a native of Sark, whose knowledge of the Guernsey breed and Island farmers was instrumental in initiating the direct purchase from the Island of many of the further additions to the herd. Some of the cattle from this source unfortunately brought troubles with breeding with Johnes Disease, which took some time to eradicate.

Pigs were started in a very small way in the early 1940s with the purchase of two Wessex gilts. These were later succeeded by pedigree Large Whites, the herd increasing to some twenty breeding sows. The followers were fattened to slaughter weight.

When new construction work became possible after the war, the Duke set about modernising the estate, starting with a completely new set of farm buildings which were at the time as up-to-date as any in the country. Planned by the Duke himself, his agent and the clerk of the works, they comprised ranges of brick-built buildings for livestock and farm stores on either side of a broad concrete roadway. The milking parlour, accommodating twelve cows at a time, was equipped with a four-bucket milking unit. Covered exercise yards were arranged to eliminate draughts and provide an equable temperature. All the buildings were equipped with strip-lighting, the electricity cables being concealed underground to preserve the visual amenities.

The cattle housed here were, primarily, the Barnwell herd of pedigree Guernseys, of which in the early 1950s fifty or sixty were milking cows, with sixty or seventy followers. All were recorded daily, the herd average in 1950–51 being 9168 lb at 4.78% butterfat content. A useful export trade, notably to Kenya, was developing at that time.

A second herd, recently acquired at that date, consisted of the then little-known Welsh Blacks. The Duke bought about twenty cows, mated them with a Hereford bull and sold the calves at about eight months for fattening. At Barnwell they grazed on the leys of coarser grasses (cocksfoot/lucerne), grown primarily for conserving as dried grass. They were naturally hardy and lived outdoors right round the year.

These cocksfoot/lucerne leys were devised as an answer to the problem of difficult, stony land in one section of the farm. Once

The Duke of Gloucester's farm at Barnwell *Dairy Farmer*

established, they were left undisturbed for as long as possible but heavily fertilised each year with basic slag, nitro-chalk and muriate of potash. In a good year they yielded up to two tons of fodder, for conservation by grass-drier, as well as a valuable aftermath. They occupied some fifty-seven acres of the farm, the other crops being cereals, mustard, kale, roots and mangolds, as well as permanent and temporary grass for hay and grazing.

In addition to the cattle, the farm supported a herd of Large White pigs and a small stock of poultry (Rhode Island Reds x Light Sussex) kept for the supply of eggs and table poultry to the household. In due course the Duke, deeply engaged in royal duties which involved travelling and residing overseas for considerable periods (he was Governor General of Australia from December 1944 to 1947), and not wishing to have the responsibility for a large estate, sold off the tenanted land in 1944, leaving only the 500-acre nucleus.

By the early 1950s the farm was fully mechanised, all the heavy horses having been disposed of, and an excellent farm workshop, including such features as acetylene and electric welding plants, an inspection pit and a forge, had been installed. As well as the farm buildings a group of handsome new cottages, constructed of brick with Cotswold stone facing, were built to house the farm workers. Following a clearance of mature timber during the war, the woodlands, extending over about 100 acres, were tidied up and replanted. A number of new shelter belts were added and the banks of the dykes adjoining the riverside meadows were planted with cricket-bat willows. Barnwell was, in short, a thoroughly modern model estate.

The Duke continued, however, to take a close interest in the farm, receiving regular reports on its activities. And at the end of his life he went there to spend his last years against the background of the scenes he loved. After suffering a stroke he used to take daily drives around the farm in a Mini-moke, with a nurse and five dogs in attendance.

'The men working on the farm used to come up and talk to him, and we think he understood and enjoyed it, although, of course, he couldn't speak,' Princess Alice told me.

Under Prince William the former policy began to be reversed and the estate started to expand again, but not within the former boundaries. The Prince was interested in acquiring land which could be farmed by the estate and so bought farms with vacant possession

as they became available. The present farming unit is therefore fragmented, a large section of it lying four or five miles from Barnwell, in the direction of Brigstock. All of it is, however, farmed as one unit.

A field of corn on the farm, showing the manor house and farm buildings *Sport & General*

The present acreage is 2507, of which 2205 acres are farm land, 185 acres woodland and 117 acres occupied by buildings, roads, gardens etc.

THE BARNWELL FARMS

This is good fertile land with a heavy soil – excellent wheat land. The farms are mainly arable and devoted primarily to cereal crops. In the current year 845 acres are producing winter wheat and 867 acres spring barley. Another major crop is oilseed rape, of which there are 196 acres. Permanent grass occupies 162 acres, temporary grass (a mixed ley) 59 acres, and a new ley of 76 acres was direct drilled in the autumn of 1977.

Changes are taking place. Oilseed rape is a relatively new crop which has to some extent replaced the potatoes formerly grown on a fairly large scale (sufficient each year to fill a 800-ton store). Potatoes have now been dropped entirely.

THE LIVESTOCK

For many years Barnwell was the home of a noted herd of pedigree Guernsey cattle, usually totalling 120–150 head of cattle – most of them have now gone. They took prizes at agricultural shows and

197

produced a satisfactory amount of cream in their milk, but their milk production was just not high enough for them to be an economic proposition. In 1970–71, for instance, the herd average for 111 cows was 8688 lb of milk (at 4.55% butterfat content). As with the other royal farms, Barnwell is run on a commercial basis; it has to pay its way.

So now only thirteen Guernsey cows are left, and the herd consists chiefly of British Friesians, of which there are sixty-four young cows (all purchased since 1977 when the Guernseys were dispersed), twenty-four in-calf Friesian heifers, and twenty-five Friesian heifers of between one and nine months which are being reared as dairy replacements.

In addition there is a beef unit, based on eighty-one suckling cows (nearly all of which are half- or quarter-Guernsey). The beef animals at the time of my visit consisted of sixty-two of 1–2 years, fifty-five of 6–12 months and forty-four calves less than 6 months. Most of them have the white faces which establish a Hereford ancestry, and a Hereford bull is kept for mating with the heifers. Some, however, are the progeny of Charolais crosses. The beef cattle graze the pastures in summer but are fattened on a concentrate mixture, plus hay, in yards during the winter.

Some of the young bulls are not castrated but are used for producing bull beef. This is a technique common on the Continent but only marginally practised in Britain, where a prejudice against bull beef has to be overcome. Entire bulls put on weight more quickly and more economically than steers and are thus a better commercial proposition. The carcases have less fat and more lean meat.

FARM EQUIPMENT

Barnwell has one of the largest and best equipped farm workshops I have ever seen on an estate of comparable size. It reflects the great interest of Mr Victor Vinson, the estate manager, in farm mechanisation. Improvement and improvisation are the watchwords here – something new is always being developed or hatched in this workshop. I saw work in progress on a highly efficient chopper for straw and hay, to be used for the big bales that are favoured, on elevators and on frameworks for adapting tractors as fork-lift trucks.

Both the Duke and Mr Vinson speak enthusiastically of the big bale system, which rolls straw or hay into giant cylindrical bales, like

Swiss roll slices, each weighing half-a-ton. All the Barnwell hay and straw is processed by this method (using a Bamford baler), the advantage being that the bales can remain outdoors for months without any damage worth considering. Rain penetrates only a thin outer layer. Mr Vinson is now directing some of his inventive genius to perfecting, above the feeding troughs, a hoist and overhead rack from which hay from these giant bales can be pulled down with a minimum of effort.

Heavy powerful tractors are required to cultivate the stiff Northamptonshire clays, and Mr Vinson puts his trust in three huge Zetor tractors together with a Leyland International and an Ursus.

There is no irrigation by water, but the slurry from the cattle pens is stored in a 250,000 gallon tank and pumped into tankers for transfer to the fields.

Some grain is stored in Conder bins, which have a total capacity of 500 tons, the remainder in bulk on ventilated floors. All the wheat is sold, but considerable quantities of the barley, of varieties of feeding quality, are retained as rations for the cattle.

Straw bales being used to form protection for farm machinery *Sport & General*

THE WOODLANDS

The 185 acres of woodlands play no very prominent part in the Barnwell economy. They supply wood for fuel, fencing and other farm and domestic purposes but are maintained by members of the farm staff at odd times. They are mainly long-established hardwoods.

There are, however, approximately forty acres of cricket-bat willows on the estate, planted on the flood plain of the River Nene, of which some thirty acres are nearing maturity.

THE DUKE'S EMPLOYEES

The key man at Barnwell is estate manager, Mr Victor Vinson. Quiet, unassuming and obviously very capable, he has had a difficult task since coming to Barnwell in 1968. The estate then consisted of little more than the home farm, which Mr Vinson ran as a subsidiary

Harvesting corn under a 1000-year-old oak *Sport & General*

enterprise. Soon afterwards Prince William increased his interest in the estate and began a programme of expansion. His tragic death in a flying accident in 1972 left Mr Vinson with the dual role of estate agent and manager of a considerably enlarged farm enterprise, which he has filled ever since.

By way of being a mechanical genius, Mr Vinson, although he comes from an Essex farming family, made his early career in engineering and during the war he built ships in London docks. After a term in the Merchant Navy, he turned his attention to the problems of farm mechanisation, which was then proceeding at a rattling pace. Some of his work in adapting and designing farming equipment for use with tractors proved so valuable that he was offered the farm managership of the well-known Orsett estate in Essex. Here, on a 2600-acre unit, he was able to exercise to the full his flair for producing the tools for the jobs, and Orsett became a cradle of new mechanical ideas.

When in 1968 the Orsett estate was sold, he came to Barnwell and found plenty of scope for continuing his good work. Several machines of his invention have been produced commercially, notably the Carier Seed-drill Cultivator.

At Barnwell the vesting of farming and estate management in one man enables him to keep everything firmly under control without a lot of fuss.

In the office he has the assistance of a secretary, Miss Janice Chapman, and a book-keeper, Mrs Vicky Burrows, who have been with the estate since leaving school.

Mr David Neeve joined the farming staff in October 1975 to take charge of the arable side of the farming, since when he has proved himself most admirably and now manages the farm overall.

Mr Ian Hamilton, the son of a man killed by a flying bomb, left the estate to serve as an air-gunner during the war but returned afterwards to run the beef-rearing side of the farm. The dairy enterprises have seen several changes in recent years but are now under the control of Mr Richard Greenwood. In charge of the workshop is Mr Ted Booker, who ably aids and abets Mr Vinson in his pioneering experiments.

Nicholas Warliker came to Barnwell as a garden boy, returned after national service and is now head gardener. With a lady helper and a boy, he now tackles a task which formerly occupied five gardeners.

Prince Henry, the late Duke of Gloucester, spent most of his later years at Barnwell, where he enjoyed walking around the fields and woods. It was no uncommon thing on a warm June evening to meet the Duke coming home from the hayfields, a hay fork in his hand.

Dynamic Prince William was energetically enlarging the Barnwell estate and transforming it into a country base for his many activities when his life ended in tragedy, two years before his father's death.

Prince Richard, the present Duke, did not, of course, expect to succeed either to the title or to the estate and had chosen to make his career in architecture. Now co-opted to the royal team, he finds his time fully occupied with official duties, which he fulfils with ever-increasing assurance. Barnwell and Kensington Palace are his two homes, now made lively by his two small children. His mother, H.R.H. Princess Alice, the Dowager Duchess of Gloucester, shares both homes with the family.

The Duke finds a kindred spirit in Mr Vinson. The farm workshop and what goes on in it is obviously a focus of interest for both of them. As a trained architect the Duke is clearly impressed by devices which work efficiently and economically.

The children are obviously going to enjoy country life at Barnwell. From the windows of the Manor they can look out over a ha-ha to a vista of green pastures and grazing cattle. There is ample space for any activity.

The farm and gardens supply fresh food to the household – Guernsey cream, cream cheese, vegetables and home-produced beef.

The Duke of Gloucester's agricultural patronages are :–

Farmers Club	Hon. Member
Royal Smithfield Show	President 1975–1978
United Kingdom Farming Scholarship Trust	Patron
Royal Association of British Dairy Farmers	President, 1978 (for one year only)
Protection of Rural Scotland	Patron (five years to 1982)

Princess Alice, Duchess of Gloucester's agricultural patronages are :–

The Gardeners' Royal Benevolent Society	President

The Duke of Gloucester
and his family visiting the
pigsties on horseback
Camera Press

203

THE PUBLIC

Barnwell follows the country house tradition of opening the gardens on two Sunday afternoons a year for charities (in this instance, the Gardeners' Royal Benevolent Society and the National Gardens Scheme of the Queen's Nursing Institute). They are local/family affairs, with Princess Alice attending when possible, and the Barnwell Women's Institute doing the teas.

Six or seven times during the summer, parties from various organisations including Young Farmers Clubs and breed associations are given conducted tours and the grounds are lent for the annual Gymkhana and Fête. Otherwise the estate is not open to the public.

SPORTS AND AMENITIES

Consisting mostly of arable land, Barnwell is not rich in game, and no attempts are being made at present to increase the stock. No keepers are employed. Shooting generally consists of a family shoot, to which neighbours may be invited once a year.

THE DUCHY OF CORNWALL

King Edward III instituted the Duchy of Cornwall in 1337 to supply an income for his eldest son, the Black Prince. The property of the Dukedom was not among the assets handed over to the Government in return for the Civil List but is still inherited by the eldest son of the reigning monarch. It consists of 26,600 acres in Cornwall, including 2000 acres of forests; 4100 acres in the Isles of Scilly; 69,470 acres on Dartmoor; 3215 acres in Devon (excluding Dartmoor); 16,460 acres in Somerset; 3840 acres in Dorset; 3960 acres in Wiltshire; and 1240 acres in Gloucester. The West Country assets also include mineral rights, notably for tin. In London the Duchy owns 45 acres in Kensington, including the Oval cricket ground. In all, the Duchy's property extends to 128,930 acres, of which only the Home Farm, Stoke Climsland, Cornwall, is now directly farmed.

HOME FARM

The concept of maintaining a home farm on the Duchy of Cornwall estates in the West Country dates from Victorian times, when a home farm was a normal feature of a big rural estate. In particular, the Home Farm at Stoke Climsland, in the heart of the Duchy's territory in Cornwall, served the useful purpose of providing a base for the Prince of Wales and his guests when visiting the West Country. It offered a pleasant and reasonably spacious house with satellite buildings and a small park which could serve as a venue for social-

205

cum-business events, notably meetings with the tenants, as well as a haven for a few relaxing days far from the pressures of the capital.

The Home Farm at Stoke Climsland, which lies about four miles north of the little Cornish town of Callington and about the same distance west of the Tamar, was acquired and adapted to the role of centre for the Duchy's West Country estates in 1914. It then comprised about 300 acres of hilly land, to which a further 200 acres were subsequently added. The farm is on the edge of the plateau which forms the backbone of the south-western peninsula and hence does not enjoy the balmy climate of the southward-facing valleys by the sea. Although the winters are relatively mild, the rainfall averages fifty inches a year, and windy days are frequent.

The Home Farm is therefore a stock farm, concentrating on the production of grass, which grows luxuriantly, and feeding it to sheep and cattle. Such cereals as are grown are destined for consumption by the resident animals and are valued almost as much for their straw as for their grain.

HOME FARM IN 1952

The Home Farm, Stoke Climsland *Tavistock Gazette*

A summary of the agricultural activities for the year 1952 serves to illustrate the conventional pattern of Cornish farming then followed.

There were 350 acres of grassland (200 acres of permanent pastures and 150 acres of temporary leys), of which 100 acres were cut annually for hay. The crops on the 125 acres of arable – oats, dredge corn, and a mixture of vetches and peas – were cut at midsummer for silage, after which the land was sown to rape in early July for autumn grazing. The general rotation was: two years of straw crops; one year of rape or roots; then another straw crop undersown with grass seeds. The grass could be long-term or short-term leys, but when it was ploughed up it was followed in the first year by potatoes, then by the two years of straw crops.

The cattle at Stoke Climsland were the Climsland herd of Red Devons, comprising about 170 herd, all attested. The sheep likewise belonged to a West Country breed, the Devon Longwool. The flock normally consisted of 135 breeding ewes, 80–90 young ewes (as replacements for older animals culled) and the necessary complement of rams. Surplus lambs were sold fat. The farm had a herd of pedigree Large White pigs, established in 1930 and consisting of about 50 animals, including 6 sows. It also kept a flock of about 200 poultry.

CHANGES

This pattern has now been altered drastically, and it is interesting to note how the farm has been adapted to suit the new requirements of the last quarter of the twentieth century.

In the first place, the farm was given a brief in 1965 to explore the local commercial possibilities of producing meat from cattle and sheep. This was largely because many of the estate tenants were switching from meat to milk, meat production being the Cinderella of the farming industry at that time. The programme proved to be reasonably successful in that a profit was made, though whether it was of much value to the tenants on the estate, with their much smaller holdings, was doubtful.

REVIEW IN 1975

In 1975 a reassessment of the situation was made, and the particular question, 'Can the Home Farm serve any useful purpose on the Estate?' was asked. In working out an answer the role of the Home farm was summarised as follows:–

a.   To assist the estate in assessing the general prosperity of its tenants. Even in these enlightened days it is difficult to get a batch of tenants to be frank and honest in any discussion of their general prosperity – especially when the landlord's interest may be linked with a future rent review.

b. To provide facilities within the estate where the landlord can be seen to be playing a part in development and progress in the technical, marketing and co-operation fields. The Home Farm can point to, for example:

    i)   facilities provided and assistance given to carry out crop variety and manurial trials

    ii)   active participation in formation and operation of North Cornwall Seed Potato Group

    iii)   limited co-operation in the sphere of better use of machinery in such operations as silage making, potato harvesting etc.

    iv)   development on field scale of new system. This farm has developed the idea of 'Bull Beef' production from the suckler herd, and a lot of financial and technical data has been collected in conjunction with the Meat and Livestock Commission. This information is attracting interest.

c. To be the prototype of the ideal holding for the future. For seven or eight years from 1966 the Home Farm was developing along these lines. It was sufficiently large to organise a sensible working week for all staff, it was not embarrassed by staff absence through sickness, and it could also be efficiently mechanised. It also supported a big enough business to allow the incorporation of technical improvements to offset the normal annual differences in change of production costs and unit value of goods produced. Inflation has, however, produced such a rapid increase in both costs and receipts that the farm is now working in a financial environment which, even in 1973, it did not expect to reach until at least 1985 or perhaps later. Not surprisingly, the farm organisation has not been able to develop quite as rapidly. Now, instead of looking ahead ten years at a time it is necessary to set one's sights on the year 2000 or beyond.

d. To farm land as a business in its own right and a competitor to creating a tenancy

    i)   It was a deliberate choice in 1965 to keep capital invested in what were commonly accepted as the least profitable of farming enterprises. The last ten years has seen a modest yield from investment in tenant capital but a quite

substantial capital appreciation. The experience of Home Farm supports the contention that money invested as tenant capital in farming has fared very much better than that invested over a broad cross-section of British Industry.

Spring at Home Farm
Tavistock Gazette

ii) It would also be fair to say that the profit margins realised from the Home Farm farming system would make it very difficult to justify borrowing a substantial proportion of the capital in present day money-markets. As a general guide, money invested in arable cropping can be compared with a high yield–low growth share, while money invested in livestock farming will compare to a moderate yield–high growth share. The climate, soil type and general situation of this part of Cornwall conditions any farming system to be predominantly livestock with limited arable cropping.

iii) The tenant farmer requires expertise and capital. The tenant farmer of the future will require greater expertise and considerably more capital. Good candidates for tenancies may become difficult to get. Skilful staff will always be more plentiful, and it may be that the method of farming an estate will move away from the present Landlord–Tenant system. There is certainly a lot of scope for experiment and adventure.

With all this in mind the farm manager, Mr David Thompson, worked out some options for the future.

Assuming that the existing policies were continued, and that costs increased faster than prices of produce (at a ratio of 50:30), the investment income in the early 1980s should be about the same as in 1975. The amount of capital involved, however, would be much greater, and therefore the interest on invested capital would be much less.

He then looked at improvements which would be made possible by changing the farming system but keeping the farm at its current size. Limits were imposed by the nature of the farm and its soil. It was, for instance, impossible to produce more corn crops by substituting arable for grass; the climate and stony soil vetoed any such policy. As an alternative, the intensive production of fat cattle and sheep by using nitrogenous fertilizers at rates that make it possible to stock grassland to the extent of one livestock unit per acre is only possible when nitrogen is cheap. At present nitrogenous fertilizers are dear. The extra cost of manuring the grass would only just be covered by the receipts from the additional meat produced.

The logical conclusions, therefore, were that the farm should either cut its costs or increase its size, in order to spread the costs over a bigger acreage. The costs could be cut by reducing the number of enterprises, particularly by eliminating the potato crop and perhaps the cereals, thus making it possible to run the farm with a reduced staff (by replacing three sixty-year-old employees when they retired with only two younger men) and with a simpler range of farm equipment. As for increasing the size of the farm, it was calculated that doubling the acreage should at least double the gross receipts, while the fixed costs of labour and machinery would increase by only about 60%.

With these considerations in mind, it was decided in December 1975, at a meeting at which H.R.H. the Duke of Cornwall was present, both to increase the acreage of the farm and to expand the beef and sheep enterprises. What I saw at Stoke Climsland in the summer of 1978, therefore, was the farm in the process of transition.

HOME FARM IN 1978

Unexpected opportunities, arising from the death or retirement of tenants, have enabled the Home Farm to increase its size more rapidly than anticipated. In 1976 Deer Park Farm, of 180 acres, came in hand, and in 1977 Penpill Farm and Kit Hill Tenement, totalling 239 acres, were added. These acquisitions have raised the size of the farm to 983 acres.

Total cattle numbers increased from 313 in September 1976 to 550 in May 1978. In the same period sheep numbers rose from 1027 to approximately 2000. Much of the increase was due to the retention of home-bred stock for breeding. A successful lambing season in the spring of 1978 produced over 1000 lambs from 650 ewes – the first time the Home Farm had ever attained such a figure. In the meantime, the farm staff and the machinery complement remained unchanged.

At the time of my visit in early September 1978, the cattle herd stood at just over 500, of which 140 were breeding cows. All were Red Devons, except for 50 young crossbred heifers. The plan now was to retain a smaller herd of first-class, performance-tested pedigree Devons in the home paddocks and to devote the pastures further from home to crossbreeds of any promising type. Most of the cows calve in spring and suckle their calves all through the summer, the calves of course learning to graze as well. In autumn they are taken from their mothers and fattened in yards, attaining a suitable weight for marketing at the age of about thirteen or fourteen months.

Contrary to common practice, the bull calves are not castrated but go to market as bull beef. Developments in Europe in the 1960s demonstrated beyond contradiction that young bulls can reach a marketable weight (800–900 pounds) more quickly and more economically than steers. In consequence, the practice of castrating young bulls quickly ceased in the Netherlands and West Germany and was reduced to very small proportions in much of the rest of the Continent. In Britain development came more slowly, largely because of Ministry of Agriculture regulations, which required all bulls not passed for service after official inspection to be castrated. Butchers also showed considerable hesitation in buying bull beef, which tends to have a rather darker colour. Now regulations have been relaxed and the market is becoming reconciled to the innovation, though the proportion of bull beef being produced is still quite small. Once again a royal farm is in the position of pioneering new ideas and techniques.

In the autumn of 1978 rather more than 1000 ewes were due to be mated. Most of them were the traditional Devon Longwools and their crosses, but some Border Leicester x Cheviots had been brought in. The aim is to maintain a self-contained flock of Longwools and Longwool crosses. The Devon Longwool, a short-legged, deep-bodied sheep with a thick lustrous fleece carried in ringlets, is indigenous to Devon and Cornwall and very well suited to the climate and soil. Its major virtue is its high wool clip, which averages between thirteen and sixteen pounds per ewe and brings in about £7 per fleece (at present prices) which is about double the price of the fleeces of most breeds. It is, however, none too prolific, and it tends to lamb late. The rams brought in for crossing are usually Border Leicester, to increase prolificness, and Suffolk and Dorset Downs are used as terminal sires. The pig herd has now disappeared, as has the poultry.

Although the acreage of Home Farm has increased to 983, only 130 acres are still devoted to crops other than grass and forage crops. 100 acres grow cereals (80 acres of barley and 20 of oats) for consumption on the farm, while 30 acres produce potatoes. This potato-growing venture is a specialist enterprise in that it engages in the production of seed potatoes of early varieties (chiefly Home Guard, Craig Royal and Maris Peer) for the growers of West Cornwall and the Isles of Scilly. Early potatoes grown there from Stoke Climsland seed mature about a week earlier than those grown from Scottish seed, which is an important consideration for a crop which depends for its success on catching the very early market. The potatoes have to be grown at the highest elevations, normally above the 500 feet contour, which are too high and exposed for virus-carrying aphids to flourish. The Home Farm is a member of the North Cornwall Seed Producers Ltd., a co-operative organisation for growing and marketing seed potatoes.

In spite of the important role of the Home Farm in this specialised industry, the future of potatoes there is doubtful. Mr Thompson says the potato enterprise is justified at present because of the manpower that the farm is committed to employ. As men retire and are not

replaced the replacement of the potato enterprise by beef or sheep would not require any further capital, and so its days are probably numbered.

Devon Longwool ewes and their crossbred lambs
Tavistock Gazette

The power units at Stoke Climsland comprise four tractors (3 David Browns and one International). A Dania combine-harvester tackles the grain harvest but when eventually it wears out it will probably not be replaced. A combine-harvester to deal with only 100 acres of cereals is hardly an economic proposition. For silage-making the farm co-operates with a tenant neighbour, sharing machinery.

The Home Farm buildings are superficially imposing but were designed for a vanished age when all farm work was done by manual labour. In the late twentieth century they tend to be a white elephant. A reassessment of their potentialities is due. Can they be adapted or should they be scrapped?

THE STAFF

Home Farm is at present run by a manager and five men. David Thompson, the manager, is a married man with four teenage children, who came to Stoke Climsland in 1965, after spending ten years on the technical staff of the Ministry of Agriculture's experimental husbandry farm at Liscombe, high on Exmoor. The son of a Bristol policeman, he did his national service in the Royal Army Veterinary Corps and subsequently gained his degree (B. Sc. Ag) at Reading University, also taking a postgraduate diploma in animal husbandry.

All the men have spent most or all of their working lives at Home Farm. Mr W. H. Dawe and Mr D. Easterbrook, both tractor drivers who have worked there for forty-three years and twenty-four years respectively, have been awarded the Royal Victorian Medal for long service. Mr M. Gliddon, the other tractor-driver, began work at Home Farm in 1965, and Mr W. E. Weskett, the shepherd, in 1961. Mr H. Crago, who looks after the cattle, has done so since 1953. In addition, Mr S. Philp, who has recently retired at the age of sixty-five, started work on the farm when leaving school at fourteen, his long service winning him the Jubilee Medal. He excelled as the cattle

Shepherd W. E. Weskett feeding the sheep
Tavistock Gazette

showman in the years when the Stoke Climsland Herd of Red Devons exhibited regularly at local and national shows and won many trophies.

PRINCE CHARLES AT STOKE CLIMSLAND

Prince Charles gets down to Cornwall to see his farm when his other commitments allow, though he keeps in touch with what goes on in the meantime. As in so many other matters, the versatile Prince is well informed about things agricultural and digs below the surface in more senses than one. For instance, on the slopes of Kit Hill I was shown a field with a luxuriant sward of grass and clover but with a bare spot in one corner which looked like a stone heap.

'I left this spot to show Prince Charles what the soil was like and why the field couldn't come into an arable/grass rotation,' said Mr Thompson. Prince Charles looked doubtful that this stony spot could be a fair demonstration of the whole field and, taking a soil auger, tried taking borings elsewhere. He convinced himself.

ST MARY'S, ISLES OF SCILLY

For two decades from 1948, when it was taken over from a tenant, the Duchy also had a Home Farm on St Mary's in the Isles of Scilly. A thirty-acre holding, to which ten further acres were subsequently added, it was envisaged as a demonstration and experimental farm for the benefit of the Islanders. A new set of buildings was erected and Ministry of Agriculture trials were carried out there.

In 1952 the Home Farm, St Mary's, had a herd of attested pedigree Guernsey cattle, consisting of eight cows and heifers, two stock bulls, three heifer calves and a bull calf. It also had a flock of Rhode Island Red hens for producing hatching eggs. The crops grown included early potatoes, asparagus, narcissus and other bulb flowers.

The farm has now been re-let.

10

BROADLANDS

Broadlands, the home of the late Admiral of the Fleet Earl Mountbatten of Burma, occupies one of the loveliest reaches of the delectable valley of the Test, in southern Hampshire. The park, house and grounds lie behind the brick precinct wall on the southern outskirts of Romsey and the estate extends on either side of the river almost to Southampton Water. It has all the ingredients of a perfect country estate, including woods of towering trees (1500 acres of them), lush riparian meadows, productive arable acres and a broad, placid river. The woods are full of pheasants and the flat lands towards the Test estuary are an unsurpassed haven for wildfowl.

EARLY HISTORY

In common with most of the lower Test valley and the surrounding countryside, Broadlands was in medieval times a part of the estates of Romsey Abbey. The original house was built in 1536. When the ecclesiastical estates were split up by decree of King Henry VIII, the house and adjacent land were bought for £900 by John Foster, the Abbey's Steward. That was in 1544, but by the end of the century the property had passed to the St Barbe family, who retained possession of it for nearly two hundred years.

BROADLANDS UNDER THE PALMERSTONS

Henry Temple, the first Viscount Palmerston, purchased the estate from the St Barbes in 1736. He and his grandson, who succeeded to the title, made extensive alterations to the house and grounds, adding here and demolishing there and creating the appearance which it still

The front of Broadlands house *Edward Haydon Wood*

largely retains. With Capability Brown as landscape artist and probably architect and Henry Holland as builder, the second Lord Palmerston, a man of artistic temperament, spent more than £23,400 on the work between the years 1766 and 1779. The task completed, he set about designing the interior to match. Robert Adam, who designed much of the furniture and interior decorations, was one of the artists he employed. In subsequent years Broadlands became a centre for the artistic and literary world of the late eighteenth century. Lord and Lady Palmerston enjoyed entertaining, and among their frequent visitors were Ruskin, Joshua Reynolds, Garrick and Sheridan besides numerous scientists and refugees from revolutionary France.

It was in this stimulating atmosphere that the third Lord Palmerston, who became one of Britain's greatest Foreign Secretaries and Prime Ministers, was reared. He succeeded to the title and estates at the age of eighteen, on the death of his father in 1802. During his long life Broadlands continued to be the venue for social events

Side view of Broadlands
D. J. Swinburne

attended by leading figures in the political and cultural life of the nation.

As the result of two childless marriages Broadlands came by inheritance into the Ashley family. Wilfred Ashley, who on being created a peer revived the title of Lord Mount Temple, was succeeded in 1939 by his daughter Edwina, who in 1922 had married Lord Louis Mountbatten. During the period of their residence the house has been largely restored, by the demolition of twenty-eight rooms, to its original eighteenth-century plan, and indeed in contemporary photographs, taken from across the river, it appears to be virtually identical with eighteenth-century prints.

THE SHEETED CATTLE OF BROADLANDS

Among the Broadlands assets inherited by Lady Mountbatten was a remarkable herd of 'sheeted' cattle, reputedly imported from the Netherlands by one of her ancestors, Sir William Temple, in about 1690. The allegation regarding their origin is disputed, for from 1666 onwards the importation of cattle from Europe was forbidden by law, though it is possible that Sir William's cattle were brought in a few years earlier than 1666. However, it is also possible that the ancestors of the Broadlands herd were indigenous, for cattle with the same colour scheme were once quite widely distributed in England, notably in East Anglia, Lincolnshire, south Yorkshire and Somerset. Dr David Low, Professor of Agriculture at Edinburgh University, wrote in 1842 that 'the Sheeted Breed of Somersetshire . . . has existed in the same parts of England from time immemorial', though he added that the breed had then become rare.

The somewhat spectacular colour pattern of the sheeted cattle consisted of a broad white band across the middle of the body, as though a white sheet had been thrown over the animal. The colour of the rest of the body was usually black, though in the Somerset cattle it was a light reddish brown. A similar colour scheme is still to be found in the Belted Galloways of Scotland, the Lakenvelders of Holland and on certain animals of the Welsh Black breed. It is clearly a very primitive pattern which could act as camouflage in the wild (as, for example, in the similarly-coloured tapir and giant panda).

The Broadlands animals had their white sheets on a black background and were cattle of dairy type, though, to judge from photographs, they were of lighter build than the modern Friesian. The first documentary reference to them is in a letter dated 13 August 1785, from Lord Northington to Lord Palmerston in which he writes :–

The famous sheeted cattle of Broadlands *reproduced by kind permission of the late Lord Mountbatten*

219

The fame of your Dairy having extended itself far, as well as near, and the beauty of the Broadlands Sheet Cows being universally acknowledged and admired, I have engaged to try my interest with your Lordship and, relying on your goodness, have flattered her (Lady Salisbury) with the expectation of her being able to obtain, if you can conveniently spare one, a Calf of the Black and White Sheet Breed.

Further correspondence revealed the fact that there were also red and white cattle in the herd.

Later documentation is scanty, but in a painting by Thomas Sidney Cooper, commissioned by Queen Victoria, of the Royal Guernsey herd at Osborne an unmistakable sheeted cow appears intriguingly in the background. Nothing is known of this animal, but that she

Mr Derek Fowler, the farm manager, adjusting new irrigation equipment
Edward Haydon Wood

existed is almost beyond doubt, for Queen Victoria saw the detailed sketches he made for the painting and approved of them. The likelihood that the sheeted cow originated in Broadlands herd seems strong.

The sheeted cattle survived at Broadlands well into the present century, but during the campaign to eradicate bovine tuberculosis in the 1930s they were found to be heavily infected with the disease and so had to be sacrificed. The last were disposed of at some time in the 1940s. At Broadlands they were replaced first by Guernseys and latterly by Friesians.

THE CONTEMPORARY ESTATE

The Broadlands estate now has a total area of just over 6000 acres. It has shrunk a little in recent years, owing to the urgent demands of the urban areas all around for land for development.

Until 1960, the only land farmed by the estate was in accordance with the prevailing pattern of agricultural estates, the Home Farm, of 360 acres, all the rest being let to tenants. After the death of Lady Mountbatten in 1959, Lord Mountbatten decided, as so many other rural landowners were also doing, to reverse the policy and to take land in hand as it became available. Eight farms have now been acquired in this way, allowing the estate to farm rather more than 2000 acres.

THE SOIL

Lying on the floor of the Test valley, the farmland is in general light and easy to work. On either side of the alluvium by the river are deposits of valley gravel, with a surface stratum of silty loam. The north-eastern sector of the estate, including the house and park, overlies a deposit of brick earth. On the ridge to the east the soils vary from London clay and plateau gravel to Bagshot and Bracklesham beds. In the mid-nineteenth century Lord Palmerston, who took a keen interest in farming activities on the estate, had most of the land thoroughly drained.

THE FARMING SCENE

After several changes around the middle of the century the farming policy has now settled on the basically simple system of cows and corn. A large pig unit, for which three big specialist houses had been erected, was discontinued first, and then beef and potatoes were cut out in the early 1970s.

Of the 2000 acres about 1100 are devoted to arable crops, of which wheat is regarded as the most important. In 1978 the farms produced 460 acres of wheat, 341 of barley, 130 of oilseed rape, 100 of herbage seed, 42 of maize for silage and 26 of mixed crops for game cover. As in much of Britain, a marked swing to autumn-sown cereals is occurring. With many farmers this is in response to the weather pattern of recent years, characterised by dry, sunny autumns and late, chilly, wet springs, which favour autumn-sown corn and discourage spring-sowing, but Broadlands has an additional incentive. Oilseed rape, which is a crop of considerable economic importance, has to be sown in late August or early September, and about the only crop which can reliably be harvested before that date is winter barley. So winter (or autumn sown) barley is taking the place of spring-sown varieties. The oilseed rape is usually followed in the rotation by two successive crops of wheat.

The rest of the farmland is devoted to grass, of which about 425 acres are permanent pasture and 500 acres temporary leys. Of the permanent meadows, most lie in the Park and along the banks of the river Test. They are devoted to the rearing of heifers as replacements for the milking herds. At any one time there will be around 450 of them in the pastures, representing all ages from calfhood to the first calving, which is planned for $2\frac{1}{2}$ years.

The milking cows, now all Friesians, are divided into four herds, each of just over 100, comprising a total of 446 animals. Two herds are managed to calve in spring and two in autumn, to procure a relatively level supply of milk around the year. The cows are artificially inseminated with semen from pure-bred proven Friesian sires, using the latest techniques involved in what is known as oestrus-synchronisation; groups of heifers are inseminated to ensure that they calve at the required date.

It all adds up to a thoroughly modern commercial farm, scientifically managed and poles away from the old style of country estate home farm, with its house cows, pigs and poultry all geared to keeping the family supplied. At Broadlands there is no longer even a house cow. All the milk goes directly to the wholesaler, and the milkman calls with his bottles in the early morning, as at every suburban home.

Each dairy herd is based on a milking parlour, with facilities for milking ten cows at a time, adjacent to yards with cubicles for 120 cows. It is managed by one man, with a relief milker to give him time off occasionally. Each unit has its own calving pens, its own silage clamps and its own slurry catchment lagoons.

On the arable side there is a full complement of machinery for the efficient running of the business. Tractors number fifteen, of which the most powerful is a huge 115 hp machine with four-wheel drive. There are two massive combine-harvesters for the cereal and oilseed rape crops and adequate forage-harvesting equipment to cope with the harvesting of over 3000 tons of silage (grass and maize) annually.

It is probably axiomatic that farms of this calibre are expected to earn profits, which the Broadlands farms do. They were farmed as a partnership by the late Lord Mountbatten and his eldest grandson, the Hon. Norton Knatchbull. In 1978 other junior members of the family also became shareholders in the business, which operates under the trading title of Broadlands Farms. Some years ago Lord Mountbatten initiated a system of estate committee meetings, held at six-weekly intervals, which were usually attended by the Lord and Lady Brabourne, the Hon. Norton Knatchbull, the agent, the accountant and the farm manager, with Lord Mountbatten himself presiding. At these meetings all matters relating to the estate and the farms were discussed and decisions on policy taken. On the technical side the farms make full use of such aids to efficient management as the Milk Marketing Board's Herd Management Control Scheme and I.C.I.'s Dairymaid costing scheme.

THE STAFF

The estate agent at Broadlands is Mr Stuart Wyatt, O.B.E., and the farm manager is Mr Derek Fowler. The farm staff comprises nineteen men, plus a small maintenance gang engaged on work on the farm buildings and houses, and several girls in the office.

To care for the 1500 acres of woodlands Mr A. Grossert, the head forester, leads a team of five forest workers.

SHOOTING AND WILDLIFE

Broadlands is one of the great pheasant shoots of southern England. With its well-arranged blocks of woodland, arable fields and a few

Mr Harry Grass, the head keeper, attending to the pheasants *Edward Haydon Wood*

strategically placed cover crops the environment is ideal for the birds, and the estate is alive with them. Partridges are also quite plentiful in favourable seasons. Until 1976 the shooting was carried out by eight guns, of which Lord Mountbatten retained three in order to be able to invite two guests; the other five were fee-paying. Nowadays, the first day's shooting over the various beats is let to overseas visitors, and extra birds are reared to leave an adequate stock for the family shoot later on. The number of fee-paying guns in the family shoot has been reduced from five to three.

The head keeper is Mr Harry Grass, who is now in his seventies, and came to Broadlands from Northumberland in 1957 when the shooting was at a very low ebb. Within a year of his arrival more pheasants were killed in a single day than previously in a whole season. Now Broadlands provides between twelve and fifteen days' shooting each autumn and winter, with a total bag of 8000–10,000,

the best day's shoot yielding over 2000. Prince Charles who, like other members of the Royal Family, often comes down to Broadlands, is an excellent shot.

The lower reaches of the Test are also the haunt of large numbers of wildfowl, especially in winter, and the southward-facing valley provides a favoured route for migrating birds.

FISHING

The Test is, of course, one of the few remaining unpolluted rivers in England. The southern reaches are famous for their salmon fishing, while to the north of Romsey and especially near Stockbridge it has an international reputation as one of the finest trout streams in the world.

Some years ago the main drainage carrier through the estate was

The late Lord Mountbatten discussing farm affairs with his farm manager *Edward Haydon Wood*

widened, deepened and stocked with trout, greatly improving the fishing. Salmon are quite frequently caught. The construction of the M.27 motorway resulted in the creation of several new large lakes, where gravel had been excavated, and these have been stocked with coarse fish.

The head water keeper is Mr Bernard Aldrich, who after service in the Merchant Navy and the Police Force, moved to Romsey in 1956 and soon afterwards took over the fisheries at Broadlands. Under him the trout stream has been developed; the first rainbow trout, of over 10 lb, was killed there in 1968. A lake resulting from the M.27 gravel extraction is at present shaping well as a coarse fishery and has so far yielded specimens up to the following weights – carp 14 lb; tench 6 lb; pike $26\frac{1}{2}$ lb; golden orfe $4\frac{1}{2}$ lb (a world record); roach 2 lb; rudd 4 lb. Coarse fishing is available to the public at a charge of £1.20 a day.

Mr Aldrich, incidentally, is making a name for himself as a writer and broadcaster on freshwater fishing matters and in 1978 was busily filming for a BBC programme, *A Year in the Life of a River Keeper*.

ROYALTY AND BROADLANDS

Lord Mountbatten in his later years spent perhaps half of his time at Broadlands and was thoroughly conversant with all that went on. He was, however, until the time of his death, still deeply engaged in public affairs, entailing much travelling.

As is well known, Broadlands was placed at the disposal of the Queen (then Princess Elizabeth) and the Duke of Edinburgh for their honeymoon in 1947, and they and other members of the Royal Family have paid numerous subsequent visits. In the grounds are mulberry trees planted by the Queen and Prince Philip in 1957 on the occasion of the 350th anniversary celebrations of the granting of a Charter to the Borough of Romsey. The trees flourish near others which were planted by King James 1 in 1607 when he granted the original charter and which still bear fruit annually.

THE PUBLIC

The great occasion when the public flock into the Park is Romsey Agricultural Show, held in early September. In 1979, for the first time, the House itself was opened to the public on certain days throughout the summer.

11

WHY ROYAL FARMERS?

Questions beginning with Why? never have a simple answer.

Royal delight in farming seems to have begun with King George III. Before his time many monarchs attached great importance to the produce of and revenues from vast agricultural properties, but there are few indications of any personal interest in the farming of the good earth. In his own era, too, the King was a unique phenomenon among royalty. None of his fellow monarchs in Europe shared his passion for scientific agriculture to anything like the same extent.

He was, of course, largely a product of his age. As discussed in Chapter 2, political considerations projected him towards identification with the powerful class of Tory landowners. The previous two reigns had seen the Whigs in the ascendant, to the virtual exclusion of their Tory adversaries, many of whom, in any case, had instinctive sympathies with the exiled Stuarts. For a generation or two these numerous, able and wealthy men had had to confine their attentions to their own estates, and the natural consequence of such a concentration of energy was a tremendous surge of agricultural progress.

When the crunch came in 1745–46, the rural magnates found that they were not such dedicated Jacobites after all. In a conflict of interests between the somewhat nebulous cause of the Stuarts and the well-being of their own parks and fields their personal properties won easily. Settling down after the upheaval, they found, too, that they had as a monarch one of themselves, – a King who, above all else, desired to be an English country gentleman.

After the failure of his venture into personal government King George participated wholeheartedly in the agricultural revolution that was going on all around him. The great estates were being enlarged and consolidated by enclosures of open fields and waste land; so the King set about creating farms by enclosures in Windsor Great Park. Successful experiments, based on sound principles, were revolutionising domestic animal breeding, so he had to make his contribution, which consisted primarily of the introduction of Merino sheep. New ideas in crop rotations, agricultural machinery, farm buildings and crop husbandry were being tested; he tried them all. The agricultural scene was at last being comprehensively surveyed and the surveys published by the newly established Board of Agriculture, and agricultural matters were being vigorously discussed in Arthur Young's periodical, *The Annals of Agriculture*. The King enthusiastically joined in, indulging in correspondence for publication under the pseudonym of Ralph Robinson.

Few of the many books on the agricultural revolution of the second half of the eighteenth century give adequate credit to the part played by King George III. It is true that he joined a tide that was already flowing strongly, but his identification with the cause of agricultural progress must have helped it immensely. The influence of the Crown was perhaps greater than it is today, and in his middle years the King was exceedingly popular.

The pattern thus established by 'Farmer George' has endured to this day. After the short reigns of King George IV and King William IV the royal estates again became patterns of good management and agricultural progress under that other able farmer, the Prince Consort. And so through successive reigns the tradition has been maintained, that the royal estates be worthy examples of contemporary husbandry and that their royal owners be the proud possessors of some of the best farm livestock. King Edward VII's delight in his prizewinning racehorses was matched by that in his magnificent Shire stud. King George V was likewise 'a Shire man'. Queen Elizabeth II refuses to countenance any reorganisation at Windsor that would disperse her beloved herd of Jersey cattle.

The involvement of royalty in farming is never more evident than in times of war. When food production has periodically assumed a paramount importance our reigning monarchs have been prompt to set an example of good husbandry. None was more dedicated than King George VI, under whom much of the Windsor parkland was ploughed up, the fields of Sandringham made more productive than ever before, and the Flitcham flax factory did an immense public service by publicising and processing an unfamiliar crop.

Sir Walter Gilbey's assertion that 'an account of the work done on the royal farms during the twenty years of the Prince Consort's control would be a history of the agricultural improvements of all the soils in England' has been quoted. The same reflection could be extended to include all the royal farmers for the past two hundred years. The royal farms have at every period faithfully illustrated the best in contemporary agriculture. They still do so.

The royal farms are probably more extensive now than ever they have been. That is because, as a general rule, the larger an agricultural unit is the better its chance of being viable. As I learned from investigating many a demonstration farm in the Third World, it is useless to try to teach new techniques to farmers unless it can be shown that they can be profitable. With the world ordered as it is at present, when a farmer ceases to make a profit he soon ceases to be a farmer.

So, in the interests of greater efficiency, the royal farms have been enlarging their horizons. At Sandringham, Balmoral, Barnwell, Broadlands and Stoke Climsland, farms formerly tenanted have been taken in hand and incorporated with other units. There is increasing specialisation and streamlining, as unprofitable enterprises are jettisoned. Simultaneously, some of the poorer land, which gives the lowest returns for effort, is being withdrawn from cultivation. It will act as a reservoir of grassland, replenishing its fertility against the time when, as in 1939, it may be urgently needed again to meet a national emergency.

Present policies have achieved, in most instances, the solution of a problem that eluded previous royalty. On page 56 Nathaniel Kent laments that, although all the recommended improvements have been carried out for King George III, he is perturbed by the failure of the farms to make a profit. King William IV on his farm in Bushy Park had urgent need for profit, in view of his inadequate income, and vacillated like a gyroscope in pursuit of it. The Prince Consort scathingly criticised the Isle of Wight farmers for their inefficiency, but whether or not he would have made a profit on his farming if normal interest had been added to his enormous investment in buildings and other improvements must be distinctly doubtful. In present-day royal farms, however, it is an axiom that they must pay their way, and they do so, though in most instances the profits are ploughed back in farm improvements.

Neither the commendable desire to set a good example nor the wish to make a profit, however, can be advanced as the prime reason for royalty being engaging in farming. There are other industries equally meritorious and certainly with greater scope for financial gain. The true explanation lies deeper.

Contrary to what happened in most of the rest of Europe, the English aristocracy was never divorced from other social classes. From at least Tudor times, the younger sons of noble families went into trade and quite often married into merchant families. Successful merchants and, later, industrialists acquired country estates, intermarried with their longer-established neighbours and within a generation or two became indistinguishable from them. As the centuries passed, many a rich and titled family of landowners could trace its ancestry back to local peasants and, conversely, many a noble family, hit by hard times or bankrupted by spendthrift heirs, sank back to peasant level. The links were there and were widely known.

This is still so, although the links are now between a predominantly urban populace and a diminished rural one. Though the British now live mostly in towns there are few of them who cannot claim a grandfather or great-grandfather who as a farmer or a blacksmith or a gamekeeper or some rural craftsman earned his living in the countryside. Two hundred years ago, before the enclosures hit hard, almost all were countrymen, as they had been since the beginning of time. In such a vast panorama two centuries is a short space of time, not nearly adequate to suppress the instincts inherited from so long a line of rural ancestors.

The estate-owner with his broad acres, the peasant with his paddock, cows and geese, and the suburban householder with his rectangular garden plot are motivated by the same instincts. Their love of the land and its fauna and flora is innate. Few urban residents who possess a garden can ignore the urge to cultivate it. Those who have no garden find an outlet for their instincts in window-boxes and house plants. And every foreigner knows that the crazy British are insane about animals.

In making the most of their rural inheritance, therefore, the Royal Family are doing exactly as most of the Queen's subjects would do if they could change places. Their attitude in this respect is typically British. Heads of state, whether hereditary monarchs or elected presidents, in every nation have their parks, estates and mansions,

231

but few identify themselves with the rural way of life as wholeheartedly as the British Royal Family. The British people, sprung from the same stock, know just how they feel. They vicariously enjoy the activities of royalty, so comprehensively reported in the Press.

There was a time when everyone in Britain enjoyed a rural heritage. As children, everyone picked primroses in the woods and cowslips in the meadows. All were familiar with the dawn chorus of song-birds in May, the eerie yells of love-lorn vixens in January, the practice flights of swarms of young swallows and martins preparatory to autumn migration. All were appreciative of rain in the order of things, of the inestimable value of good harvest weather, and of the contentment that comes from possessing an autumn store of apples 'in a little heap under the stairs'. All were involved, through the breeding of domestic animals, with the cycle of birth, mating and death.

For many, the heritage that was once on the doorstep is now a luxury. It has to be enjoyed at a token level, such as by cultivating an allotment or breeding pigeons or budgerigars or by visits to the countryside on holidays. Millions certainly seek an outlet for their instincts by keeping a dog or cat. But they take pleasure in seeing pictures of and hearing about the Queen and her dogs, especially when there is a hint that the latter are not always as well-behaved as they might be. They can appreciate what the Queen must feel when one of her cows wins a prize at an agricultural show. They like to see the Duke of Edinburgh bowling along with his carriage and four horses through a park. A nation of naturalists is delighted to know about the huts on the marshes from which he watches birds. They are full of respect for that highly popular grandmother, Queen Elizabeth the Queen Mother, in her late seventies, wading waist-deep in the chilly Dee to cast for salmon, and for the Dowager Princess Alice, Duchess of Gloucester, weeding her garden at Barnwell. The younger generation of royalty has more exciting things to do than engaging in manual work on the farm (as King George III made his children do, before they were old enough to rebel!) but they have a country background and love country sports, and already Princess Anne and Captain Mark Phillips have decided that farming is going to be their career.

So the feeling that the Royal Family is their family flourishes in the hearts of the British people. And the opening of Sandringham, Balmoral, parts of Windsor and now Broadlands to the public at certain seasons is helping to foster that sense of a common identity. The bonds between the Royal Family and their subjects have never been stronger, and nothing strengthens them more than the obvious love of the Queen and her family for the abiding things of the countryside.

A contribution made to the publication Annals of Agriculture *by King George III under the pseudonym 'Ralph Robinson'.*

Further Remarks on Mr Duckett's mode of Cultivation

Sir,

The early attention you have given to my attempt of laying before the Publick through your useful Channel, Mr Duckett's System of Agriculture, fully entitles you to expect from me a compliance in the request you have intimated in a note at the end of that publication that a particular account whould be given of the course of Crops usually addopted by that original Cultivator as well as his sentiments on fallow and his mode of treating a field when full of couch Grass.

Mr Duckett has no fixed rotation of crops; he seems to think that every farmer ought to study in cropping his land what Grain will pay him best, which is the only rule he follows unless prevented by bad seasons. All he requires is to get a feeding crop between those of Grain, and renew his Soil by alternate deep and shallow ploughing. He does not regard cross-cropping his land, yet avoids sowing wheat after Barley, nay, thinks Wheat after Wheat less prejudicial; he does not object to Wheat after Oats, but Oats after Oats and Wheat following Barley he thinks are ever weak crops, and that a continuation of such successions would at last produce nothing. On the contrary Barley after Barley does very well; indeed he has known Barley succeed well with alternate deep and shallow ploughings and proper dressings when sown two years successively.

If land requires rest, he lays it down with grass which prepares it after proper culture to produce the Grain most called for in the Market.

He seems of the opinion that the most profitable plan of Culture a farmer can follow is to examine which sort of Grain will pay him best and to vary his changes of Crops according to the demand of that particular kind of Grain, instead of laying down a regular rotation of Crops.

An untoward Season may prevent his following the rotation or succession of Crops he had proposed: but he deems it, as one of the material advantages of his mode of Culture that his land is ever ready for the occupation of such Grain or Seeds he may on such an occasion judge best suited to supply the place of the original intended Crop. He therefore recommends the use of his Ploughs and his mode of Ploughing with intermediate Seeding crops; then Grain may be cultivated in any variation or succession, but he does not think his mode of cropping ground can succeed if attempted by the common Methods of husbandry.

As an Experiment he for three years successively sowed Siberian wheat on the same land, and is convinced it will answer, and if the price of wheat was so high as to pay better than other Grain he would reduce it to practice; but does not imagine this mode of Culture can be successful but with Farmers who work his Ploughs and practise his method of using them. He recommends the Siberian Wheat as the only Species that will answer to be thus cultivated, as it is of quicker growth, does not exhaust the Soil so much as common Wheats, and nourishes Grass Seeds sown among it equally with other Spring Grain.

He has reaped Siberian Wheat on the 25th of July, which has given him a good Season for Turnips as an intervening Crop, which being fed off by Christmas, he has sown the ground immediately with Siberian Wheat and by pursuing this method has taken off the same land three Crops of Siberian Wheat successively.

If the harvest is likely to prove late, he sows his Turnips when the Wheat is in full ear, and has large Turnips at Christmas. He sows this seed broadcast among the Corn, when there is a prospect of Rain, which buries it sufficiently in the ground to produce Vegetation without other assistance. His method of alternately deep and shallow ploughing the ground with his French and double-furrow ploughs contributes to the success of this practice by furnishing every other Crop with fresh food and a new Soil, which when assisted with proper dressings and an intermediate feeding Crop will he thinks prove successful in taking Siberian Wheat many times successively off the same land.

He thinks fallows necessary for stony Soils, as the clods of earth cannot be well broken to pieces without laying sometimes exposed to the Air, but would in general reject this practice on light Soils, as feeding Crops are better from the Cattle while consuming the Crop treading the Soil and rendering it more compact and firm, which a light Soil requires. He would not let the ground lay any longer idle than while preparing for the feeding Crops. This enables the Farmer to keep a larger stock of Cattle, which increases his quantity of Manure.

Many soils may be improved by Winter fallows. This may be practised by ploughing immediately after the Grain Crop is off, in a dry season, and by being well Water-furrowed during the Winter and proper Dressing in the Spring; but he does not think this method equal to a feeding Crop of Rye, Turnips or Tares.

The method he constantly pursues for destroying Couch Grass is by French Ploughing it into the Ground, where it dies when buried deep; that left on the Surface is destroyed by hoeing.

Grain of quick and luxuriant growth sown on the Trenched ground also assists very much towards the destruction of this troublesome weed; but a change of Rye, Tares and Turnips when produced by his mode of Culture will the most effectually destroy Twitch Grass.

He confesses that this practice which he has successfully pursued for many years is condemned by many persons, yet he is convinced it answers perfectly, is less expensive and quicker done than by any other method.

I have wished to be as pointed as possible in attempting to answer your enquiries which may have led me into greater length than I should have wished; I shall therefore only add that

I am, Sir,

Your most humble Servant

Ralph Robinson

Windsor

March 5th, 1787

(*RA Add. 32/2014–5*)

Plans submitted with great deference to His Majesty King George III on the present state and future improvements of the Great Park at Windsor.

Nathaniel Kent 1794

All pasture land derives more benefit from being fed by different cattle than by having one sort of stock only kept upon it. The effect is visible though the causes not generally known. The reason is, deer are fond of one grass, sheep of another, neat cattle of a third, and it is apparent that most animals seem to spare the stem and seed of those plants, the leaves and blades of which they are most fond of and which is most fit for their nature. This gives the different grasses the means of renewing themselves by shedding their seeds every year, but when land is wholly fed by one kind of cattle, they devour the seeds of those grasses the lateral blade of which they do not effect and by sparing only their own favourite grass check the general succession and by length of time greatly reduce the value of the herbage.

This in a great measure will account for the state in which most old parks are found, the most abundant grasses being creeping Bent and Vernal grass, and but little of the annual meadow Fox and Crested Dog-Tail. This, therefore, is a very strong argument for reducing the number of deer by about one third, and increasing the sheep and neat cattle in proportion.

The first thing to be done in point of improvement is draining and the Essex method should be prefered, not only because it will be the cheapest in the long run, but because it leaves no deformity. A great deal of this should be done and as there is plenty of wood upon the spot, it will reduce the expense very much, and as this work may be done entirely by measure it may be performed without imposition.

In addition to draining, the rushes should be mowed three or four times a year, which would weaken and soften them so that the neat cattle (which I recommend to be either young Scots or Welch) would not disdain eating of them in the spring of the year, when they first shoot up, which for some time they will do, and this will also attend to their effectual destruction.

Another very necessary improvement would be that of paring off all the ant-hills, so as to lay the surface smooth. These excrescences should be laid in heaps to rot and be mixed with a certain proportion of ashes and chalk and any sweepings of roads that can be accumulated, and this compost when well incorporated should afterwards be spread upon the coarsest parts, which will help more than anything else to fine and sweeten it and

render it productive of the white honeysuckle commonly called dutch clover.

Some very rough and uneven parts will, however, require breaking up and new laying down, but this should be done with caution and only in such parts as are past recovery by other means.

When this is done a very heavy roller of cast iron should be procurred and not suffered to stand still, as they too often are, but kept in motion in all seasonable weather. Rolling is wonderfully beneficial on all grass land. By pressure only and no other means the Suffolk pole or annual Meadow Grass is called into action. The seeds everywhere pervade the whole earth, there is not need to sow them, having encouragement is all they want. But the root being shallow and striking horizontally can acquire no nourishment on a hollow, loose or springy soil. If, however, the earth be pressed close to its roots this most valuable grass triumphs over most others.

Fern is another object deserving attention and though some of it is certainly ornamental in so fine and extensive a park as this (as it gives a wild, forest-like appearance) yet too much of it loses that effect, carries a slovenly appearance and sours the grass. I presume therefore to recommend its being shaped into large bunches and left only on elevated parts, having it on the plains and lower parts totally extirpated. In addition to this, I hope it will not be impertinent in me to advise the making of a large plantation on top of Bromley hill. This is a most beautiful spot and one of the most striking features of the park, and if the top of it were richly planted and the sides smoothed I persuade myself it would give additional grandeur to this conspicious object. Several other parts of the park require, here and there, a new plantation to cover objects which do not afford beauty and to break and divide some of the large flat savannah parts, and throw them into more variety and contrast. And all these new plantations should consist of a greater proportion of Spanish chestnuts and of larch than of any other plants, not only because there are but few of them at present in the park but that they would thrive more than any others and come early to use for hurdles, which will be much wanted and which in a few years may be made from the occassional thinning of the same.

What I've hitherto observed will apply chiefly to that part of the park that lies north of the Reading road, concerning which I have but two things more to observe. One is the taking out of dead trees, which in many places injur the health and hinder the growth of other thriving trees. This should be particularly attended to, and such dead trees so taken away might be used in the preparation of fences and in such buildings as may be found necessary to errect. The other observation I have to make arises from seeing in many parts of the park trees standing in straight lines, which no doubt are the vestiges of ancient enclosures, and though the utmost reverence should be paid to an old tree in a place of this kind yet it is presumed a few stunted trees may be taken away with great propriety which will break the formality of their present appearance and show other trees to greater advantage.

The greatest part of the remainder of the park lying west and south of the lodge ornamented at the extremity by the finest water anywhere to be found will afford (If his Majesty should approve of the idea) the means of establishing a sheep walk and a farm upon a truly royal scale. The thing most like what it would be is the sheep walk at Longleat where a great tract of high poor land similar to this is very judiciously and with much taste brought into beauty and profit.

In the present style of carrying on the farm there is nothing suitable to so great an object nor is it either attended with neatness or I conceive with much amusement. The land under this description lies scattered and ill-connected and the buildings and fences are not of the kind they ought to be.

For profit and amusement and to afford a beautiful contrast I should recommend two compact farms to be formed; the one comprising all the enclosures called Shepherds Meadows and Paddock Hills, with as much of the north west corner of the park behind Bromley Hill and next to Cranborne Lodge as would make about 200 acres. This farm which from the nature of the soil and the course of husbandry that I should recommend might be called the Gloucestershire farm. The buildings which should be entirely new need not be large but neat and simple and, if they were placed on the south side of Paddock Hill Wood, they would be in a most convenient situation and have a picturesque appearance. This farm should be entirely worked by Herefordshire Oxen and would produce good wheat, oats, beans etc. and here either a dairy of cows might be kept or the oxen used in labour be fattened off, as was a certain number of Bakewell's breed of sheep. The other farm buildings should be upon a larger scale and may stand a little beyond the first piece of water in the bottom, either open or concealed as may be thought best. This farm on its congeniality of soil to that of many parts of Norfolk might be called the Norfolk farm. It might with the 250 acres now in cultivation in that quarter be increased to 1000 acres and be worked by plough with two horses only to each. The turnip system should be adopted upon it and Coke's drilling and hoeing machine may be used with great advantage. And as a most useful and valuable appendage to this farm, there should be as before hinted the sheep walk of about 500 acres which would chiefly lie south of the Lodge. Part of this sheep walk should however, be broken up and when clean laid down again with Burnett, Trefoil and other grasses most natural to a poor light soil.

Through and round both these farms and sheep-walk there should be pleasant rides and drives for carriages and several other bold plantations made.

Part of the enclosure called Bear's Rails and New Meadows lying wide of both the farms might be thrown into the park to give expansion where it is rather crampt, and the remainder may be very serviceable to His Majesty's cattle that may be kept near the Palace.

The whole number of cattle now supported in the park besides working

cattle appears to be 3160 deer, 106 neat cattle of all kinds and 447 sheep only, a number of the latter are in very poor condition. If this system here recommended should be adopted and the deer be reduced to 2000 (speaking within compass) the sheep may be increased to upwards of 2000, as three sheep may be supported with the same feed as two deer, and these may be the Southdown or Ryeland breed.

The neat cattle may be increased to 150, and as to the produce from corn I trust it would be more than doubled.

Before I lose sight of this part of the proposed alteration it may be proper to observe that I am of the opinion that 2000 deer properly regulated will afford nearly as much venison as the present number does, for I understand that in many years several hundreds frequently die, which in all probability arises more from want of draining than from any other cause that can be assigned.

A farm of the kind here described situated so near the capital would excite attention, challenge imitation and be productive of great good to the society.

The Flemish Husbandry, perhaps the first in the world, is closer followed in Norfolk than in any other part of the kingdom. The turnip system is indeed partially adopted in many other parts, but it is upon the eastern coast alone that it is in general use.

In the Western and Midland counties, turnips are partly eaten upon the spot where they are grown and partly trodden into the earth in great waste.

In Norfolk the turnips are generally drawn off the land upon which they grow and either given to the cattle in cribs and troughs in the yard or thrown before them on a clean piece of neighbouring grassland, by which means they go twice as far as they would if consumed in the dirt, do the cattle much more service and greatly enrich such grassland by the most simple and easy means.

The gardens are at present managed at a very heavy expense which may be lessened by cropping part of the lower side with lucerne, carrots and cabbage for the benefit of the cattle. The walls and borders may still be taken proper care of upon a reduced establishment and the whole may be reassumed again at pleasure without having sustained any injury from the alteration.

The lawn is quite ruined, being a mere carpet of coarse moss. There are many ways of improving it, but the best and much the cheapest will be not only to let the sheep feed upon it while the Lodge remains uninhabited but occasionally to pen or fold the flock upon it.

The game need not be diminished by anything here recommended, on the contrary the pheasants may be greatly increased and encouraged by having local spots occasionally sown with buckwheat and stacking the crop under cover of some adjoining wood. This is a practice which never fails in increasing their number, as it is the food they are most fond of.

In what I have presumed to offer it has been my aim to combine beauty with profit, but in doing this I may have been less respectful in my style and manner of expressing myself than became me but trust this will be overlooked and inputed to my want of experience in what is due in point of language and address to such an exalted personage and that I shall have credit for all good intentions. . . .'

His Majesty's most humble, devoted and faithful servant,
Nathaniel Kent

March 12th 1791   (*Royal Library,*
Craigs Court, Charing Cross.   *Kent's Journal of Windsor Great Park*)

Details of the Queen's Jersey herd at Windsor, 1978

In the past fifteen years a succession of bulls direct from the Island of Jersey have been used in the royal herd with the aim of improving conformation as rapidly as possible. The bulls, selected from families of proven females, included the following.

	Purchased
Browny's Louise Sparkler	1963
Browny's Louise Royal	1971
Royal Maisies Dreamboy	1970
Itaska Fillpail King	1972
Royal Silver Dreamer	1973

In addition, semen from other Island bulls has been used.

In 1973 Her Majesty was a founder member of the Wessex Jersey Breeders, an organisation of six breeders, with 900 Jersey cows between them, who are co-operating in the purchase and progeny-testing of young Jersey bulls. The group has also imported four splendid bulls from New Zealand and members have augmented their herds with some of the best females available from the same source.

Among the most notable show successes of the Windsor Herd of Jerseys in recent years have been the following:–

A. **Browny's Design Louise** *Elite Register, Medal Merit, Order of Merit, 100,000 lb Cow.*
Sire: Ansom Apollo
Dam: Browny's Rocket Louise
Breeder: J. P. Le Ruez (Island of Jersey)
Purchased as an in-milk heifer; she was in calf to Ceres Right Royal. The resulting bull calf, Windsor Louise's Royal, sired many good cows including one Royal Show Champion (Windsor Louise's Polyanthus) and one Dairy Event Champion (Windsor Louise's Prophecy). Amongst her many show successes were:

1st Young Cow	1964 Royal Counties
Reserve Champion	1965 Royal Counties
Reserve Champion	1965 Royal Show

1st Inspection/5th Production	1965 London Dairy Show
1st	1966 Royal Show
Winner of the coveted Loxwood Trophy	1966 London Dairy Show

In her lifetime she produced 128,450 lbs milk with 7114 lbs fat in ten lactations. She was used to suckle calves after her eleventh calf until her untimely death in 1976 at the age of fifteen years. She only had one daughter, but eight sons were retained and sold to various breeders, including one to Iran and another to the U.S.A.

Purchased at the same time as 'Browny' was a young heifer calf called 'Sparkling Natalie', the first daughter of 'Browny's Louise Sparkler' who later became the first Island-bred bull purchased by Her Majesty.

B. **Sparkling Natalie** *Elite Register, Medal of Merit, Grand Order of Merit, 100,000 lb Cow.*
Sire: Browny's Louise Sparkler
Dam: Natalie's Nanette
Breeder: T. F. Le Ruez (Island of Jersey)
Sparkling Natalie was the first 'Natalie' to enter the Windsor Herd. Because of their honest production capabilities, coupled with above average conformation, the Natalies at Windsor are a numerous and very important family within the herd. They are not top-flight show cattle, and Sparkling Natalie's appearances in the show ring were mainly at the Old London Dairy Show where she won the Loxwood Trophy in 1969. In addition she was 1st in the Production/Inspection class at the 1972 Royal Show. At the age of fifteen years Natalie still remained in the herd in 1978. Her production to date was
140,891 lbs Milk
8,891 lbs fat in 12 lactations.
She had had four daughters as well as seven sons. Four sons were sold to other U.K. breeders and the other three were sold as follows:
Windsor Natalie's Jester *sold to Wessex Jersey Breeders for progeny testing*
Windsor Natalie's Pioneer *sold to Kenya for use in A.I.*
Windsor Natalie's King *sold to Oman for use in A.I.*

C. **Browny's Louise Sparkler** (Bull) *Elite Register, Medal of Merit, Gold Medal, Grand Order of Merit.*
Sire: Itaska Fillpail Dazzler
Dam: Browny's Victorious Louise
Breeder: J. P. Le Ruez (Jersey Island).
'Sparkler' was shown extensively in his youth, culminating in his receiving the Breed Championship for Her Majesty Queen Elizabeth II at the 1966 Royal Show. He then retired from the show ring but continued to breed many good cattle until his death in 1972. Semen stocks ensure a steady trickle of daughters every year. 'Sparkler' became famous for the very many successes of his female progeny.

Windsor Sparkler's Mandolin	1968 Royal Show Champion
Windsor Sparkler's Madeline	1969 Royal Show Champion
Windsor Sparkler's Madeline	1973 Royal Show Champion
Windsor Sparkler's Patsy	1974 Royal Show Champion

His progeny, exhibited as groups of three or more animals in progeny classes, were rarely beaten and included first prize at the Royal Show in 1967, 68, 69, 70, 71, 73 and 74.

With the exception of Browny's Louise Sparkler, the above Royal Show Champions as well as the 1972 Royal Show Champion, Windsor Louise's Polyanthus, were all home-bred animals. Mandolin and Madeline can be traced back through many many generations of Windsor breeding. Patsy is a descendant of the Sandringham Herd, and Polyanthus is the grand-daughter of Hursley Riff – a cow purchased as a young heifer from the herd of N. Cooper.

D. **Windsor Sparkler's Mandolin** *Elite Register, Order of Merit*
Sire: Browny's Louise Sparkler
Dam: Windsor Royal Kanita
G. Dam: Windsor Juanita 14th
G.G. Dam: Windsor Juanita 12th
In 1967 and 1968 Mandolin was shown at at least eight shows and was never beaten in her class. Her successes included:

1967 Oxford	1st Heifer in Milk, Reserve Champion
1967 Surrey	1st Heifer in Milk
1967 South of England	1st Heifer in Milk
1967 Royal Show	1st Heifer in Milk
1967 London Dairy Show	1st Heifer in Milk, Female Champion
1968 South of England	1st Young Cow
1968 Surrey	1st Young Cow
1968 Royal Show	1st Young Cow and Breed Champion

E. **Windsor Sparkler's Madeline** *Elite Register, Gold Medal Order of Merit.*
Sire: Browny's Louise Sparkler
Dam: Windsor Postillions Evangeline
G. Dam: Windsor Imperial Cherub
G.G. Dam: Windsor Alouette
'Madeline' is one of the very few cows to win two Royal Show Championships and probably the only cow to achieve that distinction in non-successive years i.e. 1969, aged 5 years and 1973, aged 9 years.

F. **Windsor Sparkler's Patsy** *Elite Register, Gold Medal, Order of Merit*
Sire: Browny's Louise Sparkler
Dam: Windsor Royal Katesy
G. Dam: Windsor Imperial Fantasy

G.G. Dam: Sandringham Galaxy

Patsy, like Madeline, was shown on countless occasions spread over 5 or 6 years. Her show ring successes included:

1970 South of England	Reserve Female Champion
1971 Oxford	Reserve Female Champion
1972 Royal Show	Reserve Female Champion
1972 Egham Show	Supreme Champion All Breeds
1974 Surrey Show	Champion Jersey
1974 Royal Show	Champion Jersey

Aged eleven years, Patsy was still very active, milking in her 10th lactation in 1978. A very regular breeder, she calved as a heifer on 26 March 1969 and with her tenth calf on 27 March 1978. A daughter by the present senior stock sire – 'Itaska Fillpail King' – was exported to New Zealand in 1977.

G. **Windsor Louise's Polyanthus** *Elite Register (3rd Generation) Medal of Merit, Gold Medal, Grand Order of Merit.*

Sire: Windsor Louise's Royal

Dam: Windsor Sparkler's Narcissus

Still very active in her eleventh year, Polyanthus has averaged 12,062 lbs with her first eight lactations. Her show successes include:

1971 Oxford	Champion Jersey
1971 Surrey	Reserve Champion Jersey
1972 Surrey	Supreme Champion All breeds
1972 Royal	Champion Jersey
1972 Newbury	Supreme Champion All Breeds
1973 Surrey	Reserve Supreme Champion All Breeds

A son – 'Windsor Louise's Victory' was exported as herd sire for the Sultan of Oman.

H. **Windsor Louise's Prophecy** *Elite Register, Medal of Merit.*

Sire: Windsor Louise's Royal

Dam: Windsor Cardinal's Kerrie

Another eleven-year-old cow still very active, Prophecy averaged 12,941 lbs with her first eight lactations. Despite calving out of the normal show season, Prophecy gained two Championships:

1971 Newbury	Supreme Champion All Breeds
1974 Dairy Event	Champion Jersey

The lactation statistics for the past few years are:

Jersey	*No. Cows*	*No. Heifers*	*Average Cows (lb)*	*Yield Heifers (lb)*	*% Butterfat*	*Calving Index*	*Rolling Herd av. Gallons sold per cow*
1977–78	73	26	9629	7220	5·86	381	—
1976–77	63	29	9152	7544	5·58	385	848
1975–76	74	25	9855	7753	5·44	390	845
1974–75	66	22	9093	7471	5·51	392	782

Real contributions to herd improvement have been made by outstanding animals purchased by or given to Her Majesty, of which the following are examples:

a. A number of animals were purchased from the Sandringham Herd when it was dispersed in 1953; Windsor Sparkler's Patsy (1974 RASE Champion) being a granddaughter of Sandringham Galaxy.

b. The most famous purchases from the Island of Jersey include –

Fairfield Itaska	Virginia Dazzling Surprise
Fairfield Lilac 6th	Nanette's Winn Louise 2nd
Browny's Design Louise	Surprise Sparks Natalie
Natalie's Fillpail Princess	Browny's Tiny Louise
Sparkling Natalie	April Rush
Dreaming Royal LADY II	Samares Camelia's Heritage
Dream Jersey Lily	Samares Royalist Winnie
Winsome Noble Queen	Margarethe's Golden Cecile 2nd
Eagle's Dreaming Vale	

Jersey animals purchased from English herds have included
Hursley Riff *g. dam of W. L. Polyanthus (1972* RASE *Champion)*
Hursley Reverie *g. dam of W. L. Prophecy (1974 Dairy Event Champion)*
Leebarn Carolette
Bollhayes Prop's Sloe
Buscot Ada
Lugate Sparkler's Louise

Bibliography

Boalch, D. H., *Prints and Paintings of British Farm Livestock 1780–1910* (Rothamsted Experimental Station, 1958)

Bonnett, Harold, *Saga of the Steam Plough* (Allen and Unwin, 1965)

British Agricultural Bulletin, May–June 1953

 The Duchy of Cornwall Home Farm, Stoke Climsland

 The Duchy of Cornwall Home Farm, St Mary's, Isles of Scilly

 The Royal Farms at Windsor

 The Royal Farms at Sandringham

 Norfolk Farm, Great Park, Windsor

 The Barnwell Manor Estate

Brodrick, George C., *English Land and English Landlords*, 1881

Brooke, John, *King George III* (Constable, 1972)

Bryant, Sir Arthur, *King George V* (Peter Davies, 1936)

Bryant, Sir Arthur, *A Thousand Years of British Monarchy* (Collins, 1975)

Burkitt, William, *His Majesty the King as Farmer and Stockbreeder* (Transactions of the Highland and Agricultural Society of Scotland, 1931)

Buxton, Aubrey, *The King in His Country* (Longman, 1955)

Carter, H. B., *His Majesty's Spanish Flock* (Angus and Robertson, 1964)

Churchill, Sir Winston, *A History of the English-speaking Peoples* (Cassell, 1956)

Dictionary of National Biography, 1892 Edition

Donaldson, Frances, *Edward VIII* (Weidenfeld and Nicholson, 1974)

Duncan, Andrew, *The Reality of Monarchy* (Heinemann, 1970)

Fiennes, Celia, *The Journals of Celia Fiennes*, ed. Christopher Norris (Cresset Press, 1947)

Fussell, G. E., *Royal Farmers before the First World War* (British Agricultural Bulletin May–June, 1953)

Fussell, G. E., *Old English Farming Books 1523–1730* (Crosby Lockwood, 1948)

Fussell, G. E., *More Old English Farming Books 1731–1793* (Crosby Lockwood, 1950)

Fussell, G. E., *The English Dairy Farmer* (Cass, 1966)

Fussell, G. E., *The Farmer's Tools, 1500–1900* (Melrose, 1952)

Gilbey, Sir Walter, *The Royal Family and Farming* (Vinton, 1911)

Hammond, J. L. and Barbara, *The Village Labourer* (Longmans Green, 1911)

Hedley, Olwen, *Queen Charlotte* (John Murray, 1975)

Hedley, Olwen, *Windsor Castle* (Robert Hale, 1967)

Hepworth, Philip, *Dear Sandringham* (Wensum, 1978)

Kerridge, Eric, *The Agricultural Revolution* (Allen and Unwin, 1967)

Kerridge, E., *The Farmers of Old England* (Allen and Unwin, 1973)

Lacey, Robert, *Majesty* (Hutchinson, 1977)

Laird, Dorothy, *Queen Elizabeth, the Queen Mother* (Hodder and Stoughton, 1966)

Marshall, William, *Review and Abstract of the County Reports to the Board of Agriculture; Eastern Department, 1811*

Matson, John, *Dear Osborne* (Hamish Hamilton, 1978)

Minchinton, W. E., *Essays in Agrarian History*, 2 Volumes (Reprints edited for British Agricultural History Society, 1968)

Montgomery-Massingberd, Hugh (ed.), *Burke's Guide to the Royal Family* (Burke's Peerage, 1973)

Nicolson, Harold, *King George V, His Life and Reign* (Constable, 1952)

Petrie, Sir Charles, *The Modern British Monarchy* (Eyre and Spottiswoode, 1961)

Seebohm, M. E., *The Evolution of the English Farm* (Allen and Unwin, 1952)

Shewell-Cooper, W. E., *The Royal Gardeners* (Cassell, 1952)

Steane, John, M., *The Northamptonshire Landscape* (Hodder and Stoughton, 1974)

Stratton, J. M., *Agricultural Records* (John Baker, 1969)

Talbot, Godfrey, *Ten Seconds from Now* (Hutchinson, 1973)

The Agricultural History Review, various articles (British Agricultural History Society)

The Gardeners' Magazine, June 6, 1896, *History of the Royal Gardens, Windsor*

Tighe, R. R. and Davis, J. E., *Annals of Windsor* (J. R. Smith, 1858)

Trevelyan, G. M., *English Social History*, (Longmans Green, 1942)

Trevelyan, G. M., *History of England* (Longmans Green, 1926)

Trow-Smith, Robert, *A History of British Livestock Husbandry, to 1700* (Routledge and Kegan Paul, 1957)

Trow-Smith, Robert, *A History of British Livestock Husbandry, 1700–1900* (Routledge and Kegan Paul, 1959)

Trow-Smith, Robert, *English Husbandry* (Faber, 1951)

Wheeler-Bennett, Sir John W., *King George VI, His Life and Reign* (Macmillan, 1958)

Whitlock, Ralph, *A Short History of Farming in Britain* (John Baker, 1965) (revised ed. EP 1977)

Young, Arthur, *General View of the Agriculture of the County of Norfolk 1813*

Young, Arthur, *General View of the Agriculture of the County of Lincolnshire 1813*

Young, Arthur, *The Farmers Kalendar, 1771* (EP reprint, 1973)

Ziegler, Philip, *King William IV* (Collins, 1971)

Chief Sources in Royal Archives, Windsor

An Account between His Majesty and Nathaniel Kent relative to the

Improvements on Windsor Great Park and Farms, 1790

Nathaniel Kent's Journal of the Progressive Improvements in Windsor Great Park, from February 8th, 1791, to October 8th and 9th, 1792

The Farms of Windsor Great Park (26th October, 1797 to 26th October, 1798)

Windsor Great Park, March 12th, 1791

Valuation of Stock, etc. on Windsor, Richmond and Kensington Farms, October and November 1804 (by William Sedgwick and others under the Control and Direction of the Hon. George Villiers)

Establishment of Windsor Great Park, 1791

Other minor items in Nathaniel Kent file

Index

Castle
of Mey

Balmoral

Edinburgh

Sandringham
Barnwell

Gatcombe

London

Isles of
Scilly

Broadlands

Windsor

Stoke
Climsland

Osborne

Glouc

Cardiff

Bris

Stoke
Climsland

Exeter

Plymouth

Isles of Scilly